My Downward Spiral To Happiness

By

Dean Roberts

Copyright © 2023 Dean Roberts

ISBN: 978-1-916820-56-2

All rights reserved, including the right to reproduce this book, or portions thereof in any form. No part of this text may be reproduced, transmitted, downloaded, decompiled, reverse engineered, or stored, in any form or introduced into any information storage and retrieval system, in any form or by any means, whether electronic or mechanical without the express written permission of the author.

Contents

Author's Note

About the Author

My story

Chapter 1: One woman's decision destroys an entire family ... 1

Chapter 2: The fist of abuse ... 7

Chapter 3: When fear leads to hate ... 14

Chapter 4: Cultivating the seed of suicide ... 22

Chapter 5: Observing infidelity, denial and death ... 29

Chapter 6: First day of secondary school ... 37

Chapter 7: My first crush and a slaughtered goat ... 44

Chapter 8: An unwelcome marriage and a family slave ... 53

Chapter 9: Going off the rails before finally gaining a degree of control ... 61

Chapter 10: My first girlfriend ... 69

Chapter 11: Breaking up, feeling stupid and discovering alcohol ... 79

Chapter 12: My final year at school ... 87

Chapter 13: Time to escape, and time to lose my virginity ... 96

Chapter 14: Using bible study to get close to a girl, and being ousted by Aunt Beth ... 104

Chapter 15: The heartbreak caused by Sabine's departure ... 115

Chapter 16: Reduced to eating ramen pot noodles and failing the driving theory test ... 122

Chapter 17: The irresistible attraction of an older woman	129
Chapter 18: Psychosis and flying raspberries	136
Chapter 19: Cars, college and women	144
Chapter 20: Boy racer	153
Chapter 21: University life	160
Chapter 22: Getting the key of the door and starting to build some muscles	167
Chapter 23: Moving into the real world	174
Chapter 24: It's Cardboard City for you	181
Chapter 25: Getting a mortgage at the wrong time	187
Chapter 26: Out of the frying pan and into the fire	194
Chapter 27: Graduation Day and taking tips from Britain's most violent prisoner	201
Chapter 28: Finally finding out what was wrong with me	207
Chapter 29: Heaven on earth	214
Chapter 30: Sinking back into the black hole of depression	221
Chapter 31: Another crazy relationship	228
Chapter 32: Enough is enough	234
Chapter 33: Working with the she-wolves	240
Chapter 34: A fresh start	246
Chapter 35: Moving on (sort of)	253
Chapter 36: What have I gone and done now?	260
Chapter 37: Back to the Seventh Circle of Hell	266

Chapter 38: Being boiled alive in the witches' cauldron	274
Chapter 39: The original witch	280
Chapter 40: The return of the dark place	287
Chapter 41: It's a West Indian thing	295
Chapter 42: The end of the road	302
Chapter 43: Working as a reluctant drug-runner	311
Chapter 44: My worst fear realised	318
Chapter 45: The noose of death	325
Chapter 46: Hope returns	335
Chapter 47: That one opportunity	342
Epilogue	349
Acknowledgements	351

Author's Note

I have changed the names of most of the people referred to in this book to protect their identity, but all the events that happen and all the actions undertaken by the people within the book are based on fact.

My main goal has been to share my life experiences, not just to show the struggles I have encountered, but also to explain how I have overcome them against some very unfavourable odds. In this way, I hope to be of help to other men who have faced or continue to face similar struggles in their own lives. I want to show that it is ultimately possible to choose a positive path through the most challenging of times, even where mental and/or physical abuse, neglect, bullying or mental health issues are involved.

Many of us at times experience emotions caused by depression, fear, isolation, anger or resentment, all of which potentially prevent us from moving forward in life and even cause us to contemplate suicide. Suicide is a particularly taboo subject for men to discuss, but the rate of suicide in males is higher than it has ever been.

I understand that, as men, we find it difficult to put our feelings into words, and that we express ourselves differently to women, but the power of words is universal and I have decided with this book to take a stand on behalf of all the troubled men who find it hard to express their true feelings. For some time now, I have been passionate about helping others where I can, and I truly want people to benefit from my story. I want them to overcome their own obstacles and to be the best they can be by discovering their true worth and potential.

I have learned many of life's lessons along the way, too many of them the hard way. I hope the experience of reading about my journey will bring you hope and a belief that there are always choices you can make that can lead to a better life for yourself and those around you. Although I have told my story primarily for the benefit of men who find themselves in difficulty, there is much in this book that may also be of use to those men and women who belong to the same family, social or work circle as those struggling individuals. Having a better understanding of what they are going through may enable you to help them along life's path.

About the Author

Dean Roberts was born on Monday, 17 December 1984, in the Mothers' Hospital in Hackney. He grew up in Tottenham, has worked as an IT professional and personal trainer, and now runs his own business as a Life Coach and Mentor. He has a BSc degree in Computer Networking and a Diploma in Personal Training, Teaching Meditation, Coaching and Mentoring. He has a keen interest in personal development through health, fitness and philosophy. He currently resides in North London and this is his first book.

My story

Chapter 1:
One woman's decision destroys an entire family

The environment into which we are born is influenced by those around us, whether for good or bad. It is not our choice to select these people, but in time we will learn which of them have our best interests at heart, and which of them don't.

Do you remember your first memory as a child? Some people claim to remember their first moment just after being born, but my first memory was as a fourteen-month-old child in 1986, when I woke up from a nightmare, trembling. Once I had woken up, I realised I was safe in the comfort of my bedroom. At the time, I lived on West Road in Tottenham with my parents, James and Tara, and my sister Laura, who was only eight months old at the time.

Childhood for me at that time can best be described as 'normal', even if my British-Guyanese mother had named me after the actor James Dean. Toys were a big part of my life, and I was lucky enough to have many of them, including a Thomas the Tank Engine train set, a number of Matchbox cars and some Transformers figures. There were many occasions when I laughed hysterically in my bedroom while watching videos of Thomas the Tank Engine on the television. From the age of three I had a fascination with trains and cars, including Scalextric cars, which my parents also bought for me. I remember a shelf in my bedroom, which my Dad had made to store all my Matchbox cars on. On many days I played with my toys for hours on end, without a care in the world.

Since 1985 we had lived in a very small two-bedroom council house in Tottenham, which didn't even have carpet. I shared a bedroom with my sister. At the time, Dad worked for a printing factory in Central London, while my mother was unemployed. My mother's parents had been separated for many years, following my grandfather Desmond's promiscuity with many women outside of his marriage. He also had a habit of physical abuse towards my grandmother Ann, which was witnessed by their children, including, of course, my mother, who from an early age probably thought of it as normal behaviour. My grandfather was also a big drinker who liked to get dressed up in sharp suits and wear gold jewellery. He spent many evenings in the pub, where he met his other women. He eventually left my grandmother, but they were surprisingly civilized towards one another following the separation.

My grandfather Desmond and grandmother Ann had four children, three sons and my mother. Ann lived locally to us in Tottenham, while Desmond lived in Hackney. They were both born in Guyana and had migrated to Britain in the late 1960s, along with many other migrants from the Caribbean. My grandparents on my Dad's side, Peter and Lorna, lived in Hackney. They had three daughters and two sons, including my Dad. They too had migrated to Britain, but from Jamaica.

My relationship with both sets of grandparents was as normal as could be. I never felt I was missing out on anything as I was always in a family-orientated environment on both sides of the family.

Many of my memories involve time spent with cousins of various ages. I saw them on many occasions when they came to visit and when we in turn visited them. We played happily together and generally enjoyed being within a wide but close family circle.

In 1986, at the age of almost three, I attended my first day at nursery. I found it exciting, because I got to meet other children from very different backgrounds. Tottenham was already culturally diverse and this was very apparent in my nursery. I knew I was going to have to make friends and I soon started to talk to an African boy called Jay. For whatever reason, we got along very well. Nursery was a good experience generally, and the starting point of not just my education and development, but also my social life outside of the family. I also started to develop an awareness of myself at this young age, to the extent that I could already hear some kind of inner voice. This voice seemed to recognise the difference between right and wrong, to the extent that I decided to test the patience of adults just to see where the boundaries between right and wrong lay.

Not long after starting nursery, I had my first traumatic experience. Our family car had child safety locks on the inside of the rear passenger doors. I always had a thing for turning switches on and off, just out of childish curiosity, and the child safety lock on my side of the car was no exception. Any time we went anywhere in the car, I used to play with it, flicking it up and down. This proved to be a very stupid thing to do. One afternoon, with my parents in the front and my sister and I in the back, we were travelling quite fast on an A road near Edmonton. All of a sudden, the passenger door where my sister was sitting flew open and she fell out of the car. Dad stopped the car very quickly and my mother jumped out to pick my sister up off the road. Luckily, my sister was unharmed, although if there had been a car behind us, I shudder to think what might have happened. I didn't just blame myself at the time, though. I decided that my parent's lack of attention had also played a part in the near catastrophe.

Not long afterwards, I began to notice my parents having problems, becoming distant with one another. My mother then started having an affair with another man, called Tommy, who just happened to be a distant relative of my Dad's. Tommy had come across as nice when I met him at family gatherings, but it was probably all a facade to disguise the fact that he was plotting to entice my mother into having an affair. Not long after that, my mother left us for Tommy. I was aged three. To add insult to injury, she completely cleared the joint bank account she had with my Dad and used the money to set up a new life with Tommy.

As you can imagine, my Dad was devastated. My mother was his first love and the first woman he had ever been with. To make matters worse, he was left with the responsibility of two children with no wife and very little money. The initial shock of my mother telling him she was leaving led to him locking himself in his bedroom with a bottle of pills. An uncle of his that had come round to visit ended up saving his life after breaking the bedroom window and taking the pills away.

My Dad's trust in women became non-existent for a while, but, as he worked long hours to support us, we needed a babysitter. This was a young woman called Nicky, who looked after us, cooked our lunch and created a playful environment within our home.

To be completely honest, I never felt all that sad that my mother had left us, as my sister and I had always had a stronger bond with our Dad anyway. It seemed to me to be perfectly normal that it was just us three. Time passed and the spring of 1989 brought many happy times. On one occasion, Dad took us to Cornwall for a few days, and I remember my sister and I burying him in the sand while he was asleep. We were at our closest then. Although my mother had been absent from the picture for a whole year by then, it didn't stop us doing things as a family. On weekends, Dad would take us to see our cousins, who we were very close with and who we had fun playing with. On weekdays, he would drop me at my aunt's house in the morning as my older cousin Pete and I went to the same school (I went to the nursery and he went to the primary school, but it was the same building). We would often frustrate my aunt with our messing around as she tried to get us ready for school.

At school I had many friends I got along with, and I always looked forward to seeing them in class. There were never any fights amongst us, even though we were from so many different ethnic backgrounds. We just seemed able to see past this. The experience helped me to identify a person's character regardless of what they looked like on the outside, and for me this would ultimately become a vital tool to make progress later in life.

Around this time, Dad bought me my first bike, with training wheels on it. I was very excited, but Dad would try to talk me into riding it without the training wheels, which terrified me for a long time. I was always excited to come home after nursery and ride on my bike, and I used to spend hours riding around in circles in our garden.

It wasn't in fact long until my Dad met someone else, but the strange thing was that this new woman, called Julia, had been Tommy's partner at the time he was having the affair with my mother. It wasn't until much later that I realised this and, when I did, I thought it was a bit sick on my Dad's part, a bit like wife-swapping. We only saw Julia a couple of times, so we didn't have much contact with her, although I do remember one time when I walked in on them having sex and was told to go back to bed. It was a disturbing moment and not one I ever wanted to relive – there is nothing more uncomfortable than the image of one or both of your parents having sex! I knew that was what they were doing as I had seen sex acted out in TV films.

In the autumn of 1989, my young life suddenly took a turn for the worse. One evening, my sister and I were upstairs playing. She was in her bedroom playing with her dolls and I was in my Dad's bedroom watching *Thomas the Tank Engine*. My Dad was downstairs having an argument with some other people. Curious to know what was going on, I decided to walk over to the stairway and peep over the banister. I saw my mother's parents and brothers arguing with my Dad. I remember one of my uncles saying to my Dad, 'You have to let Tara take the children.'

'The kids are not going anywhere,' my Dad replied.

I ran back into my Dad's room. Looking out the window, I could see my mother in a car with Tommy. The next thing I remember was me and my sister being taken out of the house by one of my mother's brothers and walking towards her car. I don't remember how I reacted to this, or how my Dad reacted, but I do remember an overwhelming feeling of sadness. It was the second time my sister and I had experienced separation already, only this time we were being separated from our Dad, and without explanation. We were driven by our mother and Tommy to a one-room bedsit in Hackney, which is where we would live for a while. The additional shock of moving from a family house to a bedsit all added to the trauma of the occasion.

Chapter 2:
The fist of abuse

Abuse in any form can have a profound impact on a child's development and the resulting psychological scars can be permanent.

Being taken away from our Dad was very unsettling for us. It was not only traumatic, it was also confusing, because we did not understand why it had happened. Getting to grips with why we had been taken from our home, our bedroom, our toys, the life we knew and, most importantly, our Dad, was impossible to comprehend at the time. Our new environment had almost nothing of our own in it. We had none of our toys, just a few clothes. We had to get used to the fact our mother was back in our lives, and that she was with someone else. Although Tommy was a relative of the family, I could tell he was nothing like my Dad. They looked different, dressed different and talked different. In fact, they had no similarities whatsoever.

In short, Laura and I had to get used to living a totally different life. Because the bedsit was in Hackney, we had to travel to and from our nursery by bus. She was not working at that time, because she had to take care of us, whereas Tommy was a driving instructor and worked most days of the week. I can see looking back that she wanted to instil some sense of normality in our lives, perhaps to compensate for the fact that she had taken us away from our Dad, but it never really worked out that way. Even as a child, I somehow knew that the trauma I was experiencing was not going to go away.

The beginning of 1990 brought our next move, into a council property on Sirdar Road, near Wood Green. The house was split into two flats, the ground-floor flat belonging to a married couple and their son. Our flat was on the first floor and consisted of two bedrooms, a storage room, a bathroom, a living room and a kitchen. The bathroom had a stairway that led to the ground-floor garden. As there were only two bedrooms, Laura and I had to share a room, which had only one bed in it. I was not happy that I had to share a bed with my sister, not least because we had been used to having our own beds in the house where we had lived with our Dad. It was frustrating, but there was nothing we could do about it.

Our routine was pretty straightforward. At around 7.30 a.m. my mother would wake us up and make sure we brushed our teeth. We got dressed and had breakfast. She would then take us to the bus stop, where we would catch the 123 bus to Tottenham, where our nursery was. She would walk us in and then go back to the house until it was time to come back for us at 3.30 p.m. Once we got home, she would prepare dinner for us, which we ate about 5 p.m. when Tommy returned from teaching driving lessons. After dinner, we would watch *EastEnders* and then get ready to go to sleep.

Tommy was also of West Indian descent and was the third eldest of the six boys and one girl born to his parents. He appeared to be a nice enough person at first, certainly in my mother's eyes, but also to me and Laura after a while. As time went on, we started to adjust to our new living environment.

One night I woke up when I heard my mother making odd noises in the next room. After listening for about five minutes, I figured out she was having sex with Tommy. It was a disturbing experience and I felt disgusted because it was Tommy and my mother who were doing it. From this point onwards, I started to develop a strong dislike towards Tommy. I felt that this outsider had come into the picture from nowhere and was basically taking my Dad's place.

Not long after we had settled into our new council flat, my parents were involved in court proceedings regarding me and my sister. The conclusion reached was that an arrangement should be made for our Dad to collect us on weekends. This did not go down too well with Tommy, who clearly felt he should have had a say in the matter and who considered any contact with our Dad to be a huge bone of contention. My mother also disapproved of the decision and I often heard her discussing the matter with Tommy and others in an angry tone, which made me very uncomfortable. Once the final decision was made, though, my Dad would pick us up on Saturday mornings and bring us back home on Sunday evenings. Dad was living with his parents at the time in Hackney and that's where we would spend most of our weekends. Once we had arrived at our grandparents' house, Dad would spend time with us for a short period and then leave us in the afternoon to go off to the car garage to see his friends. He was very much into the car-modifying scene and devoted a lot of his time and money to it, even owning a few cars himself.

My grandmother made us breakfast, which consisted of boiled eggs with toast and a cup of tea. My grandfather had a cabinet in the living room where he kept a packet of mints and, usually when all of the cousins were there, he would give us some, although he got cross if one of us went in there without asking. We got to see all our aunts, uncles and cousins most weekends, but there would be times when my Dad was not around for most of the weekend and my sister and I would have to find things to do, like watch cartoons on TV, but after a while that got boring.

My grandparents were a firm but fair couple and came from a poor working-class background. They worked very hard to support their children after settling in the UK, as did many migrant workers from the West Indies at that time. All the cousins feared and respected them at the same time. On Sundays, my grandmother would always cook rice and peas and chicken, which at first was fine, but after a while it became monotonous and I got bored of that as well.

Usually around 6 p.m. on Sundays, my Dad would drop me and Laura back home to our mother's. Our routine of going to school on weekdays and seeing our Dad at weekends was pretty much what happened most weeks.

Everything seemed to be on a fairly even keel until late one evening. My sister and I had just gone to sleep when we were suddenly woken up by my mother and Tommy shouting at each other. The shouting became louder and louder, so we decided to get up and see what was going on. As we came into the passageway, we heard Tommy hitting our mother over and over again. At the time I genuinely thought he was trying to kill her. As we opened the living-room door, we saw our mother laid out on the floor with Tommy standing over her. He had an angry look on his face, which scared me and Laura no end. When my mother saw us, she said, 'everything is okay, just go back to your room'. She was crying, but we knew there was nothing we could do about it. Laura and I just looked at each other in shock, as we had never seen anything like it before. We went back into our bedroom and tried to sleep, but the arguing continued and I covered my ears in an attempt to block it out.

Not surprisingly, that experience developed a fear inside me towards Tommy. Why was he abusing our mother? What did she do to deserve it? Why did we have to go through this? These were the questions that kept coming up in my six-year-old mind. My mother certainly didn't want to talk about it, and Tommy now seemed to be making his presence felt to a far greater extent – physically, mentally and emotionally – whether any of us liked it or not.

A few weeks after that particular incident, I began wetting the bed at night. As my mother could see no logical reason for it, she took me to the doctor to have me assessed. The doctor suggested that it could be down to me drinking fluids too late in the evening, which was not the case. My mother purchased a bedwetting alarm, which was a mattress cover linked to a bedside alarm box, which would go off whenever the cover made contact with fluid.

That alarm made things worse for me. One night it went off and, although it was very loud, I didn't wake up, because I was a heavy sleeper as a child. The next thing I knew someone had grabbed my shoulders and pulled me out of bed. Once I opened my eyes and came to my senses, I realised it was Tommy who had pulled me out of my bed and was now shouting at me for not waking up. He then told me angrily to go to the toilet, which, of course, was embarrassing. From that night onwards, every time I went to sleep with that alarm next to my bedside I would be a bag of nerves, worrying that Tommy might pull me out of bed again. I also began to think about the possibility of Tommy abusing me as he did my mother, which, I think it's fair to say, no six-year-old child should have to worry about.

After a while I calmed down and my bedwetting stopped for a while, until one night it happened again.

The alarm went off, only this time Tommy did not come into the bedroom and I managed to get up and go to the toilet. I felt relief that Tommy hadn't woken up, but what I didn't know was that I had already urinated on my bedsheets without realising it. The following afternoon I was playing in my bedroom when I heard Tommy's voice from the living room, 'Dean, come in here!' I had no idea what he wanted until I walked into the living room and saw him holding my sheet. He walked over to me and said, 'You need to stop wetting the fucking bed!' As my mother was in the kitchen down the hallway, she couldn't hear what was going on. I suddenly felt Tommy's fist punch my chest, and it hurt so much I started to cry. He punched me again and then grabbed me. With a threatening look in his eyes, he said quietly, 'Stop crying now! And don't tell your Mum, you hear me?' My reaction was indeed to stop crying and I wiped my tears away, having got it into my mind that Tommy would probably hit me again when he got the chance if my mother walked in and saw my crying. I went back to my bedroom and tried to think of something else to take my mind off the pain in my chest.

Being hit for the first time by someone who was not a direct relative was a frightening experience. This man, who seemed to have come out of nowhere into our lives, began to make his presence felt in ways which caused me to experience real fear for the first time in my life.

My mother did not have a clue what had happened, and I didn't want her to know either, because I was too scared of what the consequences might be. Tommy would do no more than shout at me and my sister when my mother was around, but there were times when my mother was not in the same room that he either pushed me, grabbed me by the shirt or hit me. He never hit my sister; it was only directed at me. As my fear grew, I became wary whenever Tommy came through the front door after work, collected me from nursery or was in the same room as me. Just being in the same house as Tommy was enough to worry me, whether my mother and sister were at home or not. Although I would not have recognised it as such at the time, a survival instinct had been awakened in me at the age of just six. I became defensive and I learned to be on my guard at a moment's notice, never knowing when the fear and pain inflicted by Tommy would strike next.

Chapter 3:
When fear leads to hate

I'm pretty sure child abuse went mostly unpunished at the time I was growing up. It probably still does.

My first day at primary level in Parkhurst School in Tottenham in September 1990 has always been a good memory for me. I got to meet new friends as well as being able to mix with old ones. Jay was in the same class as me, which was a real bonus as we had already established a strong friendship at nursery school.

School was an outlet from the abuse I suffered at home. I never told any of my teachers or friends about what went on at home, as I feared what Tommy might do to me if I did. I remember seeing Childline posters on walls, always with a picture of a child holding a phone to their ear. I already understood that Childline was a charity that supported children who were being abused by parents or other legal guardians, and I was tempted from time to time to take the number down and call them. However, I could never bring myself to do it, because a mixture of fear and survival instinct always kicked in. My young brain calculated a scenario in which social workers came to our house, my mother defended Tommy, nobody believed me and the consequences from Tommy were severe.

Primary school was a nice experience, though, and I have fond memories interacting with other children from all backgrounds of life. Tottenham was a poor area and most children enjoyed the basics and not much more, so you never came across spoilt children and some even had refugee status. In my eyes, at least, we were all the same. I think, looking back, that my time there taught me how to interact with people from all walks of life and to accept people just as they are.

Tommy often hit me in the morning before I left for school. When he was not hitting me, he was shouting at me or giving me angry looks just to scare me, but never within sight of my mother. I tried to deal with it as best as I could, but my fear continued to grow. It was as if Tommy had implanted a seed of fear into my mind that just kept growing and growing. His presence was always intimidating and just one of his looks was enough to make me feel fear deep inside my chest and leave a huge weight hanging over my head.

Some weekends we used to spend time with our grandmother Ann (my mother's mother), who we felt very close to. She always meant well, and she cooked for all her grandchildren whenever she could. Another bonus was that she lived close to where many of my friends from school lived, including Jay, so I got to see him quite a few times when I was there. On many occasions, my grandfather would come from the pub to have lunch at my grandmother's house, and we enjoyed seeing him too. Although he was still not living with my grandmother, they continued to maintain a civilised relationship. They never knew what was going on with me and Tommy, but I later learned that their story was not far off what was happening with my mother and Tommy. My grandfather had always been a drinker and womaniser, and he had been violent towards my grandmother. He used to beat her up regularly, but he didn't beat his children for whatever reason. My mother's idea of what a relationship should be was probably based on what she saw as a child and I often wondered later whether she left my Dad for Tommy because my Dad was the quiet type, whereas Tommy fitted into the same abusive mould as her own father.

As Christmas drew closer that year, the weather became really cold and the snow outside our house was about 4-feet deep. It was a struggle to walk in it and we had to wear as many layers as possible to stay warm whenever we left the house. One Saturday afternoon, my mother called me and Laura into the living room to announce that she had some news for us. As we sat down, Tommy came into the room and they looked at each other with uncertainty. Together, they explained that my mother was pregnant and that we were going to have a new sister. What seemed funny to me was that they didn't appear to be exactly over the moon about it. They then explained that things around the house were going to be different, such as me and Laura needing to be responsible around the baby. I looked at my sister and it was clear that we were both confused and didn't know what to say.

Their own uncertainty may have had much to do with the fact that we were only surviving on Tommy's income and Mum's benefit money. Another child to support in the household was going to be an added pressure.

I do remember after digesting the news that my stomach felt as if it had suddenly dropped. I didn't know what this new child would bring into the picture, but I felt as if I had to put on a happy face. In reality, I felt nothing but resentment, because this child was associated with Tommy and anything related to Tommy I hated with a vengeance.

My mother went into labour that December and was taken to North Middlesex Hospital, where she gave birth to a girl. They named her Sarah. At the time, Laura and I were staying with our grandmother Ann and when we finally met our half-sister I felt pretty indifferent towards her.

Within a month of Sarah's arrival, things started to change for me and Laura. I started to notice that we couldn't play as much as we wanted to around the house as this would cause a disturbance if Sarah were asleep. I also noticed that Tommy didn't let us get too close to Sarah, which I assumed at the time was him just being protective of her. However, as the months went on it appeared we were indeed being separated from Sarah. We didn't get to hold her that much and we weren't allowed to feed her. With most of the attention being on Sarah, Laura and I were feeling more and more left out as time went on and I didn't have anyone I felt I could talk to about that. When you throw into the mix that we were still visiting our Dad on weekends, it just became the norm that Laura and I didn't have one family but two, although we didn't really feel as if we fully belonged to either.

School helped me to channel some of my confusion and at the time I was getting into drawing and physical education, including running, gymnastics, rope climbing and using the other bits of apparatus in the gym. Running was my favourite hobby at the time, and I developed a degree of confidence when I realised that I could be competitive with the other children. Any chance I got to race someone, I took it, as I wanted to be the best runner in the school. Running against your classmates at that age was an adrenalin rush, so we would race almost every week. I was one of the fastest in my class. Another activity we enjoyed was swimming, which we used to do at Coleraine School in Tottenham, which was only a ten-minute walk from our school. It was one of the few schools in the borough which had a swimming pool at the time.

Alongside these physical activities, we often went on school trips to parks, museums and the countryside. Just before bank holidays, we had parties in school with all the other classes. In the playground, our favourite games were tag and piggy-back fights, which were exciting as the larger children usually carried the smaller children on their backs when we challenged each other. School life helped to release the negative energy I was building up at home.

Many relatives in my family were heavy drinkers and Laura and I would always be with the other children in one room at a family party while all the adults were drinking in another. One of my first experiences of being around adults while they were drinking was at my mother's birthday party in April 1991. Tommy had arranged it as a surprise and had invited my mother's family as well as his own. I was seven and I thought the adults drinking and having fun was okay at first, until an argument broke out involving Tommy and two of my uncles, which led to Tommy spending the night in the police station. From what I remember, the confrontation led to the police arriving at our house and Tommy, instead of keeping his calm in front of them, began to shout aggressively, which led to him being taken away. I began to understand that night that alcohol can have a negative effect on some people, especially if they can't control the aggression that it often brings out in them. Tommy being drunk was a scary sight, because it was clear that he certainly couldn't control his aggression, and I was happy he was taken away that night. It wasn't the last time I would witness a drunken feud between the two families.

Not long after my mother's birthday party, Sarah started to crawl everywhere, which meant my mother needed to fit a child safety gate near the top of the stairs which led down to our front door. One Saturday afternoon, while my mother and Tommy were in the kitchen, Laura and I were playing catch on the stairs. I was at the bottom and Laura was at the top. As we were playing, Sarah fell down the stairs. As soon as my mother heard her crying, she ran downstairs in a panic to see if she was okay. I remember being in total shock, unable to understand how Sarah had managed to get past the locked gate and into the passageway. Once my mother had checked that Sarah was okay, she put her to sleep and both she and Tommy told us off. Once my mother had gone into the kitchen and Laura had gone off to play in the bedroom, Tommy decided to take it out on me. He hit me on the arm and then delivered a hard blow to my chest. When I couldn't stand the pain and began to cry, he told me to go to my room.

The abuse from Tommy became more frequent from that point onwards. He hit me on the head whenever I walked too close to get past him, or he would suddenly grab me aggressively, which scared the hell out of me. I remember becoming frustrated that I couldn't defend myself against him and all I kept asking myself was why was he hitting me? The more Tommy abused me, the angrier I became. I started to fantasise about dropping something heavy on Tommy's head while he was asleep and hoping it would kill him. I had already seen violence on the television by that time, so I knew it was wrong, but in my situation of being constantly bullied it felt justified. I hoped that he would be run over in the street, that someone would kill him, that my Dad would attack him or that he would just get arrested by the police and be sent to prison for a long time. My Dad didn't have a clue that I was being abused and I felt as if Tommy was controlling my mind by now. Physical and mental abuse go hand in hand and Tommy was certainly practising both on me simultaneously. He would say things like: 'Don't tell anybody or I'll fucking kill you!' I felt trapped because I knew my mother was still being abused by him and I didn't know who to turn to. Tommy's presence was like a black cloud over my head, haunting me from the moment I woke up until the moment I went back to sleep at night.

I remember one Saturday afternoon during the summer of 1991 when Tommy, my mother and Sarah were in their bedroom. They had decided to take an afternoon nap and Tommy had told me and Laura to keep quiet. I felt like I had had enough, knowing full well that Laura and I were not really a part of the family and that my mother was also suffering at the hands of Tommy. I said to Laura: 'Do you want to run away from home? We can go and look for Daddy.' Laura could tell I was serious and knew what was happening to me, so she nodded and we put on some outdoor clothes.

After about ten minutes of contemplating what to do, I led us downstairs to the front door. At that moment, though, I realised that I did not know how to get to my grandmother's house (where my Dad lived) by foot. We always went there by car, so I didn't have a clue where to go. While we were trying to figure out how to get there, my mother came out of her bedroom to go to the toilet and heard us at the doorstep.

'Running away, are we?' she said. She had known instantly what we were up to.

My heart stopped for a few seconds, before I replied: 'No, we were going to the shop.'

As I walked back upstairs with Laura behind me, I could hear my mother laughing with Tommy about it. I went straight into my bedroom and changed my clothes. I couldn't believe that I was stuck in a family I didn't belong to. What was even more bizarre, though, was that my mother couldn't really have cared less. She didn't kick up a fuss about our escape attempt, and she never made any effort to find out why we had been about to run away from home.

Chapter 4:
Cultivating the seed of suicide

The idea of suicide can grow from the seed of abuse.

Although I desperately wanted to run away from home at the age of seven, in the hope of gaining freedom from a life that promised me nothing but abuse, I persevered because I had no real choice in the matter. I held so much pain and anguish deep inside of me, but there was nothing I could do about that either.

I started to notice that my mother and Tommy were making an increasingly big fuss over Sarah, presumably due to her being their first child, and so it became clearer and clearer that Laura and I didn't fit into their family unit.

In September of 1991, a change to my life at school made things even worse. I had progressed to Year 2, which had caused me to be separated into another class away from my old friends. I had to mix with a new set of children, but I felt out of my comfort zone and couldn't cope with socialising outside of my established circle. I would only look forward to playtimes, when I got to see old friends like Jay. For the majority of the time, though, I made the most of my schooldays, because I was at least safe from Tommy while I was there. It probably didn't occur to me too much at that age that my social skills were becoming increasingly weak.

The lead-up to Christmas that year did see an improvement, though. Things had started to calm down at home and I wasn't experiencing as much abuse from Tommy. My mother clearly wanted Christmas to be special, being that we had Sarah with us. Christmas Day was traditional, in the sense that we had Christmas dinner, a tree, presents and Christmas television programmes to watch. We all enjoyed it, considering the circumstances, and it made a change to see that Tommy could actually be happy, which was undoubtedly fuelled by the joy of having Sarah in the picture.

Around this time, the film *Terminator 2* was broadcast on television, and it was the first time I had seen Arnold Schwarzenegger on screen. From that moment on, I was mesmerised by his immense physical shape, believing him to be superhuman. I saw that he couldn't be hurt or killed, and that he was physically strong enough to defend himself against anyone or anything. I wanted to be him, as many other children did at the time, I'm sure, but for me it was different. If I could be like my hero Arnold Schwarzenegger, I thought, I would no longer have to suffer. Nothing would be able to hurt me, not even Tommy.

As we moved into 1992, communication between my parents began to break down and much anger was directed towards my Dad when he started to miss some of the weekends he was due to collect us. This had a knock-on effect, as arguments between my mother and Tommy led to more abuse towards me from Tommy. Anything to do with my Dad was a reason for Tommy to hit me.

After about a month, Tommy went missing for a few days. I had no idea where he was, and I didn't much care. I then came home one Thursday after school to see Tommy on crutches, and with a cast on his leg.

'What happened to your leg?' I asked him.

'Tommy was in a car accident,' my mother replied, and I didn't question it any further.

I was just happy that Tommy had been immobilised and that it would be easier for me to escape his physical abuse, especially as he would be in sight of my mother a lot more, although by now I was convinced that she would never protect me anyway – she might have been scared of him, but she was probably more scared at the thought of not having him around. I later learned that my Dad and Tommy had met out in public one day and that it had led to my Dad smashing Tommy's leg. Blaming it on a car accident was just a way to cover up Tommy's embarrassment.

After a few weeks, as the pressure of Tommy started to ease, I began to enjoy going into school and even coming home. I also enjoyed going to see family on the weekends. Occasionally, Laura and I stayed at my grandmother Ann's house during the week, so that my mother could take care of Tommy and Sarah. For me, it felt perfect just to be away from home.

When we came back from school to my grandmother's house, we could watch children's programs such as *Fun House*, *Count Duckula*, *Transformers*, *Sesame Street*, *Rolf's Cartoon Club* and *Rainbow*. I also got to play in the front garden with my friends and often go to Jay's house.

In the mornings, my favourite breakfasts were Kellogg's Frosties, Coco Pops, Crunchy Nut Cornflakes and Rice Krispies, especially because they often included a toy in their promotional boxes. Along with many other children whose parents were on low incomes, we had mass-produced school lunches and at times the food was horrendous. Dishes like sliced lamb with mashed potatoes and greens never went down well with me or most of the other children, but I used to enjoy turkey legs, chips, burgers and soups. Trying to get me to eat vegetables was hard, because for some reason I only enjoyed non-green vegetables such as carrots, sweetcorn and cauliflower. Waiting for lunchtime at our school always had a sense of mystery about it, at least, because we never knew quite what we were going to get. Dinner at my grandmother's house was more varied, though, including dishes like stewed chicken, fried chicken and chips, curried chicken and spaghetti.

Nutrition is important for a child's development, but my mother did not take this seriously. We were not fed properly at home and, because I couldn't always bring myself to eat the more disgusting of the school lunches either, I ended up being malnourished. I remember perfectly being so underweight that my ribcage was visible. I realise now that the worry I used to carry with me because of Tommy would also have been a contributory factor to my not eating properly, as stress and loss of appetite often go hand in hand. There were days when I could eat more, but usually they were the wrong kinds of things, like chocolates and sweets. It is not uncommon for stress to lead to a craving for unhealthy foods, because they can provide a stimulant otherwise lacking in an unsatisfactory existence.

During this year, my mother announced to me and Laura that she and Tommy wanted to go to Jamaica to visit Tommy's father. They wanted to take Sarah with them and leave me and Laura in London. The real shock, though, was that they were going for six weeks during term time and that their solution was to re-school me and Laura in Hackney near our grandfather Desmond (i.e. her father), which meant we would have to stay with Desmond for the entire duration of their trip. We begged our mother to let us remain at our local school in Tottenham near our grandmother Ann, but she didn't want us staying there as she didn't like the fact that we were so close to her mother, who was still supportive towards our Dad. We were duly registered at the school in Hackney and within a few weeks our mother and Tommy had flown off to Jamaica with Sarah.

I was seven years old and just about getting used to my new classmates at my school in Tottenham. Now I had to endure six weeks of a totally alien environment where I did not know anyone. On top of that, our grandfather's flat had just one bedroom, which meant Laura and I had to sleep on the floor. My grandfather was seeing a woman called Patricia at the time, so there were four of us sharing this flat. As you can imagine, it was very crammed at times. I didn't make any new friends at school and got told off for not participating with the other children. I truly started to hate my mother from that point onwards, as it was clearly her wrongdoing that had caused this latest predicament, which could easily have been prevented if she had let us stay with our grandmother in Tottenham.

I am more than positive that if our mother had had her way she would have stayed in Jamaica and left us at our grandfather's forever. However, she came back with Tommy at the end of the six weeks and we moved back to Wood Green, where life continued as before, including the abuse from Tommy towards my mother and me. One evening, I remember being awakened by another argument between them. My mother was screaming very loudly and she was calling for me and Laura, so I ran into the living room to see her on the floor crying, with Tommy standing over her with clenched fists.

'Go back to your room!' Tommy said in a raised voice, and I did. He had by now established total control within the household, with my mother stupidly defending his behaviour in between bouts of abuse at his hands.

Christmas of 1992 was another opportunity for my mother to put on the pretence of playing happy families, cook a Christmas dinner and share presents, but I knew about the ongoing abuse underneath the cover-up. Women like her felt it best to brush these things under the carpet, because God forbid anything should jeopardise their relationship with their husband. During that Christmas period, however, my mother got upset because my Dad didn't turn up to collect us for a few days as promised. When I started to get upset about my Dad not coming for us, she then decided that the best thing for it was to tell us how bad our Dad was and that he had left us when we were little. It was a pathetic attempt to try and brainwash us into thinking our Dad was a bad person, especially when I could remember everything she had done to break up our family for her own selfish purposes.

While processing all of this alongside the continual abuse from Tommy at that time, I began once more to fantasise about what it would be like if Tommy was dead. I started to visualise his funeral as his abuse took an increasingly psychological toll on me. I also thought of disappearing, but logic always kicked in because I had nowhere to go and nobody to turn to, because I knew what Tommy would do to me if I told anyone about his actions.

I then went from thinking about Tommy's funeral to my own funeral, which is when my thoughts of suicide began, around the time of my eighth birthday. I was becoming immersed in the idea that this was the way to get revenge on my mother and Tommy. If I was dead and the truth was read out to everyone at my funeral, Tommy would surely be put away in prison. I found comfort in the idea of my own death, because it would mean an end to the abuse I was suffering and a way to be free. I didn't give too much thought about how I might kill myself, as the end result was my main focus.

At school, I carried on as normal, free from the situation at home. When I got home at the end of each school day, however, I had to shift quickly from an educational mindset into a defensive one. I didn't really know if it was normal to be contemplating suicide at eight years of age, but I was somehow managing to develop survival strategies in any event. I tried everything I could think of to hold on to the hope that one day I would be free from my situation one way or another, and I can only assume that some divine presence kept me going throughout those long years of darkness. I somehow knew at that tender age that I had to abandon childlike innocence if I was to succeed in staying at least one step ahead of my enemy.

Chapter 5:
Observing infidelity, denial and death

Most adults don't appear to realise that their behaviour is observed very closely by the children around them, or that those children often go on to replicate that behaviour in their own life.

Although my life remained the same in the sense that the abuse continued at home and that school remained my only outlet from that, the next couple of years in many other respects were really quite eventful.

Tommy had begun to sleep with other women behind my mother's back, some of whom were related to her. It began with rumours at first, but when it did come out, my mother simply defended him. She simply saw these other women as a threat to her own happiness and she was determined not to let them take the love of her life from her. Regardless of what he did, she would rather have him with all his faults than be alone without him. One of the women that Tommy slept with was my mother's cousin, my Aunt Jane. Instead of just tackling Tommy about his betrayal, though, my mother decided that her cousin was the real enemy of the piece. She set about convincing the family that the cousin was to blame.

I knew all this because I often heard Tommy and my mother arguing about it at the top of their voices. It just made me hate the man even more, and I also resented my mother for sticking around and putting up with it.

Tommy also had problems handling himself as a driving instructor and the stress he brought home with him was always channelled towards me or my mother.

Whenever they argued with one another, though, he would threaten to leave and she would stand at the front door begging him to stay. Drinking also remained a problem for Tommy, in that it brought more of his aggression to the surface. I always had to be careful not to walk into a room if he was drunk in there, because that would put me right in the firing line.

Tommy was not the only person who embarrassed himself while under the influence of alcohol, because this was something that plagued my mother's family also. At family gatherings, most of the adults would drink to the point of shouting, fighting, passing out or throwing up. To me it seemed perfectly normal at the time, because I was used to seeing adults in this state and I was oblivious to the risks involved with drinking to such excessive levels.

My behaviour around this time started to evolve into a hyperactive and disobedient state, which of course tested my mother and Tommy's patience. My mother assumed my behaviour was down to spending weekends with my Dad, so she reverted to her futile attempts to convince me that my Dad had left us when we were little.

The year also brought with it our first holiday to Florida, which was spent with family in Miami. The experience as a whole was okay, but there were also moments of discomfort. If, for example, any of our relatives in Miami bought gifts for us children, my mother and Tommy immediately declined them on our behalf. I have always assumed that was down to their own guilty conscience about hardly ever treating us themselves. It became normal for me as a child to think twice about accepting gifts from people just in case I would get into trouble for it. The holiday was fun at times, though, especially when we got to go to Universal

Studios in Orlando, but my bedwetting continued the whole time we were in Florida, because Tommy continued to exert complete psychological control over me.

Not long after we returned to London, we were rehoused by the council to Tilson Road in Tottenham. This had the advantage of being closer to our primary school, which meant we didn't need to catch the bus any more in the mornings. Our journey to school now was a twelve-minute walk. The terraced house we got had three bedrooms instead of the two we had before, which meant that I could have my own room. The house was in need of complete renovation, though, and we didn't even have carpet anywhere in the house, which was a hazard, especially with young children around. When work got underway, one of the bedrooms was used for storage, so all three children were soon enough sleeping in one bedroom again.

One day my Mum told me that my Dad had received some bad news, which was that his father (my grandfather Peter) had died from a heart attack while he was in Jamaica. My mother told me that she did not want me or my sister to go to the funeral, which was to be held back in London, but those members of my mother's family who were still civil towards my Dad's family told her that we could go with them. My mother reluctantly agreed that I could go, but only on the condition that I was not allowed to talk to my Dad at the funeral. Laura was not allowed to go, but I went with my grandmother Ann and my mother's brother Byron.

The day of the funeral was a very sad one for my Dad's family and, as it was the first one I had been to, I got to see at first hand the effect that funerals can have on people. Everyone was dressed in black and it was very well attended, because my grandfather had known a lot of people. When we arrived at the cemetery in New Southgate, I saw my cousins Warren and Pete crying for the first time. I felt sad inside, but I didn't shed a tear, because I'd never had that much of a connection with my grandfather.

When it came time to bury my grandfather, I saw everyone throwing roses into his grave. It looked like the kind of event I wanted to be a part of, not least because I was curious to see where the roses had landed. My uncle Byron put a rose in my hand and I approached the grave when it was my turn to throw a rose in. I walked so close to the edge in order to look down to see my grandfather's coffin that I nearly fell in, but my Dad pulled me back in time. The understanding of death I got that day was not so much to do with the loss of a loved one, but more about the curious sight of a dead relative in a wooden box surrounded by the grief of his family and friends. I suppose I just saw it for what it was, which seems cold now, but at the age of eight it's hard to take these things in.

After a couple of months, we had a flood in our house in Tilson Road, so the council decided to move us into a flat in Northumberland Park while it got sorted. The flat had two bedrooms, the same as our previous house in Wood Green, but it was smaller in overall size. In the communal area outside the flats was a small park with a climbing frame and slide, but our neighbours in that deprived area were not exactly welcoming and the other kids made fun of us. It was the first time I had encountered bullying from other children and I found it so intimidating that I soon stopped going outside to play in the communal area. Being self-conscious for the first time as a child was traumatic and turned me into something of an introvert for a while.

While we were living there, my mother and Tommy had to go to the hospital and my two sisters and I were sent to stay at my grandmother Ann's house. We had no idea why they'd gone to the hospital, so we were pretty surprised to return home and have our mother introduce us to a new baby sister, Sophie. We didn't exactly have much choice in the matter, so we just accepted the situation on the spot and got on with our lives. Laura and I got to hold and feed Sophie, which we'd never got to do with Sarah, so I felt an instant bond with Sophie. After a while this role-playing became more of a responsibility, because our mother's priority remained looking after Tommy. Laura and I started to assume the roles of parents to both Sarah and Sophie.

The abuse I suffered at the hands of Tommy remained the same, though. One night, after I had got Sophie to sleep, I fell asleep next to her in the bed and the next thing I knew was Tommy's fist punching me in the side of the head. When I came round, he told me to shut up because my snoring would disturb Sophie. There were other instances when he pulled my ears so hard that I could feel and hear the cartilage splitting. It was so painful that I used to worry that my ears might fall off because of the strength he put into yanking them so hard.

We had a spare room in the flat, which we used as a playroom and to store our toys in. There was other stuff in there too, stuff which really had no place being there, like tools and a snooker cue. The snooker cue was broken, leaving the metal ferrule exposed where it would normally have had a soft tip attached to it. One Saturday afternoon, we were all playing in the toy room when Sarah got hold of the snooker cue and began swinging it around. I knew it was dangerous for her to be doing that, so I told her to give it to me, but by the time she heard me she had swung the cue around and it sliced under my right eye. I started to cry and Laura shouted out when she saw blood running down my face. My mother panicked and rushed me to the hospital. Because I had kept my eye closed for so long, I wasn't sure after a while if I would be able to see out of it or not. However, the doctors cleaned my cut and luckily the slice was underneath my eyelid. They told my mother that if it had been three centimetres higher, I would have been blinded in my right eye. The doctors then used a glue to seal the cut and put an eyepatch on me to protect it.

When we got back to the house, my mother got mad with Sarah, but I was angry with my mother because I knew the broken snooker cue shouldn't have been in the playroom to begin with. The following week, my mother took me to school to explain what had happened and told them that I would need to be absent until my eye had healed. While we were there, some younger children in the playground asked me what had happened to my eye and whether I had lost my eyeball. I enjoyed the attention I got from them. The cut healed after just a week and I was able to remove the eyepatch and get back to school.

When 1995 arrived, we were able to move back to our house on Tilson Road and I was able to put the council flat to the back of my mind along with the bullies. When we returned to the house, it was dry but still in need of repairs as a result of the damage caused by the flooding. For most of that year we lived in what could only be described as a hazardous building site, with sand and cement everywhere, power tools all over the floor and plaster lying around in buckets. We all got sick and for a while I couldn't breathe properly, resulting in me having to take an inhaler, even to school. Thinking about it now, it strikes me as a ridiculous decision by my mother and Tommy to accept these living conditions at that time, especially with a newborn baby in the house.

Once all the building work was finally complete, I got to move into the box room and no longer had to share a bed or bedroom with Laura. I could finally have my own space again. The box room could only hold a single bed and single wardrobe, but it had a window facing the garden and I loved it. I was away from everyone in there, especially Tommy.

By this time Tommy had been out of work for a while and my mother had found a job in Islington as a legal secretary. As we lived just seven minutes' walk from our school, I was given the responsibility of taking Sarah and Laura to school in the mornings and bringing them back home at the end of the day. Tommy stayed at home to look after Sophie. School remained my only place of peace and freedom, but I now had to finish my final year at junior school while simultaneously carrying out a guardian role towards Laura and Sarah.

In my last year at junior school, I did manage to make some new friends, including Tre, who would later become my best friend. Tre lived around the corner from my grandmother Ann, so on the weekends I was staying there I went to visit him and we played video games and went swimming at our local leisure centre. Tre was a real comedian and, in a way, he mirrored my own personality, because we seemed to have the exact same sense of humour. We talked to one another about personal things, cracked jokes and overall had fun together at school and whenever possible on weekends also. What I didn't know was that Tre had been going through a similar experience to me, in that his father physically beat him. He never showed any obvious signs of this, and neither did I. What we didn't know until later was that we were enjoying much-needed carefree time around each other, away from the torment of our respective abusers. Tre even stayed at my house a few times, which was the first time I ever brought a friend home, and Tommy would put on an act that everything was perfect. I never told Tre what I was going through, and he never told me about his own experiences.

It wasn't unusual for Tommy and my mother to take Sarah and Sophie out for the day and leave me and Laura by ourselves in the house. On one occasion, I was left alone in the house for the whole day and my mother told me before leaving that there would be someone coming to drop some money off and I had to make sure that I opened the door to them. During the afternoon, a man did come to the door, but only to say that he would need to stop by another day as he didn't have the money at that moment in time.

When everyone returned, I told my mother that the man had stopped by and the next thing I knew Tommy had told me to come upstairs with him. I followed him up to his bedroom, where he said very aggressively: 'I told you not to answer the door to nobody!' Before I could answer, he punched me in the stomach so hard that I dropped to the floor immediately. I was winded so badly that I could only lift my hand up towards him as a way of asking him to stop, but instead he began to kick me in my side ribs while I lay on the floor. I was in such pain from the stomach punch that I couldn't even feel the kicks to my ribs. He then warned me not to tell my mother what had happened. When I went back downstairs, I had to pretend that I was fine, and my mother seemed none the wiser about what had just occurred upstairs in her bedroom.

Chapter 6:
First day of secondary school

The first days of secondary school can be anything between life-affirming and traumatic. Much depends on which side of the tracks you come from.

Our first Christmas in the renovated house in Tilson Road was pretty much the same as all the others in terms of the traditions that were followed. My mother had another disagreement with our Dad over visitation rights, though, and we did not get to see him. He decided to drop our presents off at the door anyway. My present from him was a game for the Sega Mega Drive console I had at the time. As I had my own room now, my mother bought me a small 14-inch television and, once I had connected my game console to it, that was it for me. I could isolate myself from the family and Tommy in particular.

In 1996, I finished my last term at junior school and moved on to secondary school. As junior school had been my only place of refuge for several years, I was very apprehensive about leaving it behind. I would not see many of my junior school friends again and the thought of having to make new ones unsettled me.

At home, Tommy was becoming increasingly frustrated due to being out of work and claiming benefits. Following the disagreement my mother had had with my Dad, she decided to request child support payments via the courts. All of this resulted in us not seeing our Dad for a while, as we became little more than leverage to be applied to secure financial gains for my mother and Tommy.

As I approached my final days at junior school, I had mixed emotions. I would even miss a lot of the teachers who had looked out for me over such a long period.

One of my older cousins, Elle, had been going to Greenfield Secondary School in Edmonton and her mother had advised my mother that this would also be an ideal school for me. There was an open evening at the school, and I went there with my mother to look at their facilities. I was impressed, because they had a drama theatre, science labs, an all-weather football pitch, a massive field for other sports, basketball courts, three huge playgrounds, a different lunch hall for every school year and a tuck shop. While I was walking around, I saw Tre with his mother and that helped to alleviate my anxiety. If Tre and I were going to go to the same secondary school, then maybe it wouldn't be so daunting after all.

On that same evening, I saw my cousin Warren. He had become a hyperactive child and it was decided by my mother that I was not to be put in the same class as him, because she thought it might be distracting to have family members in the same class.

When I saw Tre the following day, we agreed about Greenfield as our main choice for secondary school. On our last week of junior school, there was a leaving party for our year, with party food, sweets, biscuits, fizzy drinks, games and music. I remember dancing to an R&B CD and everyone watching me party like there was no tomorrow. After the party I went to Tre's house and we played on his Sega games console. It had never really sunk in until that day that there would be a big difference in my life after junior school. When it did dawn on me, I felt a real sadness to be leaving the place I had spent most of my childhood in, having fun, learning and, of course, escaping my torment at home.

During that summer break, Tre and I became members at our local leisure centre in Tottenham and mostly used the swimming facilities. The swimming pool had a wave machine and we used to go swimming every weekend without fail. It was good for getting me away from the house and gave me another interest in life. During this period, my Dad was back in contact with us and he got me my first mountain bike. What he didn't tell me was that the frame was stolen and that he had ground off the serial number, stripped and resprayed the paintwork and put new brakes and tyres on. I was very happy to have a new bike, but Tommy wasn't too pleased because he felt uncomfortable about me getting a gift from my Dad. I didn't care, though, because for me it symbolised the idea of my independence.

Having a brand-new bike is one thing; having one that was stolen and rebuilt is another thing altogether. One day I decided to pedal really fast on the way to Tre's house and the bike chain came loose. The bike buckled on to the pavement, and I landed on my right thigh. The pain was excruciating, but I was more concerned about somebody seeing what had just happened, so I managed to pick myself up and limp the rest of the way to Tre's house. The problem with the bike was that my Dad had fitted the wrong chain to it, so anytime I pedalled beyond a certain pace, the chain would come loose. My bike-riding days were over as quickly as they had begun, because I just left my bike in the garden after that incident and walked to Tre's house instead – it wasn't far to go from my house anyway. I spent a lot of time there and my mother got worried if I didn't get home by 6 p.m., but I didn't care because I was having fun. One day I lost track of time completely and it was approaching 7 p.m. when I panicked and ran home. When I arrived, I found out that my mother had been driving around the neighbourhood looking for me, so Tommy beat me up for worrying her and I was grounded. I ignored my mother for two days until she caved in and allowed me to go to Tre's house on condition that I let them know where I was and always got home by 6 p.m. I felt that I had won a small victory against my mother and I felt the strings between us starting to loosen.

As the summer came to a close, we needed to go to Greenfield to purchase my new school uniform, so my mother and I headed off there. There were lots of children there with both their parents, picking out and paying for their new uniform. My mother picked out my uniform and stuffed it straight into a white plastic bag and, before I knew it, we were in the car heading back home. She had walked out without paying for my uniform and got really uptight when I asked her about it. She just said that it was too expensive and that she couldn't afford it. It was the first time I had witnessed theft in front of my own eyes, and I have to confess it gave me a bit of an adrenalin rush. I remember thinking that if she could just go and take something and not pay for it, then I could do the same thing. Luckily, I did not resort to theft straight away, but it did open my mind to the idea if circumstances warranted it.

I remember clearly my first day at secondary school that September. I had to go to the bus stop and get on the bus by myself for the very first time. I was very nervous travelling by myself, not least because I didn't know what to expect when I got to my new school. I somehow made it into my form class, which was H6. You went to your form class for morning and afternoon registration. The letter H was for Humanities, due to the class being located in the Humanities block, and 6 was the classroom number. Our form tutor was Mrs Carter, who was very slim, had grey hair and wore glasses and a long dress. When I walked in, I saw Tre immediately, which was a great relief because neither of us knew anybody else.

When Mrs Carter started to read out our names for registration, she also asked each of the students if they had a pencil case with pens, pencils, rulers, rubbers, sharpeners and a calculator. To my surprise, I had none of these things, presumably because my mother had decided not to purchase them for me. It was very embarrassing being the only student in the class without a pencil case. Tre lent me a pencil for the day, but Mrs Carter and I had started off on the wrong foot and she told me in front of everyone that I shouldn't be attending lessons without the right equipment. As I was sitting right at the front of the class, I could feel the snickering coming from the students behind me and I could not have felt smaller than I did at that moment.

We were then left alone in the class to socialise with each other, which was a bit daunting at first because many of these children lived locally and had different social backgrounds to me and Tre. The harsh reality was that we came from broken families who lived in council properties and on the benefits system, whereas the other students in the class probably had both parents still living with each other and both in work, which meant they could afford things that we couldn't, such as designer shoes, trainers, jackets and even a sports rucksack to carry their books in. There was me standing there in a stolen uniform, with no pencil case and no rucksack. In actual fact, the other children probably came from a wide variety of backgrounds, but I was too paranoid to figure that out at the time.

Once the day had ended, my mind kept going over what had happened. I told my mother that I needed a pencil case as it was going to get me into more trouble with Mrs Carter if I didn't have one. My mother told me she couldn't afford it and that I had to wait until her benefit money came through. This added extra pressure to the humiliation I had endured on my first day.

As the week went on, I tried to keep my head down and not be noticed for not having a pencil case. I became familiar with my new classes, including English, Maths, Science, Humanities and Physical Education. PE looked interesting because we had such a wide variety of sports facilities, but I didn't have much passion for playing sports at the time. On a typical school day, we had morning registration followed by our first lesson, then a fifteen-minute break when we could purchase something from the tuck shop, then our second lesson before lunch at 12 p.m. As I did not have a packed lunch and my family was on benefits, I was eligible for free school lunches. Lunch ended at 1 p.m. and we then had to go back for afternoon registration before our last lesson of the day. One problem for me was that I couldn't afford anything from the tuck shop, so I had nothing to eat between my breakfast at 7.50 a.m. and my lunch at 12 p.m. This four-hour gap left me hungry and affected my concentration during lessons. It bothered me a lot that the other kids (except for Tre, of course, who also had nothing) brought food with them to school as well as being able to go to the tuck shop to buy something extra. I didn't even ask my mother for money, though, because I knew she didn't have any to give me. After three weeks, Mrs Carter asked me about my pencil case and this turned into a bit of an argument between me and her to the point where the other kids started to laugh at me. It took my mother another week before she went to a stationery shop to purchase my pencil case and I was so relieved, not just because it would help me in my classes, but also because it stopped Mrs Carter humiliating me and the other children laughing at me.

Luckily, I still had Tre at least. Although we were not in the same classes, every playtime and lunchtime we met up to play games and crack jokes.

Our older cousin Elle was in Year 11 when Warren and I started at Greenfield and she used to check on us at our break times, which was cool. Warren quickly settled into his class and his hyperactive nature started to draw in a group of similar-minded friends. Warren's behaviour started to change towards me, which was not a surprise considering the extrovert nature of the friends he kept around him, so we never said much to each other apart from hello whenever we saw each other around the school.

Fights were a common occurrence at the school, which used to make me nervous because I never knew if one day I would end up in one of them, or if I was going to get beaten up. I felt as if I needed to grow eyes in the back of my head whenever I was walking around the school. Some of the older students in fact came from backgrounds much worse than my own, displayed violent tendencies, dabbled in drugs and alcohol, practised sexual harassment towards female students and were the cause of teenage pregnancies. Bullying was also a daily occurrence. These issues became the primary focus of my attention, because self-preservation will always be more important than education.

Chapter 7:
My first crush and a slaughtered goat

A boy's first crush is often his first romantic disappointment.

Music was a big part of my life when I was at secondary school, and I was very much into hip hop at the time. I used to record albums on to audio cassettes so that I could play them on my Walkman stereo. Tupac Shakur in particular was a very big influence, because his lyrics seemed to connect with me and even helped me deal with rough days at school and at home.

One weekend, while my mother and Tommy were away for the day, I came across a video tape in a cupboard in the bathroom. I was intrigued because it was covered in towels, so I took it and put it into the video cassette player. I was surprised to see that it was a porn video, which more than likely belonged to Tommy. In any case, I was fascinated to see one for the first time and I immediately knew that I wanted to have sex with a woman similar to the one on the video. At school, I had been very shy around girls and never really spoke to them much, although I was aware of feeling more attracted to the girls in the years above me.

In our class, we had an equal mix of male and female pupils and after a few months everyone began to form their own groups. Tre and I were always hanging around with each other, but we did make an effort to socialise with other students, including a whole group of boys who already hung around with one another. The girls also formed their own groups, but one girl in particular still caught my eye. She was called Janine and she had short blonde hair, freckles and a lovely smile. She was one of the first girls in my class I ever spoke to. The attraction turned out to be mutual and before we knew it we had started talking a lot to one another.

Whenever I was busy getting along with Janine, Tre usually spoke to her friend Jill. Tre was a slow developer in this respect, though, so he and Jill were friends more than anything. The four of us got along well as a group, so we decided to meet up one weekend to go to the cinema together. For me and Janine, it was more of a date, so I was very nervous. Tre was very cool about the whole situation and had decided that he and Jill would be there to support me, which was a big help in my nervous state. I didn't tell my mother that we were going to meet girls from our class, just that we were going to the cinema.

Having bought Janine a rose with the pocket money I had, because that's what I'd seen done in films, I met up with Tre on the Saturday around 7 p.m. and we took the bus to Picketts Lock cinema, where we met the girls. When I got off the bus and saw Janine, I was excited and nervous at the same time. I gave her a hug and a kiss on the cheek and handed her the rose. 'I got you this,' I said, shaking like a leaf. She took it and looked at Jill and smiled, but Jill seemed to find it very funny, which made me even more nervous, because I wasn't sure then if I'd done something wrong.

We headed into the cinema and bought popcorn, drinks and tickets to watch a disaster film called *Twister*. Janine didn't say much while we were watching the film, which raised questions in my head about whether she liked me or not. Once the film had finished, we headed towards the bus stop to part ways. I gave Janine another hug. Jill started to laugh again.

I asked Tre what he thought had gone wrong and why the whole experience had seemed a bit weird, but he didn't know either. Back at school, word got out in our class about me and Janine and everyone was talking about it. I felt embarrassed and just tried to keep my head down. Before I knew it, though, Janine came to speak to me and said, 'I don't think it's a good idea that we see each other, because everyone knows and I don't want people to talk about me, so let's just be friends.' I felt humiliated. Not only was I a laughing stock in my class, but something that might have blossomed into something, at least in my mind, had suddenly come tumbling down. Janine and I did not speak for a long time and I became more annoyed than upset in the end. I began to think that all girls must be like Janine and so I felt an element of resentment towards them.

I became apprehensive about dating, so I took a step back and focussed more on school and having fun with Tre. After a while, though, Tre developed a personality trait where he would make fun of just about anyone, including me. At times it was funny, but at other times it was way over the top and I took offence. Tre making fun of me in front of our classmates opened up opportunities for others to do likewise, which made me self-conscious to the point that I could not walk down a corridor without feeling as if the other students were looking at me and making fun of me behind my back. When it showed no signs of stopping, I started to socialise with other students in different classes to take the pressure off a bit.

Back at home, Tommy received bad news about his brother, Ronald. He had been in a car accident in America and had been put on a life support machine as a result. It was decided that Tommy would go to see him in hospital there. Ronald had been a black-cab driver in

London before meeting his wife and moving to America, where he continued his taxi career. Tommy had six brothers, but Ronald was the oldest and the closest to Tommy, so it hit him hard. I was just excited that Tommy was going away, because that meant I could relax more around my own house.

While Tommy was away, I was happier than I'd been for a long time. I even had Tre over to the house to play videos games and listen to hip hop. One Saturday afternoon, we were listening to the radio when we heard the tragic news of Tupac Shakur's death. I was truly shocked, because no other artists resonated with me to the extent that Tupac had. After a few weeks, Tommy called to tell my mother that Ronald had passed away, but all I could think about on hearing the news of Ronald's death was how much freedom might I have left until Tommy returned, so I made the most of it while I could.

When Tommy did return, the mood in the house nosedived. His aura had changed from his usual aggression to one of sudden loss. I honestly did not feel any sympathy whatsoever for him, though, just a deep-rooted disappointment that he was back. After years of abuse, I had built up a mental wall between myself and Tommy.

I kept my focus on school as per usual, but on weekends Tommy began to harass me by coming into my bedroom early in the morning, pulling my duvet cover off and making loud noises with a metal spoon and a cooking pot. It was the only place he could get to me, because I spent most of my time in my bedroom when I wasn't at school. He would also put the dirty bowls that he had used for his breakfast on my bed, which not only smelled but meant also that I needed to clean my bedsheets on a regular basis.

Things in the house started to calm down slightly towards the end of the year and Tommy began to back off. My mother had a new job as a legal secretary in Central London and, as Tommy had been out of work for a very long time, he wanted to try his hand at being a black-cab driver like his brother Ronald. To obtain a black-cab licence you need to study London's roads and pass a very strict test known as 'the Knowledge', but Tommy had other ideas. He had brought Ronald's belongings back with him from America, not just his clothes, shoes, pictures and some jewellery, but also his identification papers, including his passport, birth certificate and taxi licence. Tommy proceeded to shave his hair off to look more like his brother and then use Ronald's ID to become a taxi driver. It never occurred to me to report Tommy, but I hoped he would get caught and be sent to prison for fraud.

Not long after Tommy got his fraudulent ID, he began to work as a black-cab driver. The great thing about this for me was that he always worked nights, so after a while I hardly saw him around the house. With both Tommy and my mother working, they began to save for a holiday. They decided that during the summer break from school we would all go to Jamaica to stay with Tommy's dad. Two weeks after school broke up, then, we were on a plane heading to Jamaica. The flight was the most exciting thing about the whole experience for me, because I got a rush of excitement before take-off, similar to the feeling you get waiting for a rollercoaster ride to begin, and as we took off I got a rush of adrenalin from the acceleration and climbing. As soon as we landed in Jamaica, though, things went rapidly downhill.

The house belonging to Tommy's father was located on a farm he owned, but it was still being developed. In fact, it was pretty much a concrete shell with no windows, no paint, no carpet and no floorboards even. There was no boiler in the house, so there was only cold water throughout, including in the shower. Tommy's father, Cuthbert, had a cow, a goat, some chickens and three dogs, which were used as guard dogs. This meant they were not allowed in the house and always stayed outside. This is common in Jamaica, but it means the dogs are generally more aggressive and bark a lot. Cuthbert also had two servants on the property, an old Jamaican lady called Betty and her son Justice. Betty cooked and cleaned around the house, while Justice took care of the exterior, including the farmland.

For the first few days I found it hard, because I had to sleep in a bed with a mosquito net attached to it in a bedroom with no windows. My body also remained on London time, so I would find myself awake before everyone else at 5 a.m., often being woken by the roosters. Although it was hot in Jamaica, I did not find the cold showers at all pleasant, but I soon overheated like everyone else when the sun got higher in the sky. The only thing to keep us cool during the day was a metal fan, which had no cover attached to it. One afternoon, I had an accident when one of the blades nearly sliced my finger off. The cut was deep, but all anybody had to cover it with was a plaster, so that's what they did.

Most days we were stuck on the farm and didn't go anywhere, so I got bored very quickly and really wanted to get back to London as soon as possible. On the odd occasion we got to travel somewhere, most of us had to sit in the open back of Cuthbert's Toyota pickup truck, which was really quite dangerous as there were no seats for us to sit on. Some days we went to the beach and on other days we went into town, where it was even more dangerous than the back of the pickup truck. While driving through downtown on one occasion, we saw a man being robbed at knifepoint. The weirdest thing about that was that everyone seemed quite casual about it, like it was an everyday occurrence.

One evening we took a trip to a Chinese restaurant on the other side of the island, so it took us over two hours to drive there. By the time we had finished eating, it was dark and the temperature had dropped considerably, which meant it was freezing at the back of the truck. My mother and Tommy were sitting with Sophie and Sarah right by the driver's cabin, where it was nice and warm. I asked my mother if Laura and I could sit there as well, because we were cold and the only place we could rest our backs was on the rear flap of the truck, which was dangerous because it wasn't that secure and it could easily have dropped down. She told us 'no', so for the whole two-hour drive back Laura and I froze while leaning on a piece of metal that could have retracted at any moment. Luckily, the flap stayed upright and we got back safely, but I considered my mother to be the cruellest person in the world at that point in time, because her actions really brought home her negligence towards me and Laura and her favouritism towards Tommy and their two daughters. Laura and I were clearly the outcasts in that group and from that moment on a deep-seated resentment towards my mother began to develop within me. For years on end she used me and Laura as babysitters for our two young stepsisters, because we had to look after them during holidays and after school until she or Tommy got home from work, but she never showed us anything like as much love as she showed them.

Two days later, I was walking around the farm by myself, having a look at the land and the animals. When I started to walk back to the house, the dogs started to growl at me as if they were about to attack. As I was still quite a distance from the house, I got nervous and I started to run as fast as I could. I was scared that I was going to be mauled and I could even feel the fur of one of the dogs at my ankle as I ran. I buckled over suddenly on to a rock and slid off it to the ground, slicing my right thigh on the concrete when I landed. The dogs ran away as I lay there screaming and the cut in my thigh was so deep it was gushing blood down my leg. I managed to get myself up and limp back to the house, where I showed my mother what had happened, and we headed off to the local hospital. The cut was stinging so much I could barely stand it. When we got to the hospital, they washed a purple antiseptic dye over my wound to prevent infection and ease the pain. There was no doubt, though, that I was going to have a permanent scar on my thigh.

I was so nervous throughout my time on the farm that I wet the bed quite a lot, which meant that I had to start many of my days there with hard punches to the head or chest. It was Tommy's way of 'teaching me a lesson'. I had taken about as much as I could take for one holiday and just wanted to jump on a plane and fly back to London, but I had to endure the rest of the holiday for another few days before that happened.

The day before we were due to leave, Cuthbert decided to have a big dinner and to invite a number of locals to join us for that. At around 2 p.m., a truck full of men turned up at the farm, walked towards the goat, tied it by its legs, hung it upside down and chopped its head off. Although I ate meat on a regular basis, I had never seen an animal being slaughtered and I found the sight of it quite sickening.

The men then proceeded to skin the goat and completely butcher it, cutting out its insides, slicing through its flesh and throwing different cuts into different pans. They cooked different dishes with it, including curried goat and goat soup. I felt so sick that I completely lost my appetite, but my mother told me that I had to eat something. I tried the soup, but because I couldn't get the image of all that blood pouring out of the goat's throat from my mind, I couldn't finish it and I was told off for that. It didn't put me off eating meat, but I knew that I didn't want ever again to see animals slaughtered in front of me before eating them.

Finally, we flew back to London and all I could think about on the journey was that I never wanted to return to Jamaica and that I certainly never wanted to go on holiday with my mother again.

About a month after we settled back into London life, my mother told me and Laura that our Dad and his girlfriend Julia had recently had a baby girl. I assumed that I would now be put to one side by my Dad, just as I had been put to one side by my mother after she had children with Tommy.

Following on from the dreadful holiday in Jamaica, the news about my Dad left me feeling trapped. With no one to turn to, I felt like I was walking with a heavy heart into a very dark corner.

Chapter 8:
An unwelcome marriage and a family slave

There were a million and one other places I wished I could have been rather than at my mother's wedding.

I didn't say much about my holiday in Jamaica to anyone when I got back to London. The summer holidays were soon over, and I started Year 8 at Greenfield. Laura was also starting at Greenfield, in Year 7, which meant we got the same bus to school in the mornings. I made my presence known when she had her first day at the school by walking into her class with her. That way her classmates knew who I was and knew that if they had any problems with her that they would need to deal with me as well.

When I settled back into the school routine, everything was pretty much the same as it had been the previous year, except I now needed to look out for my sister as well. There were many incidents of bullying towards students in the year below us, so every lunchtime I checked to see that Laura was okay. I also spoke to Warren to make sure he told the students in his class that my sister (his cousin) was in the year below and that nobody was to bully her.

Tre was still trying to find himself and continued to make fun of everyone around him. At times it was funny still, but there were other times when he took things too far and we soon fell out over something silly that he said. This caused an atmosphere between us and we started to sit at separate tables and mix with different students. I think because we had been friends for so long, and had never argued until then, that maybe we just needed a bit of space from one other. It wasn't exactly uncommon to see students fall out with one another and go off to mix with a different group of friends.

Another break-up of friendship that occurred around that time was with Warren and some of his classmates. Warren was becoming very disruptive in his classes and was hanging around with other disruptive students. He was very bright, but he found it hard to concentrate for too long and was always looking for ways to cause problems or provoke a situation.

As I had fallen out with Tre, I knew I had to make friends with someone else, which led me to talk to Hassan, another student in my class. His family was from the Turkish part of Cyprus, and he hung around with a group of boys who were known as the 'nerds' in our class. He and his friends were indeed smart, and they helped me with my schoolwork to the extent that I started to understand my classes much better. Tre, on the other hand, never seemed to take his schoolwork seriously and started to hang around with a group of boys in our class who mostly played football at break times.

I got along with Hassan so well that he started to invite me to his house after school and on the weekends. It was an eye-opening experience for me, because Hassan's father owned a clothing factory and his mother had a great job working in the city, which meant the family was reasonably wealthy. The first day that I went to Hassan's house I was amazed at how big it was and how it had everything my house didn't have. They had a big-screen television in the living area, a separate dining area, a spare living room and a huge kitchen. Hassan's bedroom was the largest I had ever seen, and in it he had different games consoles, a PC, a large television and a cool stereo player. To me it was like something out of these TV shows that let you see how rich people live. I was so grateful just to be in that environment, because Hassan's parents seemed to like me and Hassan and I had a lot of fun just playing on his games consoles and eating food. We got along so well that I used to go to Hassan's house in the mornings so we could walk to school together and talk about different things (Laura was okay to get the bus on her own by this time).

On the home front, things calmed down because Tommy was busy working as an illegal taxi driver. My mother often took us all to a Chinese restaurant on weekends, which I certainly didn't mind because I loved Chinese food. On one visit to the restaurant, Tommy had got dressed up and seemed excited about something. He said he wanted to ask my mother a question. He then took a small box out of his pocket and proposed to my mother right there in front of us. He didn't get down on one knee or anything, he just gave her the ring and asked her the question. My mother happily accepted and I simply didn't care, because it didn't feel particularly relevant within the little bubble I inhabited at the time. It never dawned on me what the significance of them getting married might be, and I wasn't really sure how to take it all in, apart from being repulsed at how my mother continued to be taken in by the evil Tommy.

As my birthday approached in December that year, I really wanted a stereo to be like Hassan and asked my mother for one. She couldn't afford it, so she asked my grandfather Desmond, who luckily got me one for my birthday. Once I had set it up in my bedroom, I felt like I had the complete entertainment system and was able to fit in more with Hassan. It also gave me the opportunity to listen to the music which I had a passion for.

In February 1998, I was having lunch at school when a group of boys from my class were sitting next to me. We were having an argument about something or other, which turned into us all saying some pretty nasty things to one another. To my surprise, Tre came out of nowhere and defended me. It was weird, because we had not spoken for months, but we began talking again and it was good to have my old friend back. Having settled our differences, we started to hang around Hassan's group together.

My mother and Tommy wanted to have their wedding at Easter and began looking for venues. They decided on an old building that used to be a children's nursery in Tottenham Hale. I had images in my mind from television of weddings being held at glamorous venues, so when I saw the place they chose I was taken aback – it looked like a complete dump. I thought about the house we had stayed in over in Jamaica and assumed that the wedding venue must have been found by Tommy, because everything associated with him seemed to turn into a complete disaster.

When the day of the wedding came around, I was more excited about dressing up in my suit than going to the ceremony or reception. We began the day by heading to the registry office in Wood Green and had our pictures taken in a field nearby. Then we went to the ex-nursery for the reception. Overall, it was just a bit boring for us children and I found it a bit weird to see my mother and Tommy's families in the same place together.

My mother's brother, Uncle Stewart, gave a speech. He said that Tommy was a good man because he not only supported his own family but had also taken on responsibility for two children that weren't his, meaning me and Laura. I thought the speech forgot to mention the years of abuse that we all had to endure and the cheating with other women that Tommy had indulged in. I just wanted the day to come to an end so that I could go back home and listen to my music.

A week later, the newlyweds flew off to their honeymoon in Jamaica and, luckily for us, my sisters and I got to stay at my grandmother Ann's house. My mother and Tommy spent two weeks in Jamaica, and we had a lot of fun while they were away.

When they returned, it was time to go back to school following the Easter break. I began to take a keen interest in drama classes, where we acted out scenes involving characters that included the Native Americans of the Wild West and astronauts in space. Drama gave me an outlet I could channel much of my energy into, and it taught me how to become someone completely different, someone who wasn't Dean, a vulnerable and abused child. I enjoyed drama more than any other class, because I could physically and emotionally venture off into a completely different realm. Even if these escapes from reality only lasted fifteen minutes at a time, they were still fifteen minutes of living a life away from the other problems that surrounded me.

One afternoon, my mother and Tommy took us for a drive in Tommy's taxi to visit family. While Tommy was driving, my mother looked at Laura and me and told us that she needed to ask us something. 'Tommy wants to know if you would like to have your surnames changed to his?' she said. She said it was because they were married now, but I think the real reason was that Tommy was embarrassed that he couldn't address us as his own children whenever visitors came to the house. There was also an element of him trying to cut our Dad out of the picture, I think. In any event, the first thoughts that popped into my mind were anger and irritation. This man who had abused me for so many years wanted me to have his name and the thought of that disgusted me. I firmly declined my mother's suggestion and said that I was perfectly happy with my own name. Laura followed suit and Tommy looked sad, but I didn't feel an ounce of sympathy for him. I felt that the suggested name change was another way for him to control us, and also a way to pull the wool over people's eyes about what he had done to me.

As Tommy's taxi work was becoming very demanding, and Laura and I had more and more homework to do, chores around the house such as cleaning and maintenance were not being carried out. Instead of hiring a cleaner, Tommy had the idea that we should get one of his relatives to help out, so he called his father in Jamaica to discuss the possibility of bringing his uncle John (his father's brother) to the UK. John's nickname was Barrel, and he lived in a wooden shack in Jamaica and didn't have much in terms of material possessions or wealth. Tommy thought that, in return for paying for a plane ticket and allowing him to stay with us, Barrel could help around the house. So, not long after that conversation, the flight was booked and Barrel on his way to London.

Barrel had long black hair, dark brown skin, a scar on his face and a strong Jamaican accent. He was in his late fifties and had an intimidating but frail look about him. His clothes were wrinkled, and he had an odour due to the fact that he never showered much. I didn't know what to make of him, and neither did my sisters, but it was certainly weird having a complete stranger living amongst us all of a sudden.

As there were already six of us occupying a three-bedroom house, there was no room for Barrel to sleep in. Tommy told him to sleep downstairs on the floor, but we didn't have any spare blankets, so Barrel just slept in the clothes he arrived in. Laura and I would see him in the mornings lying on the floor, and the rest of the time he just seemed to sit in absolute silence. He wasn't used to a house with modern technology like a television or kitchen appliances, and he certainly wasn't comfortable amongst people, let alone teenagers, so we never even said good morning to each other. After allowing him a short settling-in period, Tommy began to instruct his uncle on the things that he needed to do around the house and the garden.

After a while, Tommy asked me if his uncle spoke to us in the morning and I told him that he was very quiet. Eventually Tommy started to talk down to Barrel as if he was a child, telling him that he needed to say hello to me and Laura in the mornings and that he needed to shower on a regular basis because he smelled. On the surface, it looked pretty much like slavery, because this man was sleeping on a floor with no covers but had to do whatever he was told around the house and garden.

Once, when Tre stayed over, he asked me who Barrel was and I told him that it was Tommy's uncle. Because it didn't look that way to Tre, the following day in school he told the rest of our classmates that I had a butler from Jamaica. This was Tre's way of putting a comedic spin on the situation and I found it hilarious, so I just ran with the idea. Tre even went as far as to make out that we were rich, knowing full well that there wasn't another student in our school that could question the story. No matter how rich the parents of some of the other schoolkids might have been, there had certainly never been any talk about anyone having a butler at home. The idea spread like wildfire around the school and the comedic element that attached to a Jamaican butler made me popular with everyone. Without knowing it, Barrel was changing my life, at least for a while at school. This shift in dynamics boosted my confidence and I found myself socialising with students from different years.

For Barrel, however, life had taken a very different turn. Tommy managed to get him a job with the local council through a friend of his. It was a cash-in-hand job so that the taxman wouldn't clock on to Barrel's increasingly long stay and illegal employment in the UK. The job at least helped Barrel to get away from the house for a while, but you could see the increasing resentment he felt towards Tommy, who was, after all, treating this family member as a slave. I can't begin to imagine how embarrassing it must have been for Barrel to be treated so disrespectfully in front of his own nephew's family.

Chapter 9:
Going off the rails before finally gaining a degree of control

It's not abnormal for children to go through a rebellious phase at school. It's like you've been led into a world where it's fun to break the rules.

In September 1999, I began Year 9 at Greenfield. As it was the year prior to working towards our GCSEs in Years 10 and 11, it was more like a preparation year than anything else and our classes became mixed with different students according to the subjects we were taking. I didn't really understand the significance of the preparation year and I became distracted and disruptive, easily influenced by some of the students in the years above me. Drugs and alcohol were popular and readily available, and Warren began to bunk lessons in order to smoke drugs with his gang of friends. I, on the other hand, developed a fascination with money and began to bring things into school to sell to other students. When my birthday came, I asked for small items, including a Walkman, computer games, video films and CDs. I stored these in a shoebox under my bed and then took them to school to sell to my friends.

Prior to my mother's wedding, she and Tommy had their hen and stag parties respectively. As was traditional, they had each received a number of gifts, many of which were stored in the attic of the house. One Saturday afternoon, when I was at home alone, I went to check in the attic for anything that I could sell. In one corner, I saw a couple of bags that looked new, so I peered inside and saw all the gifts from my mother's hen party. There were sex books, sex toys and porn films. I didn't want to make it obvious that things were missing, so I just took a couple of the porn films and two sex books. The books were every bit as pornographic as the films and I decided to keep them in my room for a few weeks to see if anyone noticed they were missing. After about a month, I took one of the books to show Tre. As he had never seen anything remotely pornographic before, he was fascinated by it, so I let him have it. I didn't feel bad about taking stuff from the attic, because my main driver at the time was to make some money. I made copies of the films and sold a lot of them at school for £10 per VHS cassette.

I had long since felt left out by students who brought their lunch from outside and I didn't like the school lunches much either. Tommy had a pouch in which he kept his change for the passengers that used his taxi, and I saw this as an opportunity to rectify my lunch problem. The pouch was always left downstairs in the living room and every morning I took some pound coins from it. It was easy, because there were so many of them and he never counted how much money he had in there anyway. I saw it as an opportunity to get my own back on him. I thought it was proper retribution for treating me so badly for so many years.

When Tre stayed over once, he noticed me taking money from Tommy's pouch and he said 'shit, what are you doing?'

'I don't give a fuck,' I said. 'I'm taking it. What shall we get for lunch today?'

I bought us both lunch, which Tre found hilarious. I think he could tell that I resented Tommy, but it was never mentioned.

Tre was also showing signs of rebellion at that time. He was disruptive in class and trashed our form room by leaving rubbish behind cupboards and swinging like Tarzan on the curtains, which fell off. Because nobody ever snitched on anyone else, the teachers decided to ban the whole year from using the form room at lunchtimes. It was as if the whole year had taken a crazy pill, because most of us were rebellious and really didn't care about much else. Fights were commonplace in our class, with other classes and even with students from other schools. Many of the teachers were strict enough to impose some discipline, but there were just too many of us for them to deal with.

Mrs Carter was teaching us Humanities that year and for some reason she began picking me out of the whole class as the cause of many of the minor disruptions she faced each day. It got worse and we ended up arguing with each other during most classes due to me not being able to keep up with the rest of the students. I didn't in fact understand much about what I was being taught, and I had tried to explain that to Mrs Carter, but her irritation with me was deep-rooted and she never really took what I said on board. It eventually came to a head during a parents' evening that my mother came to, and it was decided that I needed additional support.

I took after-school literacy classes, but the stigma attached to those only made me feel more stupid because I was in there with other students who had severe learning difficulties such as ADHD (attention deficit hyperactivity disorder). I knew I wasn't on the same level as the students with the major learning difficulties, but handwriting and understanding some of the educational content in class did often confuse me. I had treated school up to that point as a way to channel my thoughts and energy away from the abuse I suffered at home, so learning had always been very much secondary to that. What with my money-making schemes, the money I was spending from Tommy's pouch, having fun and arguing with teachers, I can honestly say that actual education took up a very small portion of my typical day at school.

On the weekends, whenever there was a family gathering or a party, there would be drinking involved. It never appealed to me because it smelled horrible, but with all the madness going on at school it just seemed like the right thing to do. I mean, all the adults were doing it and it looked like they were having fun, at least until the arguing and fighting started up again. When Tre stayed over one weekend, everyone was out so I suggested that we have a drink. He said, 'yeah, okay, let's try some', so I went to the cupboard and got a bottle of Jamaican dark rum. Because I had seen my uncles pour drinks, I knew what to do, so I got two glasses, filled a quarter of them with rum and the rest with coke. We said 'cheers', knocked the glasses together and started to drink. At first it tasted weird, because of the alcohol, but the sweetness of the coke soon counterbalanced that. We only had one glass, because we only wanted to know what it felt like to be adults.

At the time my older cousins were into smoking, and I wasn't sure how I felt about it, but because they were all doing it, I wanted to try as well. One day after school, I saw Warren and we took the bus back to the flat where he lived with his mother, my Aunt Mariam. By this time Warren was smoking cigarettes and weed, so I knew he would have cigarettes with him, and I asked him if I could smoke one with him. He took out a gold-coloured box of twenty Benson and Hedges and pulled one out for us.

'How do I smoke it?' I asked.

'Just inhale it by the tip and exhale through your mouth,' he told me, making it sound like the most normal thing in the world. I took the first pull of the cigarette and started to cough like crazy; it felt like I was inhaling fire into my chest.

'Your lungs are not used to it, but they will be in time,' Warren said, as if he had a vested interest in my curiosity.

Soon I started to smoke in the mornings on the way to school and sometimes at lunchtime. Whenever I was around my cousins I would smoke, but I stayed away from weed because I was scared to try it. My mother smoked at least forty cigarettes a day and, although for most of my life up to that point I had hated the smell of her smoking, I was now doing it myself out of curiosity. It did make me feel part of the crowd, but I never felt that I gained any good from it physically. Because I wanted to budget my money, I bought a cheaper brand of cigarettes and always got a pack of just ten. In order to buy them, I had to go into shops that would think I was older than I actually was and, luckily, I found a shop not far from my school. At other times I would get someone older, such as the students from the years above me or my older cousins, to buy them for me. I smoked maybe twice a day during the week at school, but it was harder on the weekends because I was at home and couldn't take the risk of getting caught.

My money-making schemes were going so well that I began selling condoms to other students in my year, which caught the attention of a new student in my class called Kos. Kos came from a Greek Cypriot family and was reasonably wealthy. He was one of the strongest boys in our class and I started to hang around with him after selling some small electrical goods to him. He was also into smoking, and he told me about a chewing gum called 'Airways', which was a strong menthol gum that was able to mask the smell of smoking.

One Saturday evening, I took a risk and smoked out of my bedroom window after I thought everyone had gone to bed. Unfortunately, Tommy came into my room and caught me. He started shouting and told my mother and they were both mad at me. Although I was nervous when I got caught, I didn't say much, which caused an atmosphere in the house. I scaled down my money-making schemes for a while, because I didn't want my mother finding out about the money I was making. Things at school were becoming out of control and I was hanging around mostly with Kos. This annoyed Tre so much that he told me I was turning bad, but I wasn't too bothered what he thought. I even found myself in detention with Kos for disrupting classes and falling behind on schoolwork.

What I was doing felt perfectly normal to me because everyone I knew behaved in similar fashion. Things got really out of hand, though, when I came into school one Thursday and Kos told me that he had a firework that he wanted to set off there. I didn't really care about the risks involved, so I just went with the idea. On our first break of the day, we went to the field near our football pitches, and I kneeled down and planted the firework. I took a lighter that Kos gave me and lit it. As we were running back to the school building, the firework let off a loud bang. Other students, who wanted to see what was going, saw me and Kos running away as they headed towards where the firework had gone off. As soon as the break was over it sunk in what had happened, and I knew someone was going to tell the teachers that it was me and Kos that were responsible.

By lunchtime Mrs Carter had found me in our form class and told me that she had heard that Kos and I had set off the firework. I understood the position I was in, so I just came clean. Because I felt loyal to Kos, I didn't snitch on him and said that the whole thing was my idea. Mrs Carter took me to the staffroom and told me to wait there while she went off to call my mother. Instead of feeling remorse for my actions, I began looking around the staffroom for something of value. I soon found a full pack of twenty cigarettes and put it in my pocket. After my mother got the call at her place of work, she called Tommy and they both came down to the school in his taxi. The senior teacher for our year told them that the school needed to suspend me for two days as punishment for setting off a firework and endangering the other students. My mother and Tommy looked embarrassed and angry, and I was embarrassed myself at having to walk alongside them in full view of the students in the playground at the time.

When we got back to the house, my mother and Tommy searched me and my room and found all my money, the porn videos, the electrical goods and the condoms. She took my favourite stuff out of my room as well, including my television and stereo. She told me that I wouldn't get my stuff back and that I needed to sort my life out. Tommy didn't say much at all.

The following day, after my mother had fully absorbed what I had done, she told me that I could do what I wanted from that point on and that if anything bad happened to me it was going to be my problem, not hers. I felt a huge weight lift from my shoulders at the thought of being empowered to take control of my life. I found my money in a kitchen drawer and took it, along with all my other things, back to my room. As my suspension happened just before the half-term break, I had a week off to think things through. I decided that I no longer had any need to rebel now that I had been given control of my own life. Looking back at it now, I can see what a clever move that was on the part of my mother.

After half-term break, things started to change for the better, although when I got back from school one day Tommy confronted me by asking whether I had told anyone about him doing his taxi driving illegally. I told him I hadn't, and he let it drop. He later discovered that his own mother had told a lot of people and that was what had put him at risk. When he found this out, it actually cleared the air a bit in our house and our relationship started to improve as a result. Tommy had to stop doing the taxi driving, though, and he started to do what he should have done in the beginning, which was to study 'the Knowledge'.

As I adjusted back into school life, I remained friends with Kos, but I started to back away from all the mad things that were happening around me and concentrated instead on my schoolwork.

On the home front, Barrel continued to get a raw deal. Any money he made from his day job he spent in buying us all takeaway food. The cost of feeding seven people in this way was horribly expensive, so he literally had nothing left for himself. My mother and Tommy never bothered to contribute and let Barrel carry on paying for everything. Because Barrel was becoming experienced working in our garden, my mother's family started to use him to work on their gardens as well, including doing brickwork, but no one paid the man. He was literally a modern-day slave. I didn't like anything about Tommy, but I thought his treatment of Barrel was deeply wrong even by his standards.

Chapter 10:
My first girlfriend

Having a relationship with a girl at school can be wildly exciting, but also very confusing!

Just before the end of Year 9 my mother agreed with me that the issues I had with Mrs Carter needed to be addressed. My mother went to the school to speak to her and, when she didn't get the answers she wanted, she gave Mrs Carter strict instructions that I should be moved to another Humanities class. It was decided that I should join the new class when I came back to start Year 10. Although I was happy to finally get away from Mrs Carter, I wasn't pleased about seeing less of the friends in my old class or joining a different class where I didn't know anyone.

Once the summer had passed and Year 10 began for me in September of 2000, I had a much more positive and grown-up outlook on school. I was coming up to sixteen years of age and Year 10 was the start of our two-year GCSE stage at school, which meant we would be working during Year 10 towards our GCSE exams in Year 11. On our first day, Mrs Carter went through our registration. As Humanities was the first lesson of the day, she told me to make my way to H10, which is where I would be taking my new Humanities lessons with my new class.

When I walked in, I was very nervous, because I only knew one boy in the class. I sat down at a desk close to the corner. The rest of the class, of course, were already familiar with the teacher, Mrs Bailey. Our first topic of discussion was on heredity, on the passing down of genetics from one generation to the next. Many of the students contributed ideas as if it was second nature to them. I, on the other hand, was worried that I would be ridiculed if I made a mistake, so I refrained from participating. After the class I told myself that I would have to make more of an effort with my education, that I would have to at least try to seem a little bit more intelligent to fit in with everyone else. It was clear to me that GCSE level in Year 10 was going to be a challenge and that I would have to concentrate more.

The separation from my old class did help in that sense. The good thing about GCSEs, of course, is that you are able to choose some of the subjects that interest you the most. I chose Media, IT, Electronics and Drama. All my other subjects, including Maths, English, Science, Religious Education, Humanities and a foreign language were compulsory. I also received additional literacy tuition to help me with my reading and writing, and therefore learning, skills. I was very embarrassed about that, but the tutor was very helpful, and the tuition was ultimately to be of great benefit to me, but it would take time.

The lesson I was most unsure about was the foreign language. I had a basic understanding of German from previous years, so I was put into the intermediate class. I found German and Electronics the two most difficult subjects to understand. I couldn't do anything about my Electronics class as there was only one level, but German classes were broken into three levels. After two weeks at the intermediate level, I tried to explain to the teacher that the class was too hard for me and that I wanted to go down to the foundation level, but this was rejected.

Tre was doing the foundation level and I asked him what the class was like. He said, 'It's all just fun, the teacher is too soft on us and we can do what we want.' After he told me this, I just turned up at the class and told the teacher, Mrs Jennings, that I was joining her class because I couldn't manage the intermediate level. Before I knew it, the intermediate teacher had marched into the class to tell me to go back with her.

'No, it's too hard,' I said. 'I'm staying here'.

To my surprise, she didn't argue.

'If that's what you want, then,' she said, 'but you're not doing yourself any favours.'

Mrs Jennings could only be described as one of the most timid teachers in the whole school. She had almost no control over the class, which was more like a circus, with no structure whatsoever. Students used to turn up late, or sometimes not at all, and everyone used to swear at Mrs Jennings just for the sake of it. One of the girls in the class was pregnant and spent her time making a list of baby names to choose from.

There was one instance when a student called James was smoking a spliff out of the window before class was about to start. When Mrs Jennings came in, she said, 'James, put that out now.'

'Okay, miss, I'm nearly finished, let me just take my last few pulls,' James said and carried on smoking his spliff as if that was a perfectly normal thing to do.

I knew that German was never going to be a place of learning for me, so I used the class as a place to unwind and ease the pressures of all my other classes.

During my drama classes we began to take lessons in 'mask work', which involved us wearing a mask and acting out the fixed expression on that mask physically through our bodies. I chose a mask that had a look of anxiety and began to get into the mindset of such a character. I imagined someone who worked in a shoe shop and was under pressure to meet the needs of a demanding and awkward customer. I really felt the pressure and even drew on bad experiences at home to get into character. The teacher was so impressed that she made notes of what I had done and told me that I had got into the character really well. From that point onwards, I began to look at acting as a tool. I realised that people in real life, whether they were policemen or teachers or anything else, were essentially playing a role when they were at work, and that the depth of their true selves was buried under the mask they wore at work.

After a while I became comfortable in my new Humanities class and I drew the attention of a girl called Dianne, who was sitting at the desk to the left of me. She had lovely milk-chocolate-coloured skin and a nice smile, wore glasses and had hair down to her neck. Our interaction began with general talk about the class and trying to understand the GCSE content. After a while, I heard rumours from other students, including my friends, that Dianne had taken an interest in me. I simply brushed them off, though, as I was still very shy following my embarrassing experience with Janine. One afternoon, when our Humanities class had ended, Dianne asked for my number. I gave her my home number and she told me she would call over the weekend.

On the Saturday afternoon, when I got home after playing pool with Warren at Edmonton Pool Hall, I was barely through the front door when my mother told me that Dianne had called. She had left her home number, but I became nervous about the prospect of ringing her back. After an hour, I finally plucked up the courage, but there was a nervous hesitation in my stomach, which seemed to pulsate all the way to my fingers as I dialled the number. After a few rings, Dianne picked up and said 'hello'. Her voice sounded beautiful.

'Hi, you okay? It's Dean,' I said, trying to sound controlled and confident. It soon became apparent, though, that Dianne was more experienced in these kinds of situations, and she simply led the conversation from that point onwards. We spoke about me playing pool with Warren and about what she had been doing, and soon we were talking about the cinema and other dating options.

'Would you like to meet up next weekend and go see a film together?' she asked, sounding very enthusiastic.

'Sounds good to me,' I said, trying to disguise the excitement I felt.

During the following week, when I arrived for my Humanities class just after lunch, Dianne was already there and was sitting by herself at a desk built to seat two students.

'Hey, come and sit next to me today,' she said, as if it was the most natural thing in the world.

I smiled and sat down next to her, trying to look composed. As the lesson began, we worked together through the topic of hereditary behaviour patterns, and I tried hard to come across as smart in order to impress her. It seemed to work, but the content of the work truly racked my brain. Once class was finished, we smiled at each other and headed back to our own form classes. I felt a combination of excitement and nervousness, thinking maybe there was more to life than just turning up to school and learning. I hadn't ever envisaged enjoying schoolwork with someone I liked a lot.

As it drew closer to the weekend, I thought long and hard about what to wear for my date with Dianne. At the time, I was going through a baseball cap phase and always wore one whenever I was out and about. I had a navy-blue Tommy Hilfiger cap that I had received as a gift from my cousin Elle, so I decided that I would wear that with a navy sports jacket, navy jeans, black jumper and smart shoes. Dating attire was as alien to me as the Japanese language, but I thought if I just threw together the best clothes I could find then I'd probably be okay. I didn't try to coordinate my outfit as such, because I had no idea what went with what anyway.

The big day arrived and I told my mother that I was going to the cinema with Tre. She probably knew I was lying, because I had taken a bath, combed my hair and got changed into my smartest clothes. When I called Dianne, she said: 'Come to my house first and we can go to the cinema from there.'

I headed out at around 7 p.m. As Dianne lived just ten minutes from our school, I pretty much took the same route that I always took on schooldays. I was very nervous, and when I got there I was amazed at how nice the house was. It was detached, with new double-glazed windows and a tidy front garden. I hesitantly rang the doorbell. When Dianne opened the door, she looked amazing. She was wearing a tight black top, black skirt down to her knees and black shoes. She invited me in and introduced me to her mother, Delores. I was a bit taken back as I had never met any girl's mother before.

Dianne told me that she was going to finish getting ready upstairs, so I sat down and spoke to her mother. We spoke about my family background and what I liked to do in my spare time. Delores began to speak about her daughter and asked me if Dianne had told me about her singing and music. I said that she had never mentioned it, just as Dianne walked back in and blushed when she realised that we were talking about her.

On the way to the cinema, I asked her about her singing, because I was genuinely curious about it.

'I got into singing at the age of thirteen and it's been a passion of mine ever since,' was all she said.

When we got to the cinema, we bought tickets to see a comedy called *Blue Streak*. We got drinks and popcorn and headed to our seats to watch the trailers. When the film started, I was too distracted by Dianne to concentrate on it very much.

Suddenly, she whispered: 'Give me your hand.' She took it and wrapped my arm around her neck. My hand came to rest on her breasts, and I completely froze. I had no idea what to do, so I just smiled at her.

'Take your cap off, I want to see your hair,' she then said.

I took it off and she rubbed my hair and told me that she preferred me without the cap. At that point we gazed into each other's eyes and began to kiss. Almost instinctively, I began to squeeze her breasts, which quickly resulted in my intense arousal. That was my first kiss, and it would probably not have happened at that time without Dianne leading the way. Dianne had been out with a couple of guys before me and had more experience with the whole dating thing. I think she felt comfortable around me due to my easy-going, submissive approach to whatever she instigated.

Once the film had ended, we walked out of the cinema hand in hand towards the bus stop. It was my first serious date, and I was mesmerised by it. It was the first time a girl had shown that sort of interest in me and it was the first truly intimate moment of my life. It felt great. As we parted ways at the bus stop, it was obvious that we were very attracted to each other, and things began to blossom from there.

At school I began to develop headaches in the afternoon, so I started to take paracetamol tablets to ease the pain. The problem was I began to depend on them very quickly. It was only when I went to see an optician that I discovered that I needed to wear glasses to prevent the eye strain that was causing my headaches.

Dianne and I hung around together a lot and on one occasion I went up and hugged her from behind while she was standing outside the tuck shop with her friends. To my surprise, she moved away from me as if it was some sort of inconvenience for her, and her friends just stared at me as if I was mad. Dianne eventually turned around, said 'hello' and smiled awkwardly at me. I didn't say anything, because I was confused, and then the bell rang so we headed back to our classes.

That evening, when we were on the phone, Dianne explained that she didn't want people to see us at school doing anything affectionate, because she thought it drew too much attention from the other students. I knew she was popular in our year, but I hadn't realised she cared so much about what others thought of her. I was a bit taken back, as I had been under the impression that we were okay to act naturally around each other. I went with her suggestion, but I remained confused. I had completely opened up to a girl for the first time, only to discover that there was a condition attached to the relationship, a condition that required me to be discreet.

In a way, it felt like I was being told not to express my true self and I quickly became a bit wary of the whole situation. Instead of confronting Dianne about it, though, I tried my best to brush it under the carpet and carry on as if it hadn't happened.

After a while, Dianne began to come to my form class at lunchtimes, when she would also converse with Tre. In the beginning, Tre and Dianne were okay with each other, but they had very similar personalities and it was not long before they began to argue. One lunchtime, one of their arguments over something really quite petty escalated to the point that Dianne stormed out back to her own form class.

I felt stuck in the middle between them. Tre did respect my wishes to keep seeing Dianne, but she, on the other hand, tried to coax me away from him. I made it clear that was not an option, so she had to find a way to navigate around me whenever I was hanging out with Tre.

In spite of Dianne's requirement for discretion and her attitude towards Tre, our relationship, surprisingly, continued to progress. I realised I would need to tell my mother about my girlfriend. When I approached my mother about this, I was nervous and hesitant, because I felt that the family would make too big a deal about it.

'I want to know if my friend can come over on Saturday,' I finally asked her.

'Yeah, of course your friend can come over. What time will he be here?' she asked.

'Well, hmm, it's not actually a male friend,' I said.

'Oh, so you have a girlfriend coming over! Yeah, that's fine. So, who is she? And what's her name?'

The questions kept coming and I eventually got over my embarrassment. In fact, it felt as if a weight had been lifted from my shoulders once it was out in the open. It was also a bit of an eye-opener for my sisters, as they had never seen me in that light before and had probably never imagined me having a romantic interest.

When the day arrived, Dianne came over to my house and my mother decided to cook for us all. Dianne, it turned out, was even more shy than I had been meeting her mother, to the point that she refused to even take off her jacket. I hadn't realised that it was her first time meeting a boyfriend's mother and so the situation was as alien for her as it had been for me. As the day progressed, Dianne came up to my bedroom and we chilled and watched television while we spoke about the day. It was the first time we had been by ourselves and after a while we began to hug and kiss each other. I felt very aroused by the touch of her lips and the feel of her body, but I was still too shy to take it any further than that.

Chapter 11:
Breaking up, feeling stupid and discovering alcohol

If you are not on the same page as your girlfriend, one of you will need to find another book to continue your story.

As my sixteenth birthday and Christmas 2000 drew closer, I began to feel some pressure and a level of unwanted responsibility due to my relationship with Dianne. There were definitely benefits to having a girlfriend at school, but there were drawbacks as well. I started to feel a heaviness over my head and around this time I also developed paranoia over Dianne's behaviour.

The paranoia stemmed from my impression that Dianne was flirting with other boys in school, which I thought I had seen her do on a handful of occasions. I bottled it up without saying anything, which caused me to have headaches. I was also feeling under pressure to meet Dianne's every need, which included meeting her at every opportunity at school, speaking to her over the phone every evening and seeing her every weekend. My headaches became so bad that not even my glasses helped, so I started taking paracetamol tablets again. I became so dependent on them that I was it was becoming an addiction. All this worry over the relationship also began to affect my schoolwork and I turned back to my computer games as a means to escape the pressure.

A few weeks before Christmas, I went to Dianne's house and managed to trick her into letting me know her ring sizes, as I wanted to get her one for Christmas. I kept a mental note of them and the following day I headed to a jewellery shop in Walthamstow, where I found a nice diamond band. At the time I had some pocket money saved up, which I used to buy the ring. As it was the first gift I had ever bought for a girlfriend, I wanted to get something precious.

On my birthday, which falls the week before Christmas, I bunked off school and stayed at home to play on my computer console and watch television. Dianne called me when she was on her lunch break and wished me a happy birthday. In the evening she stopped by to drop off my birthday present, which was a nice surprise. When I opened my gift, I was amazed to see that Dianne had bought me a 9-carat gold sovereign ring. I had never worn jewellery, but I was delighted with it.

I spent Christmas Day at home and got a call from Dianne. 'Merry Christmas,' she said, 'and thank you so much for my ring, I love it!'

It made me happy just to hear her happy over the phone.

Once the Christmas festivities wore off, my mother decided to throw a party to mark the start of the new millennium. She invited the extended family and we played music and ate loads of food. We also had a large selection of alcoholic and non-alcoholic drinks, so I decided to make the ultimate cocktail. I got hold of a giant plastic cup (it was a promotional cup from a cinema) and poured in vodka, rum, whisky, lemonade, cider and beer. I shared it with whoever else wanted to try it and we drank it down like it was water, with me drinking most of it. I was soon throwing up in the bathroom and the next day, presumably because of the high sugar content of all the different drinks, my hangover was so bad that my head pounded, and I couldn't eat anything until evening. Drinking was a big thing in my family so no one thought there was anything too abnormal about a sixteen-year-old knocking that much alcohol back in a single evening. None of them were ever going to explain the health implications of excess drinking, that much was certain.

One afternoon early in the new year, my mother was getting ready to go and collect Sophie from my grandmother's house when she tripped on the bottom stair while trying to grab hold of her shoes. She screamed so loudly that I could almost feel the pain in her cry. She had twisted her ankle out of its socket, and it was obvious even to the naked eye that she needed medical attention. Tommy called for an ambulance, but instead of waiting for it to arrive he decided in the meantime to twist my mother's ankle back into its correct position. The sheer stupidity of this became immediately apparent when she screamed even more loudly than she had when she fell in the first place. When the paramedics turned up, they told Tommy in no uncertain terms that he should not have done what he did and that he had caused further damage to the ankle. She was rushed to hospital, where her foot was put into a cast. They told her that the severity of the dislocation would result in a long period of recovery and that she would be off work for quite some time.

On the school and relationship fronts, everything was fairly stable at the time, but the mounting pressure of schoolwork soon led to Dianne and I having disagreements over petty issues. The more I stressed, the more we argued, and it began to affect my sleep.

One day, I forgot to put on my sovereign ring before leaving home. Dianne immediately noticed I wasn't wearing it and ignored me for our whole Humanities lesson. I had no idea what I was supposed to have done wrong and I was even more surprised when Dianne stormed out just before the end of the lesson. Everyone knew we were a couple, including the teacher, who looked at me and said: 'It looks like you're in the doghouse.' I had no idea what that meant, but I knew I was somehow being mocked by her and I felt embarrassed because everyone was staring at me.

At the end of the day, I tracked Dianne down to find out what the problem was.

'What's wrong?' I asked her.

'Don't talk to me; I don't want to see you right now,' she said as she walked off, leaving me just as confused and red-faced as I had been in class.

Later that evening, we finally spoke on the phone.

'Why were you not wearing your ring today?' she asked me.

'I forgot to put it on before I left it home. It's no big deal,' I replied, but that was clearly not the right answer.

The more I thought about her reaction, the angrier I became, and the pressure I was already under at the time started to feel unbearable. A few weeks later, after yet another disagreement, I decided that I had had enough and that I wanted to end the relationship. I called her one evening and asked her to bring the computer games I'd lent her to school the following day. She didn't ask why I wanted my games back, so I knew she had pretty much figured out that I was done with the relationship.

The following day she came into my form class at lunchtime and dropped the games off without saying a single word. From then on, I sat at another table in the Humanities class, but the atmosphere between us remained intense and it was clear that we resented each other following the breakdown of our relationship.

I was inundated with questions from friends who knew us both. They all wanted to know why we had broken up and they even began to take sides depending on whose story they believed. I became self-conscious on account of all the unwanted attention I was receiving, and I started to despise the idea of going into school most days. It took a heavy toll on my schoolwork, and I drew back inside myself.

Not long after the break-up, the whole year was due to take mock GCSE exams and I had to revise for weeks beforehand like everyone else. I found Science, Humanities and English the hardest subjects to understand at that level, but I found Maths much easier because I had a teacher who was able to explain everything in a way I could understand.

The issue I had was absorbing information in pure text form, which became clear to me when my mother bought us a home PC. I was able to use the PC instinctively without help from anyone, and I was particularly drawn to Encarta Encyclopedia. Because of its combined approach using pictures, videos and audio, I was able to absorb information much more easily than I ever could with text alone. Because the way in which my brain processed information was never identified by the school, however, I just had to keep trying to keep up as best as I could.

The results of my mock exams were very disappointing, ranging from D to F. It knocked my confidence and my self-esteem hard, because I had put in a lot of effort for such poor results, and I had no way of knowing that the primary reason for my failure was the way in which my brain processed information.

I became angry at my own stupidity, especially when I saw that the popular kids who never seemed to do any work had received grades A to C. I felt that I just couldn't keep up with the pace at which we were taught and that I would continue to fall behind, no matter how hard I worked. My mother didn't take time to understand what was going on, because her attention remained mostly focussed on Tommy, and I didn't see my Dad much either. I was on my own.

Luckily, the school year was at least drawing to a close, which meant I could look forward to a break from my stupidity and also from all the unwanted attention relating to Dianne.

Away from school, Barrel continued to be used as a slave to carry out jobs for members of the family, including brickwork and gardening. Any money he got from his day job, he still spent on takeaway food for our family dinners. He was literally working for nothing, and his enslavement was clearly taking its toll on his self-worth as a human being.

Two weeks into the summer holiday, we found out that Barrel was going back to Jamaica. He began to pack his things and the atmosphere around the house felt very heavy indeed. It was sad when he left, and Laura was particularly upset, because she had grown to like him. Tommy celebrated as though it was a good thing when Barrel left, but to me the whole episode had felt wrong on so many levels.

I spent most of the summer with my cousins and began to experiment more with alcohol. We bought cheap cider or beer to begin with, but we also got hold of spirits, including vodka and rum. I found that beer made me urinate a lot, but once it was in my system it did make me feel much more energetic. Spirits, on the other hand, seemed to magnify whatever my emotions were at the start of the drinking session in question, whether happy or sad. If I felt sad at the beginning of a session, I would feel as if I was falling into a black hole by the end of it. It was as if the alcohol was bringing my deep-seated emotions to the surface, which scared me. And then there were the hangovers and the blackouts.

One time I was at a family party at the house of Warren's dad, my Uncle Stewart. There was a large selection of spirits to choose from, so Warren and I soon escalated to vodka after drinking a few beers. We initially drank it from glasses, but then we started drinking it from teacups, presumably because we thought it would be less obvious that way that we were demolishing the whole bottle. We then found a lemon-flavoured white rum and drank that as well. Warren was so drunk that he started to be violent towards his dad. I tried to calm him down, but he was too far gone by that point and his dad had to phone Warren's mother to come and pick him up. I was so drunk that I had to go to one of the bedrooms upstairs to try and sleep it off, but I threw up all over the room, including the bed and my own clothes.

When I woke up the next day, all I could see was puke everywhere. My headache was completely unbearable. I had forgotten that Warren had gone home and when I went downstairs his family asked me if I remembered anything from the previous night. I had to confess that it was a complete blackout for me. As I made my way home, my head felt heavy, and I felt hot one minute and cold the next. My appetite did not come back until the evening and, when it did, I could only eat something simple.

Although it was one of the worst experiences I had ever had, I also knew it wouldn't be my last, because I always enjoyed the stimulation that I got from the first few drinks. Self-control was an issue, though, because I couldn't stop myself and I would always drink until I either passed out or started to vomit. Drinking wasn't just fun for me, though. It was a way to escape my problems and I found myself turning to it more and more over the holidays. Although I wasn't exactly addicted to alcohol, it certainly helped me let go of my inhibitions.

Chapter 12:
My final year at school

The person who enters secondary school isn't the same person who leaves it.

On my first day in Year 11 in 2001, I felt as though I was going back as a new person with a bit more confidence. Notwithstanding the odd bout of drunkenness, the summer holidays had helped me to mature, experiment and develop my social skills. The experience with Dianne was in the past and I remained determined to avoid her at all costs, so I could focus on my schoolwork. After the failures of my Year 10 mock exams, I wanted to redeem myself by trying even harder.

In my Drama class we were often required to work in pairs before combining into groups for a final stage piece. Coincidentally, I was paired with Janine, and we got on well. We accepted that our brief encounter was in the past and that we just wanted to work hard together to do well in our class. The chemistry between us as actors seemed to always work, allowing us to draw our characters out into the open.

By now, I had learnt so much from my Drama lessons that I felt certain areas of my life were becoming acts of their own. I was learning to wear a mask to cover up the real me inside and that gave me strength and a degree of protection. Even when I felt a connection drawing me and Janine together again, I decided to keep my outer self at a distance because I still found it difficult to accept her rejection of me back in Year 7. I was conflicted between the resentment I felt for that rejection and the attraction I still felt towards her.

As Laura and I hadn't seen our Dad in a long time, my mother decided he needed to make more of an effort, so she told me to write a letter to him. I didn't really want to do that, but in the end her persistence wore me down. In the letter, I said that I felt he didn't care about me or Laura anymore and that we couldn't understand why he didn't want to see us. I was nervous when my mother posted it, because I didn't know what to expect. I wasn't sure if he would react angrily, dismiss my views out of hand or just ignore the letter altogether. I was also irritated that my mother had instigated the process with no regard for my feelings about it. A week later our Dad called and asked me to bring Laura on the bus after school on Thursday that week to our grandmother's in Stamford Hill, which was where he was living.

When we got to our grandmother's house on the Thursday, our Dad was still at work. He worked at a printing factory, managing their commercial equipment, the same job he had been doing since I was born. Our grandmother Lorna let us in and she cooked spaghetti while we waited for our Dad to arrive. It was a huge Victorian house with seven floors, including a basement. It had a very dated feel to it, and I thought many of its features and colours gave it a quite depressing atmosphere.

When my Dad turned up, we greeted each other with a degree of hesitation and nervousness. He told me that he had got my letter, but that's all he said about it. He never mentioned anything about its contents, so I figured that they must have made him feel uncomfortable. We just spoke about school and had dinner, and then he gave me and Laura pocket money of £10 each. He then dropped us back home and made arrangements with our mother for us to go to grandmother Lorna's every Thursday after school.

The general flow after that was the same old focus on schoolwork, going to see my Dad on a Thursday after school, enjoying leisure activities at the weekend and, of course, trying to avoid Tommy as much as possible, because he still never missed an opportunity to belittle me in front of others or to hit me when we were alone.

Janine and I drew closer together during our Drama classes and we were told that we would need to create and perform a play for our GCSE exam. We had to join up with another pair to form a group of four and come up with an idea that would not offend any minority groups or belief systems. We decided to pair up with Katie and Ben from another class and we were allowed to leave other lessons early in order to work with them. During these group classes, our Drama teacher Mrs Gill wanted us to consider how we are perceived as individuals just by the way we walked. She pointed out that I had a very peculiar walk and that I could develop that into any character I chose.

We brainstormed ideas about what our play could be based on and came up with the concept of a postal worker being treated unfairly by his manager, but then ends up having a senior role above that same manager. It wasn't groundbreaking stuff, but we had to bring as many emotions as we could to our characters in order to gain high marks in our exam.

Janine was also in my Design and Technology class, so we took to working together there as well. She told me she was going through a bit of a rough patch with her friend Jill following an argument, and that she was trying to avoid her as much as she could. She obviously felt by now that she could confide in me, and I found myself becoming more and more attracted to her again. Before we knew it, though, our final exams were upon us and I spent my time studying as hard as I could.

I felt even more pressure than I had with the mock exams and every evening leading up to my GCSEs I was in my box-sized bedroom trying to concentrate and revise. I was still expected to do my share of household chores, which wasn't exactly helpful, and no one made any effort to keep the usual noise down.

On the first day of my finals, I had to sit my Humanities exam and it was one of the hardest papers I had ever sat. I felt a heavy pressure on my head throughout and at times I had a complete mental block, because I didn't fully understand the questions. I did the best I could within the two hours we were given, but I had to just guess on a couple of the questions and I was relieved when it was over. The pattern was pretty much the same for all my exams and I was not left feeling confident.

My last exam was Drama and we had to perform our play in front of the whole year, followed by a separate performance in front of the examiners. Needless to say, I was extremely nervous about performing in front of the whole year; but I also wanted to give a good performance. Our group was the last to go, so while we waited we had the opportunity to watch all the other groups before us. I was very impressed by their plays and felt that our group's story was probably too simplistic. I remained determined, though, to draw as much emotion to the surface as possible. When it was our turn to perform, I soon felt immersed within the character of the postal worker, drawing on my very real feelings of being treated unfairly by my family and transferring that energy into my performance. I became almost unaware of the audience's existence and I felt surprisingly comfortable within that very public spectacle. In that one moment I felt that nothing else mattered apart from my emotions and the energy of my performance. My worries over not meeting everyone's expectations and my embarrassment at being watched had completely dissipated. For a brief moment I was fearless.

When our play had ended, the audience applauded. I felt total relief, and I thought I could even do it all again without the initial fear. As it was also my last exam, I was almost euphoric. I felt as though a celebration was in order.

Our teachers had in fact arranged a boat trip on the River Thames for our end-of-year party. Usually there would have been a prom, but for some reason we were to be treated to a boat trip instead. I used some cash I had to buy a new shirt and shoes for the occasion, because I wanted to look smart. Although Janine was in my thoughts, I wanted above all to have a good time and to socialise with other boys and girls from our year.

On the Thursday of the boat trip, we had to get to school by 6 p.m. to catch the coach that would take us to the river. When I arrived, everyone was dressed up and the girls looked amazing. We got on the coach and headed for the Thames. I was excited at the idea of being in a social setting with all the other students away from school. When we arrived at the pier, we left the coach and got straight on board the boat.

The party started right away. The DJ played pop music to begin with and while that was still going on after an hour the boat set off from the pier. A group of my friends from another class had a spliff and wanted to smoke it, so we scouted around for a hideout away from the teachers. Unfortunately, there were lifeguards around to foil our plans. I just wanted to be part of something rebellious now that school was over.

The teachers themselves began to drink alcohol like it was water and there was a creepy moment when our

Year 11 Humanities teacher Mr Humphries came up to me and said, 'Dean, have you got any gum, my breath smells like cat shit.'

I laughed and gave him a couple of gum sticks. He then turned round and gave a very suspicious look to a student named Abigail, who looked like she was entertaining the idea of getting it together with him. To escape the weirdness of Mr Humphries and his whole grooming aura, I started looking at a Turkish girl called Aisha, who I had known for a while. She was wearing a blue glittery dress and she gave me a wink. From that point onwards till the end of the night we danced together and I had the time of my life.

When it was time to head back home, we boarded the coach just as my mother phoned to say that our grandmother Ann had been rushed to hospital and that I needed to make my way there. All I could think about in that moment was that I had just come off a complete high to a feeling that was really low. It somehow didn't seem fair.

When I got to the hospital, all the family members were there, and my mother just looked at me with sadness in her eyes. I was told that my grandmother had water in her lungs, and when I saw her she was throwing up. I couldn't shake off the selfish questions that kept coming into my mind, though. Why can't I just be left alone to enjoy my life for once? Why does there always have to be sadness around me? Although I felt genuinely sad for my grandmother, I also felt plagued by negativity and was beginning to wonder if I would ever have a happy, normal life. I just wanted to be like the other students on the boat trip, who had probably gone on to parties by now. In any event, my grandmother pulled through and she was back at home recovering after a few days in hospital.

Not long afterwards, my mother told me about a clothing store in Walthamstow that was looking for staff to work on a Saturday, so I called and spoke to the manager. He explained it was a 9 to 6 shift on a Saturday and that the pay was minimum wage. At that time, the national minimum wage was £3.60 per hour, so after tax I would be earning £25 for the day, which at the time seemed perfectly fine to me considering I had never had a paid job before.

The following week I went to the store to have an interview with the manager and everything went well. The store sold mostly jeans for men and, as I was at an age when boys have a genuine interest in clothing, it was perfect for me. The manager asked very basic interview questions and I maintained a very positive and happy attitude. A few days after the interview, the manager called me to tell me that I had got the job and that they wanted me to start on the following Saturday.

I was overjoyed as it meant I would have an income just as I was about to finish school. On my first day as a shop assistant, I had to make tea for the staff, which consisted of myself and three other guys – the manager Steve, who had interviewed me, and two other sales assistants, Neil and Hadley. My day consisted of helping customers, running up and down to the stockroom to replenish floor stock as required, and pretty much standing on my feet for the whole day.

To begin with, I thought everything was fine. But as time went on, I began to feel claustrophobic with three other men in a shop that was no bigger than my living room at home. Standing all day really put a strain on my legs and after a while the novelty started to wear off. I also began to discover things about myself in a working environment, about what it was going to be like for me to work with other people. This became especially apparent when the manager started to display some condescending behaviour towards me whenever I made a mistake, such as bringing down the wrong item of clothing for a customer. The manager's way of dealing with that was to belittle me in front of the customers in order to make himself look better. This really got under my skin, but I felt that I had to put up with it.

During this period my mother and Tommy were looking at houses to buy, so that we could relocate. The only problem was that the houses they were looking at had the same number of bedrooms as our existing house. I was already stressed living in a box room and my three sisters were having to share the one other available bedroom. It was as if we were just going to relocate for the sake of it and this began to worry me and Laura.

I took to smoking roll-up cigarettes and drinking alcohol to escape the ongoing stresses of my life. I knew that I would soon need to make a decision about whether to stay on in sixth form at school or go to college, assuming my exam results were good enough to let me do either of those things. I pretty much knew deep down that college would be the best place for me, because I needed a change of scenery and I felt like I needed a new start. I headed off to Tottenham College, which was the closest one to our home, and got hold of a course guide to see what was available. Because computers seemed to come more naturally to me than most other things, I began to look for IT courses.

To add to the pressure of the last few weeks of school, my Saturday job, looking at college courses and the family's ongoing relocation plans, Tommy suddenly announced to me and Laura that we had to help renovate the existing house to make it look more appealing to potential buyers. As we didn't have much choice, we set about painting the walls in the living area, removing old furniture and moving in new furniture, which would eventually be for the new house.

About this time, my mother fell out with our grandmother Ann (her own mother). As the original plan had been to stay with grandmother Ann in between selling our existing house and moving to our new one, that caused a bit of a problem. My mother told us that we would now need to stay at Tommy's mother's house for a while, which really annoyed me because I never liked the woman and her house was in Islington, which was too far from my surroundings at the time.

When I came home from work the following Saturday, Tommy came to see me and Laura and said, 'I know you two have been working hard with the house, but we are going to need you to work even harder.' There was no real thanks for what we had done or the extra work we were now expected to do, and I began to think that I couldn't take much more of this.

The following week I had my last day of school, which was complete havoc. Some students brought in eggs and flour to throw at other students in the years below us and even at the teachers. I once again had mixed emotions, because on the one hand I was excited to be starting a new life, but I was also saddened that I would have to leave many of my friends behind. Nobody else was thinking of going to college, so I was probably going to be on my own. At the end of the school day, we signed each other's shirts, many of the girls cried and fights began to break out. It got so bad that the teachers had to kick the whole year off the grounds of the school.

Chapter 13:
Time to escape, and time to lose my virginity

When you fly the nest, you start to find out whether or not your wings are strong enough to take you where you want to go.

After we left the school premises on that final day, a girl named Sabrina invited us back to her house and most of us went. Sabrina was very close with Janine and she knew that there was a vibe between us, so she conspired to leave me and Janine alone in a room together. It felt weird, because I knew everyone else was expecting something to happen.

'What's up with Sabrina?' I asked in an attempt to break the ice.

'I think she's trying to set us up,' Janine said.

I said I was happy to talk about that, but not right there and then. We agreed to exchange numbers and speak another time.

When I got home, Laura was there alone. She explained to me that we needed to pack so we could move into Tommy's mother's house and that we were not allowed to speak to our grandmother Ann under any circumstances. This put me and Laura in a very awkward position and a voice in my head told me to call my grandmother Ann, whatever my mother and Tommy might think about that. I phoned and asked her if Laura and I could stay with her and she happily accepted. The only problem was that we needed to grab as much as possible as quickly as possible to take to my grandmother's house, as this would probably be our one opportunity to leave home. I explained this to my grandmother and she called my Uncle Stewart to come and help us. We had two hours to gather our belongings and get out.

'Are you sure you want to come with me?' I asked Laura.

'Yes,' she said with a very determined look on her face.

We grabbed a few black bags and began to throw in as much as we could. I was very nervous because I felt that at any moment my mother and Tommy could walk through the door and ruin our escape plans. After only a few minutes Uncle Stewart turned up with his little red Nissan Micra, which had a very small boot. We stuffed our bags into the back of the car until the rear window was completely obscured and hopped in. This was it, the break I had been praying for. I saw it as a release from years of abuse and neglect, pain and suffering, mental torture, not to mention the responsibility of raising my two younger sisters. I finally felt free and I knew I had made the right decision because it felt like a big weight had lifted from me as we drove to my grandmother's house.

There was plenty of space for us at our grandmother's house. It was split into two flats, the downstairs one where my grandmother lived and the upstairs one, which had two bedrooms, a shower, toilet and kitchen. Laura and I were given the upstairs one and decided to get settled in. While we were doing that, I contemplated my mother getting home and seeing that not only were we not there but that our stuff had also gone. It would only be a matter of time until she figured out where we were, but I tried not to worry about it too much because I knew she wouldn't come to my grandmother's house due to their falling out.

After a few days I felt anxious that I had only taken my clothes from my mother's house. My personal documents, exercise bench, games console, television and stereo, and also Laura's personal belongings, were still there. I didn't want to go there, but I wanted our stuff. Later that evening my grandmother finally got a call from my mother and another argument kicked off between them. My grandmother became angry and even started to cry. I couldn't bear it, so I took the phone and spoke to my mother. She told me that Laura and I had to come back.

'No, we're staying here,' I said.

'If you don't come back, I'll throw your belongings out on the street,' she said, in the hope that it would threaten me into changing my mind.

'If you do that, I will fuck you up!' I shouted.

I had never raised my voice, far less swore, in front of my grandmother. It shocked her so badly that she begged me to calm down, which I did. My mother had hung up on me anyway.

It was pretty much a waiting game after that, because I wasn't sure what was going to happen next. Two days later, however, Tommy's brother Jimmy turned up in a van with all our belongings and I was over the moon. My grandmother, on the other hand, was very upset and started shouting at Jimmy. She couldn't understand why my mother was so upset that she couldn't come to the house and work things out with me and Laura. I didn't care about any of that, I was just delighted to have our stuff. She had even sent over our passports.

With all of our belongings in place, Laura and I settled in quickly at our grandmother's. We had more space and freedom than we had ever had in our lives. Within reason, we could think for ourselves and do what we liked.

After a few days, I went back to looking at college courses and chose a GNVQ Level 2 in IT and Business Studies, with the addition of bookkeeping and accounts. I figured that if I chose a course that covered a few different areas I could decide later which specific field I wanted to go into.

It wasn't long until our Dad heard what had happened and he came to my grandmother's house to see us. He was more concerned about how the whole situation looked than anything else, and he decided that we should stay at our grandmother Lorna's house in Stamford Hill. As I felt settled at grandmother Ann's, I didn't want to go, but my Dad persisted and within a week he had taken us to a furniture store to pick out beds and a wardrobe to use at grandmother Lorna's. I still wasn't over the stress of escaping from home and moving to grandmother Ann's, so another move was the last thing I needed, but I tried to make the most of it.

Our grandmother's house in Stamford Hill was also huge, so there was plenty of space for me to spend time by myself and gather my thoughts. Grandmother Lorna was very welcoming when we moved in and everything seemed fine on the surface, but every weekend our Dad went to Bristol to be with Julia and their daughter. Although their daughter was our half-sister, we never got to see her much.

I continued to work at the clothing shop in Walthamstow and to endure humiliation from Steve. After a while, I decided the job really wasn't worth the £25 and, as I was going to be starting college in September anyway, I also wanted to have the time to focus properly on that. One Friday I called him and explained that I was about to start college and couldn't work at the shop anymore. He seemed quite taken aback and I wondered if his concern was that he wouldn't have someone to poke fun at on a Saturday.

As I was about to stop working, money was going to be a problem because I wouldn't be able to afford clothes or food for lunch. I decided to wear a denim jacket over a hoodie and a pair of jeans and trainers, all of which were hard-wearing clothes that would last me a long time. For lunch I would go to my grandmother Ann's house, which was literally a ten-minute walk from the college. My Dad paid for my bus pass. Luckily, it had been made clear from the start that we wouldn't be expected to pay for board and lodgings at my grandmother's house, perhaps because my Dad saw us staying there as an opportunity to make amends for not having been there for us very much over the years.

A few weeks before I was due to start college (my GCSE results hadn't been startling, but they had been good enough to secure my place at Tottenham College), I had been in contact with Janine and she had invited me to her house to watch a film on a Saturday morning. I took the bus from Stamford Hill all the way to Edmonton, where she lived. When I arrived, she got me an orange juice and we went into the living room. I asked her where her parents were. She said they were out and not due back until later in the evening. She asked me if I wanted to watch a film and I said 'yes, sure'. She chose *Bicentennial Man*, which starred Robin Williams.

I was sitting next to Janine on the sofa and within fifteen minutes of the film starting we began to French kiss and it felt amazing. I was becoming very aroused and wanted to take things further. I began to touch her breasts, which she was happy with even though she didn't want to get undressed. She let me unzip her jeans and she guided my hand between her legs. I felt inside her and I could tell she was really enjoying it. She said she wanted to wait to get undressed until the next time, so we just hugged and kissed until the film had finished.

On the bus heading back home, I wondered how amazing it would be to have sex with Janine – I knew I was sexually active and ready. About a week later, my grandmother Lorna decided to go away for the weekend, which meant I would be in the house by myself (Laura was staying with our other grandmother that weekend), so I invited Janine to stay the night. She said 'yes' and asked me which films to bring. I told her to bring anything she wanted, as films were the last thing on my mind at that point in time. I knew it was going to be the perfect opportunity to have sex and I was very hopeful that I would lose my virginity, so I went to the local chemist and bought a box of condoms.

When Saturday arrived, Janine got to Stamford Hill at around eight o'clock in the evening. I was in the middle of eating my dinner when Janine called to say she was at the bus stop, so I headed out to meet her. We kissed and hugged when we met and headed straight back to the house. I showed her where my bedroom was and asked her to wait there while I finished my pizza. I realised later what a strange thing that was to do, but I suppose I just needed a bit of extra time to get my nerves under control.

After I finished my pizza, I headed up to the bedroom with butterflies in my stomach. We spoke about our old school friends, how things had been since we left school and what our plans were for our further education. Then we watched *Planet of the Apes*, starring Mark Wahlberg, which we both really enjoyed. I didn't want to rush anything, so we just hugged and kissed from time to time.

I think Janine had already decided we were going to have sex, as it wasn't like we were in her parents' living room running any risk of getting caught. By the time the film was coming to an end, we were taking each off each other's clothes and I was getting very excited, to say the least. Once we were fully naked, I reached over into my bedside drawer and grabbed the box of condoms. As I had already read the instructions, I knew that I had to squeeze the head of the condom to prevent any air getting trapped inside it and I began to roll it over my penis. I was still nervous and, as I had never seen a vagina up close, hesitant about what to do next. I tried to guide my penis in, but it started to droop. I had drunk a lot of liquid and needed to go and pee, so I excused myself. In the toilet I tried to calm down and regroup, and by the time I went back into the room I felt more comfortable. As I began to kiss and hug Janine again, I became fully erect and put on another condom. I lay on top of her. This was it, the moment I had been waiting a very long time for. I was losing my virginity to the girl I had my very first crush on and it felt wonderful. I stayed on top until I climaxed, and it was the most amazing feeling of happiness, passion and sexual chemistry. When we'd finished, we just lay in bed together, hugging and kissing until we fell asleep.

When we woke up in the morning, I saw Janine next to me and immediately became aroused again. We began kissing and touching each other until we were having sex again, only this time I felt more confident. Because I now knew what I was doing, the experience felt even more intense than it had the first time. It was everything I had imagined sex would be.

After we had finished having sex for the second time, we kissed and hugged some more, until Janine told me she needed to head back home. We got up and got washed and dressed. I walked her to the bus stop, where we hugged and kissed some more before her bus arrived.

I went back to the house and put on a film before falling back to sleep. When I woke up, I thought at first that it must all have been a wonderful dream. Because it had been with Janine, it had just felt right.

Chapter 14:
Using bible study to get close to a girl, and being ousted by Aunt Beth

Sometimes it just feels as if the whole world is out to get you, no matter how hard you try.

When I began college, it felt like a fresh start for me and I was determined to progress in my education. On my first day, I found myself in a class with people of different ages and from different backgrounds, but I was relieved to see that everyone else seemed to be just as apprehensive as I was. Nobody knew anyone else and I found it very difficult to make friends to begin with, so I just put my head down and focussed on my college work for the first few weeks. As I didn't have any money coming in, I decided to send off my CV to local shops and supermarkets, including a Safeway supermarket at the corner of Stamford Hill where my grandmother Lorna shopped.

After a month in college, everyone began to relax and I made a few friends. It soon felt like part education and part fun. There was a lot of joking going on, but we were all still serious about our college work and we knew what was required of us. Although I missed my two younger stepsisters, I also knew I had made the right decision to leave home.

On the romantic front, Janine and I had not really spoken much since we made love. She called to say that she was upset about that, but I wasn't particularly bothered. I think that was partly due to her earlier rejection of me, but also because a few girls in college had already taken my eye. Janine and I went our separate ways.

One day I got home to find a letter from Safeway, which invited me to be interviewed for a job as a checkout assistant. I was very excited, not least because the supermarket was only a three-minute walk from grandmother Lorna's house. I prepared myself well for the interview, which turned out to consist of very basic questions plus some group work with other candidates to test our social and teamworking skills. I was delighted to hear a short while later that I was to be invited back to go through an induction course and to gain practical experience on a checkout desk. After a few weeks of training, my employment was confirmed and I began to make some money working there whenever I could. I was able to buy some new clothes, which meant not having to wear the same ones every day to college, and I could afford to buy my own lunch at college instead of going to my grandmother Ann's house to eat ramen noodles every day, which I was getting a bit sick of by then anyway.

On many of the days I worked at Safeway, which was pretty much every day I didn't have to go into college, a lot of sixth-form girls from a school across the road came in to buy their lunch. I wasn't used to getting attention from a group of girls, but that's exactly what started to happen. Every time I was on a shift, groups of them would queue up at my checkout. It actually felt uncomfortable at first, because, apart from the school plays I had acted in, I wasn't used to being the centre of attention. It became clear that one girl in particular wanted to strike up a conversation with me, but she was very shy. She had dark skin, black hair and was quite stocky. I can't say I was attracted to her in any way, but it did feel good to be admired, especially given all the crap I had experienced in my life previously. One afternoon, she came with a friend, who marched right up and said: 'Can I have your number for my friend?' I was taken back, because there had been no greeting whatsoever, no introduction, just a request for my personal number. Caught off guard, I wrote my number down on a piece of paper. I looked at the stocky girl, but she didn't say a word.

After two weeks, I had a call on my mobile from an unknown number.

'It's Whitney,' said the stocky girl, 'my friend asked you for your number.'

'Oh, it's you. How's it going?' I asked.

The conversation went on from there and I decided, although she was not my type, that it would be a good idea to extend my social circle. I agreed to meet her near the supermarket on a Thursday evening at a bus stop, where she would be with her friend. Her friend, Sabine, turned to be very attractive. She was a Mauritian girl one year older than me and had lovely brown eyes and complexion, black hair and a pretty face. She was thin, and she looked even thinner standing next to Whitney.

Whitney started banging on about wanting to go into the supermarket, but I wasn't interested as I had just finished working there. Whitney continued to insist that we go in, and I continued to refuse. I started to talk to Sabine instead and after a while we exchanged numbers, right there in front of Whitney, who just carried on insisting that I go into the supermarket with her. After about twenty minutes, I said goodbye to them both and headed home.

I found out later that Whitney had a crush on a guy named Billy, who worked on the deli counter in Safeway, and that her sole purpose in meeting me had been to make Billy jealous, which is why she had been so desperate to be seen in the supermarket with me.

After about a week, Sabine and I started to talk over the phone a lot and something seemed to spark between us. I became more and more attracted to her and we started going on dates together. One issue, though, was that I could never see her between 6 p.m. on a Friday and 6 p.m. on a Saturday, because that was the time of the Sabbath for her.

She came from a strict religious background, her entire family belonging to the Seventh-day Adventist Church. During the Sabbath, they attended church, abstained from meat, didn't watch television apart from programmes about the natural world, and were not allowed to smoke or drink.

Sabine raised the question of me meeting her parents, but I wasn't a religious person and thought it best not to. I discovered that Sabine met a lot of her friends, including male ones, at her local church. There were two guys in particular that she had known her for a few years. Apparently one of them really liked Sabine, whereas Sabine had always had a soft spot for the other one. I felt like an idiot when she told me all this, but I was determined to be put first among her male friends, especially as I was her boyfriend.

I raised the stakes by surprising her at church one Saturday. She was both shocked and happy to see me, and she introduced me to her parents, but not as her boyfriend. The service had meant nothing to me and my intentions remained purely fixed on the need to spend time with Sabine. As we left the church, Sabine's father, Paul, offered to drop me at my bus stop in Tottenham Hale. He didn't say much as he drove me there, but Sabine, who was also in the car, said I was interested in their religion and that I wanted to learn more, so Paul suggested that we could all do a bible study together. If that's what it takes for me to see Sabine more, I thought, I'll give it a try.

Sabine made the arrangements for us to have the bible study at her family home in Edmonton Green, so I took a bus there one Wednesday evening. I was greeted by Sabine and went into the house, where I saw religious texts covering the walls. I met Sabine's mother, Rosie, and she asked me more about myself and what I was doing at college. She herself worked at the local hospital and Paul was an IT manager for a big company. It was all very prim and proper, and Paul just wanted to get on with the bible study, which he then proceeded to lead. I could see that he adored Sabine and felt very protective towards her, and that it would probably be virtually impossible to impress him as a potential boyfriend.

At college I was also getting attention from the girls in my class, and one girl in particular, called Farah. She was Indian, and she lived in Woodford with her very rich family. Five of us in my class had started to hang around as a group: Darryl, Hassan, Shivaun, myself and Farah. Darryl and Shivaun were British Jamaican, and Hassan's family was from Turkey. Out of college, I spoke to Farah on the phone a few times, but not in a romantic way. Sabine was aware that I spoke to girls from my class outside of college, and it seemed to be an issue whenever it was brought up. It was the same for me, of course, whenever Sabine talked of her male friends. After a while, it became a tit for tat battle to her way of thinking, and she found ways to make me jealous, and even angry sometimes. Sometimes it felt like my relationship with Janine all over again. However, I never said anything for fear of having arguments or breaking up. Instead, I just bottled it up inside me.

One evening, when I arrived at my Uncle Stewart's house with my cousin Warren, I noticed a black taxi parked outside. Without taking much notice, I carried on to the front door when I heard someone shout out 'Dean!'. I turned around and was shocked to see Tommy sitting in the taxi. He asked me how I was and if I wanted to see my mother. I said I would like that and I jumped into the taxi, although I felt very awkward sitting in there with him. He drove me to a Blockbuster video store in Tottenham Hale, where he knew my mother was queuing inside. I walked in, feeling very apprehensive. She had her back towards me, so she didn't know I was there until Tommy suddenly shouted out: 'Look who I found!' He sounded like he'd discovered buried treasure.

When my mother turned around and saw me for the first time in almost a year, her eyes filled with tears. We then headed to their new house, which was in White Hart Lane, where we spoke about what I was doing at college and I also got to see my sisters. Sophie was doing fine, but Sarah had developed a thyroid disorder, which she had inherited from my mother, who also suffered from the condition. My mother and Tommy had bought the girls a family dog, called 'Lucky', which was a cross collie. I didn't stay too long as I felt uncomfortable, but we exchanged numbers and arranged to meet again. Tommy was civil enough, but I suspected it was an act to please my mother. You can't suddenly like someone you abused for years, I thought to myself.

I spoke to Laura about it and gave her my mother's number, as my mother had said she wanted to talk to her. I just wanted to stay focussed on my college work, supermarket job and relationship with Sabine, so I kept things on a purely civil basis to begin with between me and my mother. As the summer of 2002 approached, I had participated in many of Paul's bible studies and

Sabine and I continued to enjoy strong feelings for one another, in spite of our jealousy issues.

At home, however, things had taken a turn for the worse. My Dad's sister, Aunt Beth, had moved into my grandmother Lorna's house with us. Beth seemed fine at first, but she had remained bitter after the break-up of her marriage a few years back, and often got drunk to drown her sorrows. When drunk, she would say crazy things, like her intention to hang herself in a park. She was also very argumentative, which brought out a negative side in grandmother Lorna as well. The two of them would sit there and criticize the whole family one by one, which made me uncomfortable, as I felt sure that one day it would be my turn to be the subject of their criticism.

One afternoon, I invited Shivaun and Farah back to my grandmother's house to go over coursework we needed to complete before the summer break. When they arrived, I introduced them to Beth and my grandmother. Beth was polite enough with them, but I could tell she was not impressed that I had female friends coming to my grandmother's house. Shivaun, Farah and I went into the living area and went over our coursework and had a few laughs.

A few days later, my Dad called me while I was on my lunch break at college to express some concerns he had over my behaviour. Basically, Beth had told him that Farah and Shivaun had laughed at my grandmother's family photos. I tried to explain to my Dad that Farah and Shivaun would never have done such a thing, but he took my aunt's side and said that I shouldn't bring anyone else to the house.

A week later, I asked Farah to come to the house to go over some more coursework, but I told her we had to be quiet so we wouldn't be heard by my aunt and grandmother. After a few hours I walked Farah quietly to the front door, but after she left Beth came out of her bedroom and said: 'Your Dad told you not to bring people here, so you shouldn't be going behind our backs like that.'

Two days later, I was out with Sabine when I got a call from my Dad. He told me that my grandmother and aunt had reported to him that I had girls staying overnight. I couldn't believe what I was hearing and told him it wasn't true. He then said: 'Do you think I am going to believe you over your nan? Don't make me come to the house and change the locks.'

He hung up the phone before I could say anything else and I knew then that Beth had managed to spread her poison to not just my grandmother Lorna, but also my Dad. I decided to call my grandmother Ann, who at the time was looking for tenants to rent the upstairs of her house, where Laura and I had stayed before. I asked her if she had found tenants and she told me no, and also that she was totally fine with me moving back in. Even though she could have earned income from paying tenants, there was never any suggestion or expectation that I should pay her anything. Perhaps she was trying to right the wrongs of her daughter by helping me out.

When I got back to Stamford Hill, I told my grandmother Lorna that I was moving back to my other grandmother's house, because my Dad had threatened to change the locks on the front door. She tried to cover her actions by saying that I had gone against her wishes by bringing people back to her house, but I could tell by the tone of her voice that she knew she was lying and I suspected that she was also worried that me moving to my other grandmother's house was going to make her look bad.

My Dad called me the following day and asked me what was going on. I told him he didn't need to change the locks because I was moving out. 'Just make sure you only take what is yours,' he said, 'and leave my DVD player there.' I was disgusted that all he cared about was his DVD player that I had been using in my bedroom, and that he had allowed himself to be so easily fooled by Beth and his own mother.

The following day, I called Farah to tell her what had happened and she called two of her friends to come and help me move. While I was packing, my grandmother came to see what was going on. She began to cry and asked me to stay.

'No, thanks,' I said, 'it's best if I go to my other grandmother's house, where the locks won't be changed.'

I was blunt with her because her daughter had started all of the nonsense and she had allowed herself to be taken in by her. Deep down, I knew she was more embarrassed about how she was going to look to everyone because of what had happened, but I had no sympathy for her on that score. She and my Dad had both shown a different side to themselves and that made me think twice about my relationship with them.

Once I had packed everything into Farah's friend's car, I called Sabine to tell her what was happening. She agreed to meet me in Tottenham at my grandmother Ann's house. I was unpacking by the time Sabine arrived, so she came up to my room. I told her everything that had happened, but she seemed preoccupied. Finally, she asked me to sit down, because she needed to talk to me.

She said had given some thought to us as a couple and was worried that it wouldn't work because of her father, but she couldn't bring herself to break up with me either. She told me she had spoken to one of her male friends at the church about us, and that she had asked his advice about what she should do. For the third time in as many days, I couldn't believe my ears. I felt as if I was being kicked while I was down.

I told Sabine that it was up to her whether she wanted to be with me or not. She didn't answer me, she just sat there while I finished unpacking my stuff. I walked her to the bus stop, but neither of us said much. I gave her a kiss and a hug before she jumped on her bus.

The following day, recent events spun round in my head. I realised that no matter how well I did with my college work or job, my Dad would never give me any praise. He only cared about his relatives and about his other family in Bristol. It brought back memories of when Sarah was born and my mother and Tommy pushed me and Laura out of the picture. My Dad had revealed himself to be no better than my mother in that respect.

My Dad's family and Tommy's family were both of Jamaican origin, of course, and I began to wonder if they had a shared mentality as a result of that. With Tommy, I had suffered abuse behind closed doors and witnessed the maltreatment of Barrel at the hands of his entire family. With my Dad, I had suffered neglect and I had watched him take the side his mother and sister against me, his only son.

After a week of settling into my latest home, I got a call from my mother, who asked me to go and visit her. When I got there, she and Tommy told me that they had asked Laura to move back in with them, and that Laura had agreed to do so, because she didn't want to stay in Stamford Hill without me. They asked me if I wanted to do the same, because they missed me, they said.

'I have my independence now and I can never go back to how things were for me under your roof,' I told them, without going into detail. They both looked disappointed, but neither of them asked me what I meant by that. At least one of them, of course, knew exactly what I meant.

Chapter 15:
The heartbreak caused by Sabine's departure

Sometimes we just have to do the right thing, no matter how much pain it causes us.

In spite of Sabine's misgivings, we found ourselves growing stronger as a couple as time went on. Our social circles converged, so we got invited to twice as many birthday parties and other events. We were inseparable when we were together, always walking arm in arm, with our hands in each other's pockets. The flip side to all that was our ongoing jealousy and resentment whenever one of us spotted the other talking to a member of the opposite sex. Looking back now, it is clear that we both lacked the maturity required to handle such an intense relationship.

One rainy afternoon, though, we had sex for the first time, at my grandmother Ann's house in Tottenham. As Sabine was a virgin, I was extra gentle with her, and overall the experience further strengthened the bond we felt together. It was very different to the sex I had with Janine, because my feelings were much stronger for Sabine.

The more I hung around Sabine and her family, the more her father seemed to accept me, but you could never relax fully in the strict atmosphere of their home and there was certainly no way that I could be affectionate towards Sabine while her parents were around. It felt like we were two magnets in a room separated by the unstoppable force of her parents, but mostly Paul.

Sabine seemed to have more and more male friends as time went on, including a cocky guy called Pete. I was okay with him at first, but I couldn't help noticing that he tried to impress Sabine every chance he got. I bottled up my frustration once more, angry that Sabine seemed happy with the attention he gave her. Things came to a head when Sabine invited Pete over to her parents' house and he took Sabine's mother a bunch of flowers. When she told me what had happened, I lost my patience and we got into a huge argument about it. Even some of our mutual friends agreed that it had been a bad move on Sabine's part and that it had made me look stupid. Sabine finally admitted that it had been a very bad idea and she said that she was going to back away from Pete, as his intentions were clearly more than just being friends with her.

While all this drama was unfolding, my Dad called me out of the blue to ask if I wanted to go on holiday with him and his family from Bristol. I was speechless, and I began to wonder why it was that everyone around me seemed to be nasty one minute and nice the next. Tommy, my long-term abuser, had said he missed me and wanted to me to move back in with him and my mother. My Dad, who had only recently branded me a liar and threatened to lock me out of his mother's house, was now trying to bury the hatchet by inviting me to go on holiday with his other family for the first time. I couldn't bring myself to forgive him that quickly, so I declined. He did manage to convince Laura to join them and they all went off to Spain together. For the time being, I was just happy to stay focussed on college and on my part-time job at Safeway. Truth be told, I didn't really want to be away from Sabine for any length of time either.

As Sabine's birthday approached that year, I bought her some perfume, a teddy bear and a make-up set. More importantly, I decided to declare my true love for her in the birthday card I had bought for her. I spent a whole day trying to put the words together to express my love in the most romantic way possible.

Some of her friends and I had arranged a birthday party for her at one of the Mexican restaurants called Chiquito. We were a group of about twenty, several of them being friends from Sabine's school that I hadn't met before. I sat next to Sabine, all the while concealing the contents of my bag of gifts for her, because I wanted them to be a surprise later in the evening. It was a typical birthday dinner, in that we got her a birthday cake, sang 'Happy Birthday' and relaxed with a few drinks. When the evening came to an end, I shared a taxi with Sabine to drop her home first. I gave her the gift bag in the taxi, saving the card for last. When she read the words I'd written for her, she smiled and said, 'I love you.' 'I love you, too,' I said, and we kissed. I had never felt happier.

A week later Sabine invited me back to her house while her parents were out for the day. Being really into music, I took a few CDs with me so that we could listen to something other than gospel music. We spent some time watching television and attempted to make a pizza from scratch. After putting all the ingredients together, we left it in the oven and Sabine suggested that we head up to her bedroom, which I hadn't seen before. I was totally on edge, worrying that her parents might come back at any moment, so Sabine called them to check on their whereabouts, which confirmed that they wouldn't be home any time soon. We settled down to listen to an R. Kelly album I had got for my birthday the year before and just lay together on her bed listening to the whole album. As we hugged, kissed and gazed into each other's eyes, it felt to me as if time itself had stopped. Everything around us seemed to disappear, and I knew in my heart that this what real love must feel like.

We spent so much time gazing into each other's eyes that the pizza got burnt, but we didn't care and ate it anyway. As evening approached, I knew that I had to go before her parents got back. We walked to the bus stop together and I headed home, feeling on top of the world.

Sabine was in her last year of school at that time and was looking at going to university. Her parents insisted that she went to Newbold College in Reading, the only institution in the UK which was owned and operated by the Seventh-Day Adventist Church. This would be so expensive that Sabine had to get a job to help pay for her fees. Her father arranged for her to work with a friend of his, who owned a company in Tottenham. She worked as an office administrator from Monday to Friday, but I got to see her every day for lunch and I also walked her home every day when she finished work.

Her father arranged for us all to visit the college to check out the facilities. Although I wasn't happy about the distance between Reading and London as far as keeping in touch with Sabine was concerned, I was nonetheless pleased that the family had decided to include me in their upcoming trip to Reading.

The more I thought about it, though, the more anxious I became about losing Sabine once she left for university. When the day of the trip came around, my head wasn't in a great place and I thought my brain was going to explode listening to gospel music for the entire two hours it took to reach Reading. It felt like I was stuck in one of those dreadful horror movies in which a happy-clappy family sing their hearts out together just before some madman takes an axe to them. I was very relieved to get out of the car when we got there.

Although the countryside location was stunning and the college buildings were impressive, to say the least, I couldn't help putting a negative spin on everything I saw and heard. Because it's a religious institution, there are a lot of social restrictions at Newbold, including the requirement for visitors to leave by 8 p.m. and for students to be back in their dorm rooms by midnight. I knew that these rules weren't going to help my cause one bit.

Paul enjoyed the day immensely, which I ungraciously put down to him relishing the idea of separating me and his daughter. I didn't say much, not wanting to spoil the day for Sabine or her parents, but Sabine, of course, could tell I wasn't happy. Quite apart from anything else, I knew that I wouldn't be able to find the time or the money to travel to Reading on a regular basis.

Sabine also struggled to accept the idea of moving so far away, to the point where she had argued with her mother about it. Rosie actually called me to explain that she was concerned about Sabine and to ask me to try and talk her into going to college, because she thought Sabine might listen to me. Although Rosie had never recognised me as Sabine's boyfriend, I believe deep down that she understood the intensity of our relationship.

That call made me realise that I had the power to influence Sabine's decision one way or the other. I could prevent her from going by pledging my undying love and begging her to stay, or I could break both our hearts by convincing her to go. It was going to be a tough decision to make.

I arranged to meet Sabine and asked her what she wanted to do. 'I want to stay in London and be with you,' she said. To my surprise, I then heard myself telling her that she should go to Newbold, that it was far too great an opportunity to miss. My eyes filled with tears and I began to cry, which was something Sabine had never seen me do. She began to cry, too, because I think we both realised in that moment that it was the right thing to do, however much pain it might cause us. I walked her home after a couple of hours, but our conversation was punctuated with awkward silences for the first time.

Summer was fast approaching, and I was finishing my own year at college. I needed to decide what I was going to do next academically. Convinced by now that IT was something I really liked, I chose a two-year Advanced Information and Communication Technology course.

Sabine had saved as much as she could to help pay for her university fees and, when the holidays arrived, we spent as much time as we could with each other. In no time at all, though, the time came for her to start her new life on campus. Her parents helped her move there and I had to wait until the following week before Paul invited me to go with him and Rosie to visit Sabine on campus.

Two hours of gospel music later, I saw Sabine walking towards us in a pretty dress. She looked happy to see me, but she couldn't greet me as she'd have liked to, in case Paul noticed. I was really annoyed, having gone all that way to see her. To make matters worse, as we were walking towards the church on campus, another student came over to talk to us and addressed Sabine as if he'd known her all her life. I assumed they had spent some time together and, when I finally did get a moment alone with Sabine, she could tell I was not happy. She locked the door to her dorm and tried to kiss me, but I was too angry to reciprocate.

Suddenly, before we could even talk about it, someone knocked on the door. When Sabine opened it, there was Paul, giving me a look that could kill.

'Dean,' he said, 'this place has standards and you shouldn't be locking the door.'

'I didn't lock the door, Sabine did,' I said, staring hard at him.

Luckily, we were interrupted by Sabine's roommate and Paul let his lecture drop. I didn't say much to Sabine for the rest of the day and eventually headed back in the car with Paul and Rosie. You could have cut the atmosphere with a knife and I promised myself on the way back to London that it would be my last journey with the overbearing Paul.

Chapter 16:
Reduced to eating ramen pot noodles and failing the driving theory test

The aftermath of a failed relationship can drag you down into a deep hole.

After the Reading trip, I was left fuming at the many injustices the world seemed determined to throw at me, and especially at Sabine, Newbold College, Paul and the guy that had dared to come over to talk to Sabine. It was a few weeks before I spoke to Sabine again over the phone (we had been used to talking to each other every day before she left for Reading) and she took that opportunity to tell me that another guy on campus was letting her drive his car so she could practise for her driving test. That was the straw that broke the camel's back in the state of mind I was in, so I let Sabine know in no uncertain terms what I felt about it. Incapable of rational thought by now, I told her to let my next call divert to voicemail. Once she had done that, I rang again to break off what was left of our relationship (I couldn't bring myself to do it while she was on the other end of the phone).

A great sadness filled my heart after that phone call and I suffered a feeling of complete emptiness during the weeks that followed. Although it was the height of summer and the sun was often shining, there were days when I just stayed indoors, because I couldn't face seeing anyone. I stopped eating and couldn't even bring myself to watch television or listen to music for a while.

The dark place I was in began to affect my job at Safeway and I would call in sick just because I couldn't be bothered. When I did go into work, I smoked weed with one of my fellow workers during our lunch break and I began to take longer and longer breaks. Inevitably, my line manager and I began to clash, so I handed in my notice. The supermarket had been a constant reminder to me of happier times, because it was where I had met Sabine, so I figured I needed to break away from it for that reason in any event.

I started once more to direct my attention towards college, as I was due to begin my advanced course in September. The only downside was that I was out of a job, which meant I had no money coming in at all. That did worry me, but I didn't need much money to do simple things like watch television or listen to music in my own space, which I had at least started to do again. I remained stuck in my rut for the rest of the summer, though, bottling my problems up inside as I had nobody to talk to about them.

September finally came around and I started the new college term. Unfortunately, because I was the only person from the previous course to choose the advanced class, I knew nobody. In my first year, I had managed to make friends once I overcame my shyness, but my confidence was at an all-time low at the start of my second year. On day one, I settled into a corner of the class where I could be alone and that is where I stayed, head down at all times. My typical day consisted of going to college, walking home for lunch, leaving college at the end of the day and spending evenings in my room.

I should have gained some confidence after receiving a pass certificate from the basic course at the end of my first year, and I had been proud to show it to my grandmother Ann and other members of the family, but they had all pretty much shrugged their shoulders as if my certificate didn't really amount to much.

To ease the pressure on my financial situation, I applied for a local government allowance, which I was eligible for while attending college and being simultaneously unemployed. It worked out at £30 per week, but to qualify for it I had to get my college tutor to sign my application. As far as I knew, I was the only student to have this arrangement, and I felt very embarrassed about it. Everyone else in my class could afford to buy lunch and wear nice clothes, while I had to wear the same clothes on most days and eat ramen pot noodles for lunch (because they only cost £1 for four). I wasn't able to cope with getting a job, though, so I just kept my head down and focussed on my coursework.

I managed to save up some of my allowance money to take my driving theory test, because I wanted to be able to drive and maybe even get my own car one day. I purchased the theory book and began studying it every day, becoming so focussed on it that I felt the need to push some of my college work to one side for a while. Once I felt ready, I booked my test and went to the centre in Southgate to do the exam. I thought I would pass with flying colours and I knew that I would receive my results immediately following the test. I clicked away at the multiple-choice questions and finished thirty minutes before the timer was up. I was so excited to have done so well and headed over to the results room full of confidence. When my results were printed out, though, I couldn't believe my eyes. I had got only 28 out of the 35 questions correct and that was an instant fail. My heart sank and I stood fixed to the spot, totally bewildered. How could I have failed after all that studying? Why does nothing ever go right for me?

I went home with a heavy heart, but I decided that the best thing was to get straight back on the horse and try again. Within a few days, I had rebooked my exam and was studying my theory book again to find out where I had gone wrong.

College became increasingly challenging for me and I began to clash with our data analysis tutor on a regular basis. I felt that she didn't help me enough to get to grips with the content of the course and that she thought I was just being rebellious whenever I raised my concerns. My concentration began to suffer and so, to take my mind off the difficulties I was having with the coursework, I started to look at cheap cars for sale on the internet. I really wanted to have my own car and to be able to drive wherever the road took me, hopefully somewhere far away from my life at that time.

I went through the driving theory books with a fine-tooth comb to ensure I didn't miss anything this time. In November, I went back to Southgate to take the test again, more determined than ever to pass it. Once again, I flew through the questions without hesitation and went to collect my results full of confidence. When I saw that I had got only 26 out of 35 questions right this time, I asked the examiners to double-check my results, which they confirmed as being correct. I left Southgate on an all-time low, wondering how I could be so stupid that I couldn't pass a simple multiple-choice exam.

When I got home that day, my cousin Warren called to say that his dad (my Uncle Stewart) was having another party at his house, and that I was invited. At first, I didn't want to go because I felt so depressed, but something inside told me to go to take my mind off my failed test. When I got there that evening, I saw that everyone was having a good time, eating, drinking and listening to music. I didn't mingle much, I just stood halfway up the stairs looking down at the party, deep in thought about my latest failure. I woke up a bit when I suddenly noticed a gorgeous woman sitting in the living room. She looked exotic, with black curly hair, a fair complexion, beautiful make-up and a sexy figure. I had never seen anyone like her and I couldn't take my eyes off her for most of the evening. After a while, she caught me staring at her, but she didn't really react too much. She seemed to be with Shane, a long-time friend of my Uncle Stewart's.

Shane got drunk to the point of acting the fool and dancing inappropriately with one of my aunts. Shane's girlfriend, the exotic woman I was fast becoming infatuated with, did not take this lightly and tried to pull him away. It created such a scene that she had to back away, but she looked very angry. Shane began rolling around on the floor, acting like a proper clown. I thought this might be my one opportunity to talk to his girlfriend, so I walked over and said, 'Are you okay?'

She paused for a moment, surprised by my sudden appearance, but then began to talk to me about Shane and how he was disrespecting her. We then spoke to one another for the next forty minutes. She was called Carolina, she was Mauritian and she had been seeing Shane for a while. She was thirty-four years old and she worked in the cosmetics industry in Central London. The spark of attraction between us was obvious, but it also felt wrong to be speaking to her like that, considering she had come to the party with my uncle's friend. I really needed a boost, though, and she was the most attractive woman I had ever spoken to. I was, of course, still very much on the rebound from Sabine at the time. I became increasingly bold as the conversation went on and I told Carolina that I would not disrespect her like Shane did if I had a woman like her.

Shane had looked over at us talking a couple of times, but he was very drunk and I didn't much care what he thought by then. I decided it was time to leave, though, and after saying goodbye to everyone else, I shook Carolina's hand as I said goodbye to her. She smiled at me and said, 'I hope to see you again, Dean.' I somehow knew that our paths would cross again and I thought about her all the way home. I was mesmerised by her, in spite of the fact she was twice my age.

The following day, I looked at my driving test theory book again and happened to notice on the back cover that my book was not in fact the official test book provided by the examination company, but one from a third party. I headed straight to a bookstore and saw that the official book was four times the size of the one I'd been using. I really did feel like an idiot then, but I was also relieved to find the correct study aid, which I bought on the spot.

In December that year (2002), I turned eighteen, without ceremony or celebration. I received no special presents, and nobody suggested a party, in spite of the fact that my mother's family and my Dad's family both seemed to throw parties at the drop of a hat. There was, however, to be a New Year's Eve party at the Selby Centre in White Hart Lane, which the whole family on my mother's side (except for my mother and Tommy) was going to, so I decided to go as well.

On the day of the New Year's Eve party, I happened to realise that I had left a video at Sabine's parents' house and I called them to see if I could go round and collect it. Paul said that would be okay, so I jumped on the bus that would take me there. I was greeted warmly by Rosie and I found Paul cooking fish in the kitchen. He asked me how I was and I told him I was fine and that I was enjoying my course at college – I didn't want him to know that I had been having problems with my state of mind or my course. They had told Sabine since I called that I was coming and they said that she was on her way home. I decided to wait, partly because I felt great in the new clothes I had on and because I had just changed my hairstyle. I no longer felt intimidated by Sabine or her family either, so I was feeling relaxed in their home for the first time. After a couple of hours, though, there was no sign of Sabine and I got fed up waiting. I said goodbye to Paul and Rosie and headed for the front door just as Sabine walked in.

She looked like she had just had the shock of her life, like she immediately knew I wasn't the same person that used to be at the beck and call of herself and her parents. It made me feel good to think that maybe she regretted her previous treatment of me. We spoke briefly and it was clear that we felt no animosity towards each other, but I could see a curiosity and a longing in her eyes. The arrogance of youth being what it is, I felt on a complete high when I left.

Chapter 17:
The irresistible attraction of an older woman

If you feel as if you need to be the one in control of your romantic life, you're going to struggle in a relationship with an older woman.

I headed back from Sabine's house to get ready for the New Year's Eve party at the Selby Centre and then met Warren and Uncle Stewart in the pub for a couple of drinks. I ordered us a round of beers before we went on to vodka and lemonade. Shane turned up out of the blue and, with the alcohol already hitting my bloodstream, the first question I asked him was: 'Where is Carolina?' It wasn't my place to ask that, so Shane looked confused, but he answered me anyway. 'I'm not sure where she is,' he said, looking at me as if I had just touched a nerve.

We all headed over to the Selby Centre, where a Guyanese dance was in full swing. Guyanese functions usually involve music, food and much alcohol, which I have always thought a bit hypocritical as most of the people who attend them are practising Muslims, but that night I was solely focussed on having a good time at all costs.

After about an hour, out of the blue, Carolina turned up. She looked amazing in a grey dress. As I had drunk quite a lot by then, I immediately locked eyes with her and asked her if she wanted to dance. Before she even had a chance to answer, I took her hand and led her to the dance floor. We were soon all over one another and, after dancing together for a while, we took ourselves off to a corner and spoke about the first time we had met.

She also said she had been to my uncle's house again following the party we had met at, and that she had hoped to see me there. I knew now for sure that she was interested in me, especially when she added that she had broken up with Shane, which is why they hadn't come to the New Year's Eve party together. It felt like the green light to get to know her better, but for whatever reason I couldn't quite shake Sabine or Shane from my thoughts either.

As midnight approached, I led Carolina over to where Shane was standing, so that they could either reconcile their differences or get closure or whatever it was they needed to do. I left them to it and went off to find my cousins. I worried that I might be shooting myself in the foot by putting them together like that, but I also knew that it would be wrong to disrespect Shane by assuming that he was over Carolina. When it was time to leave, I saw Carolina walking out by herself, so I assumed that Shane had not been bothered about getting back with her. I put my arm around her as if she were now my girlfriend, and I could tell immediately that she was entirely comfortable with that. My cousin Elle invited us all back to my Aunt Jane's house (Aunt Jane was Elle's mother) and Shane and Carolina had both been invited.

When I arrived at my aunt's house, I got a call from Sabine on my mobile. She said she was calling to say 'Happy New Year' but I instinctively knew there was more to it than that. By the time we had told each other how we had spent our respective evenings, the conversation had degenerated into who was to blame for our separation, and I think it ended with me saying something unkind about her having blown her chance when she had it. I fell asleep shortly afterwards. The following morning I woke up with a slight hangover, and

I also felt angry at Sabine for phoning when she did. It was a bad way to start the year, I thought.

A few days after the New Year's Eve party I got a surprise text message: *Hi Dean, hope you had a good night at the dance, Carolina xxx*

I didn't know how she had got hold of my number, but I didn't care either and I texted her back immediately to see how she was. Within a minute, she called me. Apparently, we had exchanged numbers on New Year's Eve, but I had been too drunk to remember that happening. She asked me if I wanted to go for a drink that evening, and I said that I thought that was a very good idea. We agreed that she would pick me up in her car at my grandmother Ann's house, which is still where I was staying at the time. When she arrived, I got into the car and kissed her on both cheeks. We went into Wood Green and, after parking up, walked to Yates, a very popular bar that played music. I ordered us some drinks, but I had already decided not to drink too much, just in case the evening turned out how I hoped it would.

Carolina explained that she and Shane had definitely broken up for good. She also said that they were actually distant cousins, which seemed a bit weird to me. Things had not really been working out with her and Shane by the time of the party at Uncle Stewart's, she said, so she had been pleased when she noticed me looking at her from the staircase. After about ten minutes, a woman who had been sitting at the bar came over to us and explained that she was a medium and that she got a strong vibe that there was a connection between Carolina and myself. I thought that was a bit strange, to say the least, but we were both glad that she had said it, I think. We danced, often intimately, until about 1 a.m., at which point Carolina drove me home. We talked and kissed in the car for another two hours, until Carolina said she needed to go to the toilet.

I thought this might be my chance, so I said: 'If you come into the house, you will have to be quiet so as not to wake my grandmother, and I'll need to lock the door behind us in case you try to leave and make a noise.'

'That's fine by me,' she said.

We tiptoed into the house, where I directed her to the toilet nearest my bedroom. When she joined me in my room, I showed her my family photos and we talked quietly for a while, until we finally went to bed. I was nervous, never having been with a woman of Carolina's age before, but it soon became clear she knew what she was doing. We both got undressed and she got into bed first. She was wearing a leopard-skin-print lingerie set, which I thought was the sexiest underwear I had ever laid eyes on. I only had a pair of loose boxers on and, when I slid into bed, Carolina got herself into a spooning position and started rubbing her cheeks against me. I leaned over, and we began French kissing. I couldn't contain myself any longer, so I grabbed a condom from my bedside table and we were soon having great sex.

Everything about Carolina opened my eyes to the essence of a fully grown woman, which was a very different experience to the teenagers I had known before, young girls who had played games with my emotions more than anything else. Carolina raised the bar when it came to sexual expression and, after we had both climaxed, there remained a lot of affection between us. We continued to touch each other until we finally feel asleep. In the morning, which was only a very few hours after we had fallen asleep, there was a comfortable silence between us as we locked eyes and smiled and kissed one another. We talked about how wonderful the night before had been and Carolina then suggested that we go out for breakfast. We headed out to a cafe nearby.

The following day, once everything had hit me, I realised that I had been to bed with the ex-girlfriend of my uncle's friend, and that it would therefore be best to keep quiet about the situation so as not to suffer their disapproval.

An intrinsic part of Mauritian culture is sega music and dance, the latter being a belly dance performed without the feet ever leaving the ground. Carolina was a sega dancer, and she performed at various events and carnivals. She invited me to a Mauritian dance, but I said I didn't want to go as I was not much of a dancer. She told me that she would go anyway and that she would meet me afterwards. This bothered me, of course – I might have been going out with an older woman, but that didn't make me any more mature myself.

After the dance Carolina met me and, as we sat in her car talking, we arranged for her to come and stay with me again. A few days later, she arrived as planned and I sneaked her into my grandmother's house and up the stairs, just like before. My grandmother knew Shane, so I didn't want her to know what was going on.

Up in my room, while she relaxed and took off her make-up, Carolina put a CD she had brought with her into my stereo and we listened to her favourite sega music. One of the tracks had a very funny intro and I couldn't help laughing at it, whereupon she gave me a very stern look. She asked me why I was laughing, and I told her that the intro had just sounded a bit funny to me. She looked offended and the previous positive vibe in the room was quickly replaced with an awkward silence.

After a few minutes, she said, 'If you find my culture funny, I should probably just leave.' I explained that I wasn't laughing at her culture or her music, just at the intro to that one track, but if looks could kill that would have been the end of me. The atmosphere in the room eventually calmed down, but for the first time I wondered if there were going to be problems between us if something as trivial as that could cause conflict and uncertainty.

The following day we went for a drive in Carolina's car to West London, where she used to live. As she drove, she told me about her job working as a cosmetics consultant in a high-end store in Central London, which explained why she wore so much make-up and perfume, I realised, and why she wore such beautiful clothes. She then said that she was going to perform a dance at another Mauritian event and asked me again if I wanted to go. I wasn't comfortable about her performing in front of other men, but I didn't say that. I just told her I would think about it and let her know.

The following week, I was back in college, where I still kept myself to myself, but I was definitely more relaxed knowing that I had Carolina to talk to outside of college. The next time I saw her, she gave me a gift of some aftershaves she had got from the store she worked at. I never had a woman give me gifts before, and I really appreciated it. She then spoke to me about the dancing event again and, when she noticed the immediate change in my mood at the mere mention of it, our conversation quickly escalated into an argument.

'I love to dance,' she said. 'It's who I am. I don't dance with other men; I dance to perform. If you can't handle that, then I may not be for you.'

I remained quiet for a few minutes, looking out of the car window as I tried to gather my thoughts. I just couldn't come to grips with it, though, because I felt jealous at the thought of her dancing provocatively in front of other men, whatever she said about it being a performance thing. When I didn't reply, she told me me that an ex-partner of hers had been possessive of her and that their relationship had been volatile because he hadn't liked her performing either. On the one hand, I knew that I should put my discomfort to one side to please her and to keep our relationship on an even keel. On the other hand, I felt that she was selfish in putting her dancing before me.

The atmosphere eventually settled, and we continued the evening with no more conversation on the topic. There was no doubt, though, that we had a very large elephant in our room.

Chapter 18:
Psychosis and flying raspberries

You often don't see the warning signs until it's too late.

The week that followed the argument over Carolina's sega dancing went by without a hitch and it felt great to be together, doing normal things without a care in the world. It wasn't to last, though. One Saturday afternoon, Carolina drove us to Turnpike Lane to get an Indian pastry dessert. While she was parking, a good-looking tutor from my college (she was an Indian woman with deep green eyes) walked past and looked briefly in my direction, as you do when you recognise someone in the street. Not knowing her outside of the classroom, I simply nodded in her direction by way of acknowledgement, just as a common courtesy.

'Who's that?' asked Carolina.
'It's just one of the tutors from my college,' I said
'Why is she looking at you like that?' said Carolina, starting to sound aggressive.
'What do you mean?'
'She was looking at you in a weird way and I don't like it.'
'I think it was just a case of her recognising me,' I said, trying to defuse the situation.
'I don't care, I don't want her looking at you like that,' Carolina replied.

We left it at that, but I was beginning to realise that Carolina had some deep-seated issues, and the rest of the day was spent largely in silence.

I discovered in the weeks that followed that Carolina remained bitter towards Shane and was intent on exacting some revenge over his treatment of her. She still had keys to Shane's flat and car, and she was forever plotting her next move. She picked me up one Sunday afternoon and told me that there was something she needed to do. She drove to where Shane lived and said: 'I know Shane is out today at the pub and I still have the keys to his car.'

'What are you going to do?' I asked, as she got out of the car, but she didn't answer. She walked over to Shane's car, opened the passenger door, removed his tax disc and walked casually back to her own car. I couldn't believe what I was seeing. She said that she hoped Shane would be pulled over by the police when they noticed the missing tax disc, as if that was a perfectly normal explanation for what she had just done. Although I knew that their relationship had not always been a smooth one, this still struck me as a bit odd. However, I still had strong feelings for her, so I just went with the flow.

Valentine's Day was coming up and Carolina dropped off a bag of gifts for me a few days beforehand. She got me more aftershave, some clothes, chocolates, a teddy bear and a card. I had heard about a Valentine's dance at the Selby Centre and we agreed to go to that. I was a bit apprehensive about being seen out and about with her, not least because her recent behaviour had been so erratic, but I thought we should celebrate the occasion in an appropriate manner, and the dance seemed as good a way as any.

When we arrived, there were already a few people there that I knew. They looked at me strangely, presumably because of the age difference between me and Carolina. I got us a couple of drinks and the place soon got lively as most people got up to dance. While I was standing with Carolina, a guy came over to say hello to her. She introduced him to me as her friend David, explaining that he was a family friend. They exchanged a few words and he went off to dance.

After I had drunk four vodkas and coke, I felt brave enough to dance myself, so Carolina and I went on to the dance floor. I was in a seductive mood by now and started to dance closer and closer to Carolina. Suddenly, she pulled away from me, saying: 'I don't know how to dance like this, and I don't like it.' She then walked off to find her friend David and began to dance near him. I went into a complete meltdown and simply walked out of the building, feeling confused, hurt and angry. The venue was only a twenty-minute walk from my grandmother's house, so I headed off in that direction. About forty minutes after I got home, Carolina called.

'Where are you?' I heard her shout above the music.
'I went home,' I said.
'Why did you do that?' she shouted. 'Stay there. I'm coming over.'

Within ten minutes she had driven to my street and she called to say that she was waiting down the road. Still seeing red, I went out and got into her car.

'What's your problem, Dean?' she asked.

I told her in no uncertain terms what my problem was and an almighty argument ensued, which culminated in me getting out of the car and slamming the door shut so hard that the lights in some of the neighbouring houses came on not long after.

I began to walk back towards my grandmother's house, but she rolled her window down and followed alongside me in her car.

'If you don't get back in the car, I'm going to take a fucking overdose!' she screamed.

Panicking at the thought of anyone hearing her screams, I got back into the car and tried to calm her down. We eventually agreed that we should have avoided the dance altogether and sneaked back to my grandmother's house to get some sleep.

The following morning started off as a somewhat sombre affair. I went downstairs to get us something to eat from the fridge and grabbed some raspberries and yoghurt. While we were eating those, Carolina brought up the topic of the dance again and another argument ensued. She began to scream and threw the tub of raspberries at the wall to reinforce some point or other. It made such a mess that I needed to wipe it down immediately for fear of it causing permanent stains. While I was doing this, Carolina began to push me against the wall.

'Do that again and I'll fucking knock you out!' I shouted.

'So, you're going to hit me now, are you?' she shouted, packing her things and getting dressed. She stormed out of the house, slamming the front door shut. I was lucky that my grandmother wasn't home; otherwise I would have been in deep shit.

I breathed a sigh of relief that crazy Carolina had left the house, but it wasn't long before I heard a loud bang. She had come back, and she was now trying to kick the door in. I opened my bedroom window and told her to go home, whereupon she kicked the front door even harder. I shut the window and tried my best to ignore the din she was making, and she did eventually leave.

She phoned later that same day and we managed to calm one another down. She came back the following day with a pack of raspberries to replace the pack she had thrown at me, which I went out to her car to collect. My grandmother was home, so I decided to take Carolina to the house to say hello to her. As I opened the front door and walked in, my grandmother was already in the passageway.

'This is Carolina,' I said. 'She has come to say hello.'

'Dean, you are not allowed to bring her here,' my grandmother replied. 'I don't want to be seen as if I am accommodating your relationship with that woman and she is not to come here again.'

I was taken aback at my grandmother's attitude, and I argued with her over my right to have a relationship with whoever I chose. I saw a side of my grandmother that I didn't like, and it never occurred to me that she might well have a point, especially given that she had been providing me with free board and lodgings for quite some time already.

In any event, Carolina and I left and went for a drive. We realised that my grandmother probably didn't like the idea that I was with her son's friend's ex-partner, but I was still angry with her. I decided that Carolina would just have to continue coming when my grandmother wasn't home, and that I would just have to keep sneaking her in when my grandmother was home. It took careful planning, and it was a constant strain, because my grandmother was home most of the time. Some days we just had to spend a few hours in the car to have time together. It got to the point where we started to stay in hotels, which was costly, but sometimes it was the only way we could be intimate, because Carolina lived with her parents.

Carolina continued to mention that she had other male friends, but she stressed that they were just friends. There was one in particular that she spoke to on the phone, even in front of me if we were out together. I was uncomfortable with it, but I didn't say anything in case another argument broke out.

Carolina's liberal attitude to having other male friends didn't apply to me having female acquaintances, though. When we were out shopping in Wood Green one day, I ran into a girl I used to work with at Safeway and we stopped to say hello to one another. I introduced Carolina, but she didn't look at all pleased and I knew what was coming as we walked back to the car.

'It was like you and that girl had a history together,' she said, true to form. 'It was like you didn't know whether to hug or kiss each other.'

'I used to work with her and that's all there is to it,' I said. 'What am I supposed to do, just ignore every girl I ever met or worked with? You even have a male friend, who is more than just an acquaintance by all accounts, and I haven't exactly banged on about that.'

Carolina just carried on talking, justifying the appropriateness of her own relationships and the suspicions she had about mine. I decided I couldn't take her double standards any longer.

'Fuck this,' I said, 'let's just call the whole thing off and you won't have to worry about your petty suspicions anymore.'

Carolina began to cry, like a child that couldn't get its own way. She eventually simmered down, and the truth came out about her major concerns. She said she was worried about me going off to university (I had started to consider this as an option once I finished my three years at college), because she would probably never see me again once I met someone younger and more attractive. I tried to provide her with the reassurances she so desperately needed, but it was all becoming a huge strain.

The arguments continued, but each time we were on the brink of breaking up Carolina would shower me with gifts and park her car outside my grandmother's house until I came out to see her. I felt like I was being stalked.

This was the ebb and flow until things finally came to a head one weekend. Carolina had booked us into a hotel in West London and we were soon being wildly intimate, which had always been the best thing about our relationship. On this occasion, however, Carolina's sex drive was so high that I simply couldn't keep up with her. We had been having sex for so long that I was utterly drained. It dented my confidence that she hadn't climaxed after all that time, and things went from bad to worse when she told me in a very condescending manner that it was okay, that I shouldn't worry about it, that sometimes men just can't quite keep up with women. That was the cue for what would prove to be our final argument, which ended up being so loud that the hotel manager knocked on our door at one point to find out what was going on.

I asked Carolina to drop me home as I'd had enough and I began to pack my things, even though we were not due to check out until the following day. Somewhat childishly, I sat in the back seat as she drove me home. She went back to the hotel and sent me a string of text messages from there, mostly saying how lonely she was. I replied by telling her I had had enough and wanted out of the relationship once and for all.

She fought a rear-guard action in the weeks that followed, almost sweet-talking me into submission on occasions, but I held firm. When she saw that the sweet-talking wasn't working, she began parking her car outside my grandmother's house and posting letters through the door. It got so bad I had to check the coast was clear before entering or leaving the house. She eventually got the message and that was that.

I was still only eighteen years old at this time, but of course there was nothing I didn't know about women by now. Surely no one had ever had such intense relationships by the time they were eighteen? I decided with the benefit of all this wisdom that the next woman I got involved with would need to be less possessive, not at all argumentative and certainly not living by double standards. I would also pay more attention up front to the number of other 'male friends' they had. I remained impossibly attracted to women, but I wanted to avoid the petty arguments that came with relationships if I possibly could. Perhaps I should just concentrate more on the sex, I thought.

Chapter 19:
Cars, college and women

Everyone remembers the best year of their life; this was mine.

With my relationship problems out of the way, I was able to put my focus back into my college work, which I had been neglecting a bit in order to spend time with Carolina. I also got back into studying for the driving theory test, which I still really wanted to pass. I put so much effort into my coursework and into studying the driving theory that I hardly ever left the house in the evenings or at weekends. This continued until the summer holidays arrived, but, even then, I didn't go out much. I just focussed more on the driving theory test because I had finished the year at college. After eight weeks of revision, I booked my theory test and headed to Southgate to take the test for a third time. I was more determined than ever.

When I got to the test centre, I discovered that a 'hazard perception' element had been added to the test, which I had not known about. I did the 'hazard perception' part first and then moved on to the main theory test. I clicked away so quickly that I completed the whole test within fifteen minutes, which meant I still had an hour and fifteen minutes left. I was confident that I had passed the test with flying colours, so I submitted it there and then. At no stage did it occur to me that it might be sensible to spend at least some of the remaining time double-checking my answers.

I went over to the results desk to collect my score and this time the test officer produced two documents. I opened the first one to discover that I had been marked 100 per cent for the hazard perception element of the test. I opened the second one and saw that I had also passed the theory test, with a score of 34 out of 35. I had finally done it! I was so excited, but I kept the results to myself because I knew by now that no one in the family would give me any credit for passing an exam anyway. My next goal was to pass the actual driving test and to do that I needed to take driving lessons. I found an instructor within a week of passing the theory test and booked my first lesson.

My instructor turned up in a silver Ford Focus and I was beside myself at the thought of driving it. He introduced himself as Henry and began to explain the basic controls. As I wanted to get my manual licence, the car I learned in had to have a manual gearbox, as opposed to an automatic one. Henry went over the biting point of the clutch and the gear changes, then asked me to get into the driver's seat. He told me to put the car into first gear, depress the clutch with my left foot, and then slowly press down on on the accelerator with my right foot while simultaneously bringing up the clutch with my left foot. I followed the instructions and found to my amazement that we were moving. The instructor then asked me to change up into second gear, but I got confused and stalled the car. He told me again how to go through the gear changes and I kept practising until I managed to drive the car around a few streets. I was nervous, but I eventually began to settle into it. When the lesson had finished, I felt like I still had a mountain to climb as we had only gone through gear changes and braking. He said there were a number of manoeuvres I needed to learn and it all seemed a bit complex. I was forever putting pressure on myself to achieve the next goal, then the one after that, and then the one after that again. I never really took time to appreciate my gains, my moments of success.

I took as many lessons as I could until my third and last college year began in September 2003, and thereafter I juggled my driving lessons with my college work. After about eight driving lessons, I was becoming confident in my driving ability, but my manoeuvring still needed more work.

In college, I began to socialise more due to my involvement in group assignments. There were three guys in particular that I began to relax and crack jokes with: Adon, who was Greek and lived in Palmers Green; Harry, who was Nigerian and lived near the college; and Troy, who was African American and lived in Turnpike Lane. All three lived with their parents. They were the loudest students in the class, and also the funniest. We became good friends as the term went on.

As it was our final year, we had to knuckle down with our assignments, so it wasn't all fun and games. One day, though, the discussion turned to social networking sites, which were really only getting started about then. The two which caught our eye at the time were Face-pic and Faceparty. They contained the social profiles of their members and the means for those members to communicate with one another. Adon, Troy and Harry joined first, because I was a bit sceptical to begin with. After checking out their profiles, I decided to give it a try and created my own profile. After a week on both sites, I could see the profiles of a lot of young women, and I even received messages from a couple of admirers. It was fair to say that this was internet dating in its infancy. After a while, I began communicating with a few of the young women. One that attracted my attention was a girl called Kathy, who lived in

Stevenage. I had never been there, but we got to know each other really well through phone calls and messages.

I eventually managed to get my own PC for my bedroom at my grandmother's house, so I also ordered an internet connection. When I finally got hooked up, I was very excited, not least because I could now access Face-pic and Faceparty from home as well as college. I also wanted to find a way to earn some money and I had already seen a couple of guys at college on a website called eBay. Those guys had been ranting on about it for weeks, so I started to pay attention and I asked Troy to explain it to me in greater detail. He told me that it was an online marketplace, where you could sell just about anything to make some money, and he said I should bring something into college to sell and he would show me how to use it.

I went back home and looked around my bedroom for something of value and found an old camera. The following day, Troy showed me how to use the site to list the camera and I felt as if I had just discovered a gold mine. The website gave me a way to make money without even having a job and I began selling some of my old clothes. I then devised a strategy to buy items cheaply on eBay and then sell them on at a profit on that same site. It was such a good earner that I could soon afford to buy myself new clothes. I even bought clothes to wear at parties and then sold them on eBay the next day at a tidy profit.

With my financial situation picking up, my driving lessons going well and my social circle expanding, my next goal was to meet some girls. After a few weeks of talking to Kathy via webcam, she invited me to meet her in Stevenage and said I could stay at her house while her mother was away. As we had been building up a connection for a while, I was excited at the thought of meeting her. However, I had never travelled that far from home and I had led such a sheltered life that I worried that something dreadful might happen to me. I could get lost, or even robbed, I thought. In any event, we arranged to meet on a Saturday evening when she finished work, so I jumped on the train at Finsbury Park and made the forty-minute journey to Stevenage and hung around the station waiting for Kathy. No one robbed me.

After about fifteen minutes, I noticed her across the street. As she walked over to me, I could she was wearing her work uniform (it was a waitress outfit, because she worked at Whittard of Chelsea), but she looked amazing. Kathy was small, had long, straight, dark-brown hair, a nice curvy figure and beautiful olive skin. She was the same age as me, which was something of a relief after what I had been through with Carolina.

When she reached me, I hugged her and gave her a kiss on the cheek. She seemed happy and excited to see me, and we jumped straight on a bus to where she lived. I had never met someone and gone back to their house straight away and I'm not sure who was the more nervous, Kathy or me.

The house was very nice. It had a family feel to it, with lots of photos and a number of these positive family affirmations hanging on the walls I can't remember what they were exactly, but you know the sort of thing: *Family is a Gift that Lasts Forever*; *Our Family is a Circle of Friend*s). It felt a million lives from any home atmosphere I had ever enjoyed. There was also a cat and a fish pond.

Kathy got us something to drink and, after we had chatted for a while, she invited me upstairs to her bedroom. I could barely breathe; we had been flirting for so long via webcam that to be in her presence seemed like a dream come true. Her room had wall-to-wall posters of boy bands and other singers, lilac wallpaper, a huge bed and a TV with DVD player. I pointed out that she had a lot of films on DVD that I liked, especially some of the comedy ones, and she asked me if I wanted to watch one. I didn't, I had other things on my mind right then, but I said yes. She put one on and sat cross-legged on the floor to watch it. After a couple of minutes, she looked up at me and offered her lips, so I leaned over and kissed her. I became aroused straight away, but I needed the loo first and excused myself.

When I returned, we lay down on the bed and began to kiss and feel each other all over. That went on for a couple of hours while the film was playing, and when it had finished we stripped naked. I was almost in a state of panic and, as a result, I couldn't sustain an erection at first. I remembered that the same thing had happened with Janine once, and I couldn't then get that out of my mind.

We eventually fell asleep for a while. When I woke up, I felt more relaxed, so we finally had sex. I felt relieved in more ways than one. After a few more hours' sleep, we got up and had breakfast and just relaxed around the house. The day flew in really quickly and, before we knew it, it was time for me to leave before Kathy's mother came home. I packed my few things and we walked to the train station together, because that gave us more time together than taking the bus would have done. Kathy looked upset, but we agreed that we would definitely see each other again and we hugged and kissed before I got on the train home. On the journey back, I reflected that it had been my best weekend in a very long time, not least because it had been free of complications and arguments.

I definitely wanted to see Kathy again, but after a few days back home, boredom kicked in and I started to get the urge to meet other girls. I was becoming increasingly obsessed with the idea of having sex with girls just for the sake of it and wondered if that made me a bad person. On reflection, I probably wasn't the first young man to go through that particular phase, and I probably wasn't the last either. In no time at all, thanks largely to my social networking sites, I was seeing four different girls. Kathy was my main girlfriend, there was no doubt about that, but there was also Simone, an Indian girl who lived in West London; Suzanne, an English girl who lived in East London; and Chantal, a mixed-race girl who lived around the corner from me. I developed a strategy that allowed me to fit them all in every week, but I still worked everything around Kathy. I was having a ball whenever I was with any of them, but as soon as I was on my own, I immediately felt desperately lonely and bored beyond belief. I was on a roller coaster of highs and lows, and the lows drove me back time and again to Face-pic. Deep down I felt guilty, but I didn't want it to stop either.

College was going well and my relationship with my tutors had much improved. Because I was coming to the end of my final year, I needed to fill in my UCAS form to apply for a place at university. Computers remained my strong point and I had decided that I wanted to take Computer Networking at London Metropolitan University. I had seen the university four years earlier, while walking along the road on my way to a cinema in Holloway Road, and ever since that day I had nurtured in my mind the thought of going there if I ever made it to university at all, which was now looking much more likely than I had ever thought possible. It just depended on the satisfactory completion of my college coursework, as there were no actual exams to sit.

Adon, Troy and Harry had no idea what they wanted to do, or which university they wanted to do it at, so we went off together to look at different university campuses, including four in North London alone. Nowhere we visited made me change my mind about wanting to go to London Metropolitan, so I filled in my UCAS form, sent it off, and looked forward to the summer.

I had now completed twenty driving lessons and I had booked my driving test a few weeks before the end of college. When the day came, I met my instructor at the driving test centre in Winchmore Hill. I was confident, yet nervous, and I just wanted it to be over with. When we had signed all the necessary forms, I had to do an eye test by reading a car licence number from a set distance, carry out some basic car checks and describe how I would change a tyre, all of which was fine. When we finally got into the car, the whole thing felt really weird, because it was the first time I was going to drive a car without my instructor beside me. I drove off, following the instructions of the examiner.

Not long into the test, I stalled the engine at a roundabout and got so frustrated that I almost forgot what to do to restart the car. Shortly afterwards, I clipped a wing mirror driving through a width restriction. By this time, I was so stressed that I didn't even care about the outcome. I just wanted it to be over. When it was finally at an end, the examiner said, 'You have now completed your driving test, but I'm sorry to say that you have failed.' He then explained all the mistakes I'd made and I was shocked to learn of seven mistakes on top of the two I knew about. I relayed the feedback to my driving instructor, who told me that we could work on the weak areas and he dropped me back home. I was so disappointed in myself that I wanted to do the test again as soon as possible, so I got on the phone to the test centre and booked the first available slot in three weeks' time.

Chapter 20:
Boy racer

Passing your test doesn't mean you're mature enough to drive a car.

I booked double lessons with my driving instructor to improve on my weaknesses ahead of my second test. When the time came, I was pleased to see that I had a different examiner, and that he was much younger than the last one (for no logical reason, I thought a younger examiner might have more empathy towards me than an older one). I sailed through my eye test, car checks and 'how to change a wheel' test and we were soon on our way.

Luckily, I didn't have the same route as last time and didn't have to squeeze through any width restrictions or navigate any roundabouts. I completed the test without feeling as if I had made errors, but I hadn't noticed seven of my errors last time round, so I waited with bated breath for the examiner to deliver his verdict. 'That's the end of your test,' he said, 'and I'm pleased to say that you've passed. You did make thirteen minor mistakes, though, and you do need to slow down a bit.'

I thanked him and headed over to tell my instructor the good news. 'Well done, Dean,' he said, 'I knew you would pass this time.' We went into the office and I was handed my certificate to verify that I now qualified for a full UK licence. I was overwhelmed, because it meant I could get a car and drive about on my own, which would add a whole new dimension to my life.

When I got home, my mother and Tommy were waiting for me at my grandmother's house to see how

I'd done. I hadn't told them about my test, so my grandmother must have done that. When I told them I'd passed, they congratulated me. It was the first time I could remember them congratulating me for anything, so it felt good.

I began looking at car magazines and one in particular, called *Max Power*, which was very popular with youngsters because it had modified cars with big engines and expensive sound systems. I wanted to have a car like that, but I also knew that I couldn't afford one. I began ringing insurance companies to see what my premium would be on different cars and got very expensive quotes of around £2,500 for a year.

My mother knew I was looking at cars and decided to get involved, taking the more sensible approach of looking at basic cars on my behalf. In the meantime, I was already ordering speakers and amplifiers for a car I didn't even have. One day, my mother and Tommy took me to look at a purple-blue Vauxhall Corsa in West London. It only had a small engine, but it seemed to be in very clean condition and we took it for a test drive. It checked out, so my mother handed over £1,700 on the spot and that was that. I had my very own car. I was delighted, but I don't remember feeling all that grateful to my mother, probably because I continued to put any act of generosity on her part down to a need to ease her conscience.

It didn't really sink in for a while that, without a job, I wouldn't be able to afford to run a car. After a couple weeks, though, I set about installing the stereo system I had bought. I began by removing all the door panels so that I could run the wires behind them. I did really well until I got to the bit where I had to wire up the amplifiers, speakers and CD player. I drafted in a family friend called Collin, who identified where all the wires needed to be connected and, once that was done, the whole system was good to go. I was in music heaven in that car and I also had my independence, free to go wherever I wanted.

Over the next three months I drove all around, mostly in North London, picking up, dropping off or just visiting family and friends. It was also a lot easier to get to parties now that I had my own wheels. The only problem was my driving, because my need for speed totally clouded my judgement and I completely ignored the sensible advice that my examiner had given me after my test. I took corners too fast and, on one occasion, with my sister Laura in the car beside me, I went round a corner so fast that the car nearly skidded out of control. Although that shook me up, I didn't stop driving fast and I kept on taking unnecessary risks. One evening, I went to drop off a pair of shoes that Adon wanted to borrow from me for a party he was going to. On the way back from his house in Southgate, I took a bend so quickly that when I tried to straighten the car it began to steer out of control. I hit the brakes so fast that they locked. The car mounted a kerb and I saw my life flashing before me as the car stopped dead with a loud bang.

I had hit a signpost, but luckily not a human being. I pulled myself together a bit and got out of the car, only to see that the bonnet was smoking and that there was a massive dent on the front. The signpost was on the ground, because I had hit it with so much force that it had folded in the middle. As shock set in, I started to panic that I was going to get into serious trouble for crashing the car. I ran over to a phone box (because I had no credit on my pay-as-you-go mobile) and called the emergency services to let them know about the accident. I then called my mother, who also went into a complete state of panic. I told her I was okay and that I was waiting for the emergency services.

As people walked by, they stared at me and at the car. I felt like a total idiot. I was nervous that the police were going to arrest me, but a fire engine turned up. The firefighters opened the bonnet to let the gathering smoke escape and then just left again. I just stood there, confused and not knowing what to do. Eventually, my mother turned up and called the insurance company to arrange for someone to come and tow the car back to her house.

A week later, the insurance company took the car and declared it be a write-off. They paid my mother £2,000 for the claim, so at least she had made a small profit. My one and only prized possession was gone, and I was left to face some harsh realities. I had to accept that I was not yet mature enough to drive a car, and that I couldn't really afford to run one anyway. In many ways, the car being taken away from me was the best thing that could have happened. I wasn't ready for the responsibility and I didn't really want to kill myself either.

I was only halfway through the year and already I had experienced an intense and troubled relationship with an older woman; a social life that included four girls on the go at the same time; the conclusion of my college life and an application to go on to university; the passing of my driving test; and the ownership and total destruction of my very first car.

During my car phase, I had broken up with Kathy over things so trivial I can't even remember what they were, but we began to speak again during the summer and we spent time together at weekends. I still saw the other girls sometimes as well, though.

I managed to get a job as an engineer with a cable company called NTL, as a result of which I was sent on a two-week training course in Edmonton. The job involved the installation of phone, internet and cable TV services in people's homes. Once I had qualified, I was paired up with a guy called Nathan, who was about my age and had been on the same course as me. Our responsibilities as a two-man crew included driving our van to jobs, which I really didn't want to do, so I navigated and Nathan drove. When we got there, one of us had to run an external cable from the street to the customer's house, while the other installed the internal components. As Nathan wasn't very sociable, I took on the customer-facing role. I had a lot of fun for the remainder of that summer, because I enjoyed my job very much and I liked seeing Kathy at weekends. I was also earning some much-needed money.

That summer, the Euro 2004 football tournament was taking place in Portugal and the host country got all the way to the final, where they would surprisingly face the underdogs of Greece. Adon took his football seriously and he was beside himself that Greece had made it all the way to the final, as were his entire family. He invited me to his aunt and uncle's house in Palmers Green, where there was going to be a big get-together of family and friends to watch the biggest match in Greece's history.

On the day of the final, I travelled to Palmers Green with Adon and his mother and father. When we arrived, we saw that the entire house was bedecked with blue-and-white Greek flags. I was introduced to everyone, but I was still a bit shy because I had only ever met Adon and his parents before. Adon's aunt served up delicious Greek food and sent Adon and me out to sit in the garden with everyone else to eat.

As we were eating, I noticed two girls of around my age who seemed to have come out of nowhere. They were both gorgeous. Adon told me they were his cousin Stephanie (i.e. the daughter of the aunt and uncle whose house we were at) and her friend Salina. Stephanie had beautiful olive skin, lovely brown hair, and a curvaceous figure. Salina was from Egypt and had long, jet-black hair and beautifully tanned skin. They came over to talk to us and Stephanie kept looking at me, but I still felt a bit awkward in my unfamiliar surroundings and I didn't say much (although that didn't stop me wondering which one I would rather go out with).

As the evening progressed, the girls disappeared and everyone else sat down to watch the match. When Greece won against all the odds, the whole family celebrated like it was the best night of their lives. I had never witnessed such unbridled joy at a sports event and it was impossible not to get caught up in the euphoria of the occasion.

At the end of evening, I asked Adon about Salina, because I didn't want to be disrespectful by asking him about his cousin. He said there were rumours about her being a bit of a slut and that she had allegedly given some guy oral sex in an alleyway. About a week later, Adon sent me an email address for her. I added her to my MSN contacts and she accepted the connection.

We began messaging, but I had decided by then that it was Stephanie that I really wanted to get in touch with. I got Stephanie's email address from Salina and added her to my contacts. The following day Stephanie also accepted my invitation to connect and we began messaging one another. The conversation flowed nicely, but she seemed fairly oblivious to my amorous intentions, so I didn't come on too strong.

About a week later, Adon moved into his uncle's house after an argument with his mother and he invited me and Troy to visit him there. We were sitting in the front room where Adon had been sleeping when Stephanie came downstairs, wearing a very revealing pair of shorts and T-shirt. I tried to remain composed, although Troy and I did exchange glances which suggested we were on a similar wavelength as far as Stephanie's choice of outfit was concerned. As we were leaving, I heard her dad saying, 'Put some clothes on, Stephanie!'

The following day, I started to flirt a bit with Stephanie online, just to test the water. She went with the flow, so I asked her if she wanted to come to my house, and she said she would. A few days after that, I met Stephanie off the bus near my grandmother's house and we walked back there together. We went straight up to my room, where we talked about our interests and our studies. I was quite struck by her beauty, as she was without doubt one of the most attractive girls I had ever met. I had decided to play it cool, though, for fear of moving too fast. I walked her back to the bus stop after a couple of hours and gave her a hug and a kiss on the cheek before she got on her bus.

Summer was almost up, and my place at London Metropolitan University had been confirmed thanks to my college results, which included an AVCE in Information and Communication Technology (the equivalent of two A Levels).

When I arrived at the university to enrol, I saw Troy, Henry, Adon, Moe and Matt, all five of whom had been in my class in college. They had decided to do the exact same course as me, which was great news, because it meant I wasn't going to feel at all isolated when the term started. I would be able to have fun, all right, but I was determined to do well in my studies above all else.

Chapter 21:
University life

University is as good a time as any to get the hang of work-life balance.

Once I had completed my enrolment, I secured my student loan. I had no intention of squandering it and had in mind to save as much of it as I could. Along with my substantial earnings from eBay, I reckoned I wouldn't be broke like most students seemed to be at the end of their time at university.

Our gang of six met up and we headed out together for the Freshers' Fair at the Students' Union bar on Holloway Road, where we received much useful information and a goody bag of promotional products from local businesses, who obviously hoped that we would spend a portion of our student loans in their shops.

On our first day proper, we were greeted by the dean himself, who welcomed us into the fold and explained the values of the university. The university was only a direct thirty-minute bus ride from my grandmother's house, so I didn't need stay on campus, which saved me a small fortune. My lifestyle at university was pretty much the same as it had been at college.

After a few weeks of settling into my new academic surroundings, I felt comfortable with the pace of the coursework and I was able to balance it comfortably with my love life. Stephanie began coming to my house on a regular basis and we became increasingly intimate. One Monday evening, we could contain ourselves no longer and we finally had sex together for the first time.

I was head over heels in love with her at that moment and I wanted her to stay the night. You could have knocked me down with a feather when she explained that she couldn't because she had arranged to meet Salina so that they could go and buy some weed from their dealer, who was in the year above them in college. What Stephanie kept from me, I later learned, was that she was also involved with her dealer.

Having established that Stephanie wasn't entirely committed to our relationship, I carried on seeing Kathy and my other Face-pic girlfriends whenever I could. I had always imagined that having lots of girls in my life would make me happy, and it did in a sexual sense, but I still felt empty whenever I was by myself. I figured that maybe what I really yearned for was a deeper connection with one girl, but the idea of it also worried me. The more I thought about that, the more I realised that I feared history repeating itself. My Dad had committed 100 per cent to my mother, only for her to dump him with complete disregard for his happiness and the lives of the two small children they had at the time. Could any woman really be trusted, I wondered? The one time I could turn these black thoughts to my advantage was at the end of a relationship, because I was able to console myself with the thought that it would never have worked out in the long term anyway, given the unavoidable treachery of all women.

Although I couldn't trust members of the female species, I nonetheless remained impossibly attracted to them. I made contact with more and more of them through Face-pic, but not to the extent that I let it interfere with my coursework. Things between Stephanie and myself were going smoothly enough, in spite of the odd tit-for-tat moment. She was younger than me, of course, and at times she behaved like a child that needed attention, but she would soon lose interest if you overdid it. I remained a bit of a control freak, but I had to suppress that to strike the balance she seemed to need between getting sufficient attention from me and having enough freedom to do as she pleased.

That first year at university flew by very quickly, with lots of fun and games and relatively easy coursework. Our gang of six went to a lot of parties, met a lot of girls, shared ideas on how to make some extra pocket money and talked about where we saw ourselves after we had finished at university.

***

When we started our second year in 2005, things got a bit more serious. It was time to start preparing for our final exams in two years' time and we needed to get off to a good start. Matt had dropped out after the first year due to some personal problems and already had a job. This brought a sense of anxiety to the group, because we thought if we didn't take our studies seriously enough maybe that could happen to us as well.

I was aware that there was an option for students to take a year out after their second year to gain full-time work experience, before coming back to complete their degree the following year. Quite often, these students became addicted to a steady wage and never came back, and I was already determined not to go down that road. I decided that it would be better to get a part-time job related to my degree while still studying, so that by the time I graduated I would be leaving with a degree and two years' relevant work experience under my belt. I knew that employers always looked for candidates with qualifications and work experience, so I wanted to be ready for that.

I sent my CV off to my old college's ICT department and they got straight back to invite me in for an interview. Due to the fact that I used to study at the college, and that I was now studying for a computer networking degree, I was in a very strong position. Sure enough, the manager, Hussain, agreed to take me on as an ICT Technician one day a week to fit around my studies. The job included changing data tapes that backed up the college servers and physically taking them to a fire-proof safe in another building. It was an unpaid voluntary position, but I didn't care. It was my future I was thinking about. I also discovered that I was able to gain extra credit on my course for a module based on work experience, so the opportunity at my old college also enhanced my degree prospects.

My week filled up fast and I found myself juggling my studies, my eBay business, my work experience and all my girlfriends. Things got so busy that I had to have a specific day to see each of the girls, but still I never let it affect my progress at university.

I intended to save some of my second-year student loan and add it to the money I had saved from the first year, while the rest of the boys spent their money on cars, big-screen televisions, and expensive clothes. It never seemed to dawn on them that they should invest anything for the future.

Adon was being inundated with requests from the university's finance department about how he was going to fund his course for the second year and eventually his ID was blocked. He fell under a dark cloud and we didn't hear from him for over a week. I decided to go to his house (he was back staying at his parents by then) and when I got there he was playing on his Xbox. I asked him what was wrong, and he explained that he did not qualify for a student loan for his second year, because both his parents worked. His parents didn't have the funds to pay for him in spite of the fact that they both worked, so he had to drop out. I asked him what he was going to do, and he told me that he had started to apply for jobs because his parents were on his case to sort his life out.

First Matt and now Adon. Who would be next, I wondered? Adon did keep in contact at least, and after a month he managed to get a job selling cars for a Ford dealer. That was perfect for Adon, because he had the most bullshit of everyone in the group. With only four out of the original gang of six remaining, the atmosphere began to destabilise somewhat. Adon had made us laugh even on our most challenging days and I missed him, but I had to accept he wasn't coming back.

He was seeing a girl called Amy at the time, who he'd met on Face-pic. Their relationship had been a rocky one from the start, because, as far as I could make out, she applied the double standard that I was beginning to think was pretty much standard for all girls of her age. She thought it was absolutely fine to talk to her ex-boyfriend and have other male friends, whereas Adon was banned from doing any such thing. More worrying for me was that Amy had started to hang around Stephanie and take her to meet guys. Amy didn't know that Stephanie and I were seeing each other, but Stephanie did! I was seeing other women, of course, but I didn't count that as applying double standards because I was a bloke and that's what blokes did.

Eventually, Amy twigged that Stephanie and I were seeing each other, so Stephanie thought we had better tell Adon about our relationship before he found out from Amy. Stephanie spoke to him first and Adon didn't really respond much, she told me later. Amy had also thrown her weight behind our cause by the time I called

Adon and suggested that we meet up for a chat. We went to a pub in Cockfosters and the atmosphere between us was as relaxed as it had always been. Eventually, I brought up the fact that I had been in a relationship with his cousin for a while, so he asked me how serious it was. 'It is pretty serious,' I said, 'I have a lot of strong feelings for Stephanie.' He shook my hand and gave me his blessing, and I felt relieved that I could now stop hiding it from him.

With our relationship out in the open, the next challenge was going to be Stephanie's parents. It probably wasn't going to be straightforward, we thought, especially because I was a few years older than Stephanie. I had met her parents many times, but I had to find a legitimate excuse to visit more often, to get them used to the idea of my presence. I started to go round to drop off recruitment magazines, to show that I was helping Stephanie look for work. She had already told her parents that she wanted to find a part-time job.

This seemed to work okay for a few weeks, until one day her mother came home while I was sitting in the living room and Stephanie was ironing in the front room. Her parents had always made me feel welcome as Adon's friend (Adon was, after all, their nephew), but now they were clearly beginning to suspect that I had designs on their daughter. When Stephanie's mother, Joanna, saw me sitting in the living room on my own, looking like I had made myself very much at home, she asked me what I was doing there. I told her I was just dropping off some more recruitment magazines, whereupon Joanna told Stephanie that she wanted to speak to her in private upstairs. I couldn't make out the conversation, but I did hear Joanna raise her voice.

When Stephanie came back downstairs, she looked upset, so I thought I had better go. I shouted up the stairs: 'I'm going to head home now, Joanna, take care.' Joanna's reply was civil, but also ice-cold.

Within three minutes of me leaving, Stephanie texted: *Don't leave me here by myself!*

I replied immediately: *I'm just up the street, so come and meet me if you want.*

When she arrived, I asked her what was wrong with her mother.

'She has a problem with me seeing you,' Stephanie said, 'and she asked me why I couldn't date a nice Greek guy. It's a cultural thing, and she doesn't approve of, well, you know.'

I remembered the tough times I had been through with Sabine's parents, but that was nothing compared to being disliked because my skin colour and my culture didn't match somebody's expectations for their daughter. It appeared I simply wasn't good enough. I had good academic prospects, decent work experience, a thriving eBay business, no criminal convictions and no addictions, but I still wasn't, apparently, good enough for some folks.

Chapter 22:
Getting the key of the door and starting to build some muscles

Working out at a gym is a fantastic way to channel your energy in a positive way.

At university, we were briefed on the dissertation we would be expected to produce in our final year. We had to choose a topic from a prescribed list or create our own topic based on the specifics of our degree courses. None of the prescribed topics really interested me, and most of them looked horribly technical in any event. I was comfortable in some areas of technology, but others left me cold. I could see that most of the suggested topics involved some kind of analysis in the area of networking, so I came up with the idea to compare the differences between broadband fibre lines and ADSL landline connections.

We were given examples of the previous year's dissertations and told to adhere to the same structure as those. Although we had more than a year to complete our dissertations, I decided to get started on mine right away, and perhaps even get it drafted by the end of the current (second) year. If I could do that, I thought, I would just need to make any necessary changes to it based on the content of the third-year coursework when the time came. On the very day we were handed the guidance, I did some research and began to put an outline dissertation together. Within four hours, I had completed my first draft and couldn't really understand why we had been given a whole year to do it in.

I asked our diminishing gang, as well as some other students, what they were going to do for their dissertation, but they all seemed to have put it to the back of their mind, presumably because the deadline was such a long way off.

Harry had started to struggle with his coursework and even started to miss whole days. He said it was just too difficult and he wanted to try something different. This meant that there were effectively only three of us left from the original gang of six: myself, Troy and Moe. More determined than ever, I kept my attendance record immaculate and made sure that all my assignments were done on the day they were handed to me.

The year 2005 was coming to an end and my relationship with Stephanie was on-off at best. However, I had my twenty-first birthday to look forward to. I invited lots of family and friends for dinner at Nando's in Wood Green and, when I turned up, I saw Adon, Amy and Stephanie standing at the entrance. Stephanie was smoking a cigarette, which was a surprise to me as I'd never seen her smoke before. Although she said hello, she didn't look all that pleased to see me. I put it to the back of my mind and we all went in to sit down and eat. I was happy to see everyone, and I had a great time over dinner. Towards the end of the meal, Harry asked me where we were going next, and I suggested we all go to Yates bar. 'There will probably be a lot of girls there,' he said, 'we should let them know it's your birthday.'

Before I could reply, Stephanie piped up: 'As if you could get any of those girls.' I was embarrassed that she'd said it in front of my friends and family members, but I didn't respond. As we were leaving Nando's, Adon, Amy and Stephanie said they were heading back home and Stephanie said goodbye, but there was no feeling in it.

I drank so much in Yates that when my sister Laura turned up with her boyfriend Mike, I agreed to smoke the birthday spliff he'd brought for me. I eventually blacked out and the next thing I knew was when I woke up at four o'clock in the morning at my cousin Elle's house, where she lived with her husband and newborn son. When Elle got up, she told me I'd come back to her house to smoke the spliff with Mike, but I couldn't remember anything after meeting Mike at the bar. I was still annoyed with Stephanie's behaviour the whole of the next day, but I had already decided not to get in touch with her again.

As the new year dawned, I decided to join the university gym as I had some real body-confidence issues. I wanted to put on some muscle and, although I used my own weights bench at my grandmother's house occasionally, I really needed to train in a gym environment to do it properly. I decided I wanted to be more like my childhood hero, Arnold Schwarzenegger, and I began to buy bodybuilding magazines.

There was a guy studying for the same degree as I was called Abbi, but we nicknamed him 'Deebo' on account of his sheer size (Deebo was a muscle-bound character in a 1995 film called *Friday*, and our 'Deebo' had a similar physique). He was always in great shape, although much of it was down to steroid use, which was not a road I wanted to go down. He worked as a bouncer in some of Central London's high-end nightclubs and attractive women were forever falling over him. I asked him as many questions as I could about gym training and nutrition and he gave me some good advice. I figured that if I ate and trained the same as Deebo, I would get a similar physique, only a bit smaller because I didn't want to take steroids. I had heard rumours about steroid use, about how it could impair your sex drive or be the cause of aggression.

I read magazine after magazine and began to supplement my diet with protein shakes, which I made by mixing together oats, bananas, egg whites and water. I brought packed lunches into university to make sure I got my calories in.

In the beginning, muscle-building was difficult and I didn't really feel as if I was gaining very much, at least not in a physical sense. I soon found, however, that my workouts were channelling negative energy away from me and leaving me feeling more positive. I felt less stressed, less insecure.

I had another reason for wanting to build up some muscle. Although it has been some time since I had suffered abuse at Tommy's hands, the memories still haunted me and I wanted to be sure that no one could ever bully me like that again. I wasn't short of incentives when it came to working out in the gym.

I was certainly keeping myself busy, and I felt as if everything was going pretty smoothly as my second year at university came to an end. Then, one Thursday evening, I got back from university around 8 p.m. to find my Uncle Ricardo (one of my mother's brothers) heating up packet noodles in the kitchen. He had just been released from prison after a six-month sentence for assaulting his neighbour. He had a history of mental health problems and had been diagnosed with schizophrenia in his early thirties. He also had a history of smoking skunk, a strong grade of marijuana, which many family members had speculated was probably the direct cause of his aggression and medical condition. Anything noise-related could trigger a mood swing, which is what had happened six months previously at his flat in Muswell Hill.

The large property he had lived in then was split into two flats, with him occupying the top-floor flat and an elderly neighbour living underneath him. According to Uncle Ricardo's version of events, the neighbour used to bang on his ceiling with a broom, which he said tormented him. Things got so bad, he said, that he had to attack the old man to put an end to the knocking. The police were called, and he was arrested.

As part of the terms of his release from prison, he was not permitted to go back to his old flat, although he was entitled to another council property. However, my grandmother had decided that it would be better for him to move into her house, in the room right next to me. My heart sank at the thought of losing the privacy I had enjoyed for so long, especially as there was no suggestion that Uncle Ricardo should ever move out.

I was also a bit concerned at the prospect of living with someone who had been diagnosed with schizophrenia, simply because my grandmother had decided that it might be safer for him to live with us instead of getting his own place, to which he was perfectly entitled. Unfortunately, she was not a mental health professional and she certainly didn't have any of the skills or expertise needed to manage someone with his condition.

For the first month or so, Uncle Ricardo seemed to be on a fairly even keel. Then, one Saturday afternoon, he walked into the kitchen to check on the pot of whatever he had cooking on the stove and saw me putting some clothes into the washing machine. He went ballistic.

'Why are you doing in here while I'm cooking?' he screamed. 'I need my space!'

'I'm just washing a few clothes,' I said, trying to defuse the situation.

'Not while I'm cooking!' he shouted.

Feeling a bit intimated, to say the least, I left him to it and returned to my room. About five minutes later, he knocked on my door.

'What do you want, Uncle Ricardo?' I asked, opening the door no more than was absolutely necessary. He stood there smiling, as if nothing had happened, and explained calmly that he had a thing about not having dirty clothes near his food.

I raised the issue with my grandmother later that day.

'Can't you say something to him?' I asked.

'Just stay out of his way,' she said.

I tried to avoid Uncle Ricardo at all costs after that.

***

One day, on a visit to the gym, one of the members of staff, a guy called Sean, asked me what degree I was doing at university.

'Computer Networking,' I said. 'Why do you ask?'

'We're looking for additional staff to work in the new gym facility we're opening in September, ideally someone who's doing a sports degree,' he explained.

'I have a friend who plays basketball, but that's about it really,' I said, and headed on into the gym.

The following week I returned to the gym and Sean said, 'It doesn't matter what degree you're doing if you want to work with us. I'll even give you the answers to the interview questions in advance, just to make sure you get the job.'

I accepted his generous offer and agreed to fill out an application form. Two weeks later, I was interviewed by Judy, the gym manager and, needless to say, I passed with flying colours. My job title was Fitness Staff Member and the role required me to sign up new members, carry out induction sessions, clean gym equipment, manage the gym if there on my own and adhere to health and safety procedures.

Chapter 23:
Moving into the real world

There is something deeply satisfying about starting to reap the rewards of hard work.

During the summer before my final year at university, I became inundated with requests from family members to fix their computers as news got around of my technical skills. It dawned on me that I could make some money doing that privately, so I let it be known that I was available for computer work and soon began getting referrals. It was a nice little earner, but not exactly regular, so I began to apply for part-time retail jobs. I still had a healthy amount of savings and my eBay business was running nicely when I had things to sell, but I wanted to increase my earnings yet further.

A month into the summer holidays I got a job with B&Q as a cashier. The store was in Whetstone, near Barnet, and, once I had been trained on the checkouts, I settled into a shift pattern. I wanted to make as much money as possible, so I asked for more and more hours and ended up working full time for the rest of that summer.

I was still having fun in my spare time, mostly by going to family parties and barbecues. I even went to parties at my mother's house, not because I felt kindly disposed towards her or Tommy, far from it, but a party was a party. On one occasion, I met a group of three guys at my mother's house who were distantly related to Tommy. At first, I was a bit hesitant about talking to them because of their link to my erstwhile tormentor, but they were in my age group and we had similar interests, so I put my prejudices to one side, not least because we shared a West Indian background. They were called Dane, Lee and Jay. Dane worked for cable company NTL as an engineer alongside his dad, Lee worked as a supervisor in Next, and Jay managed his family's convenience store.

At home, Uncle Ricardo was up and down, but tensions really began to mount when a gang of boys who hung around a council estate opposite my grandmother's house started to cause problems in the area. They broke into cars and took them for joyrides before setting fire to them. When I left for work one morning, there was a burnt-out car right in the middle of the road. They also sold drugs on the corner of our road and intimidated any neighbours who didn't like the idea. They never troubled me, but they drove my grandmother nuts and set my uncle off by playing football on the street and occasionally kicking the ball against the side of our end-of-terrace house. My grandmother tried hard to keep Uncle Ricardo calm and not have him escalate the situation, on account of the fearsome reputation of the boys. The police were often called, but there wasn't much they could do. There were no willing witnesses and burnt-out cars don't have fingerprints on them. Sometimes the gang just stood there watching a car burn even after the police had showed, as if it was a perfectly normal thing to do. The police did question them, but no action was ever taken, and the local authorities had to keep removing the cars.

The summer came and went and my final year at university got underway. Two weeks in, Troy and Moe both decided to change to a media-based degree because they found computer networking too difficult and they wanted to study something that they would be happy to have a career in after they graduated. I was the last man standing and the gang of six was no more.

Undaunted, I studied harder than ever. If I thought the previous year had been busy, it was nothing compared to this one. In addition to my studies, I now had four jobs of sorts, plus gym workouts and girlfriends to fit in. I was loving every minute of it, though.

I had heard about an elite bodybuilding gym in Tottenham Hale, not far from where I lived, so I went to have a look at their equipment. It was called Body Works Gym, and I was amazed at how huge all the guys were. The equipment was far superior to anything we had at the university gym, so I took away a price list for different types of membership and joined the following week. I was determined to pack on muscle, partly to improve my self-confidence, partly because I was starting to get compliments from girls about my improving physique. I stopped going to the university gym for workouts, but I still worked my shifts there. Initially, I kept myself to myself at Body Works, because I still felt a bit weedy compared to the other guys who went there, but after a while I began to copy the exercises of the huge muscle guys.

I was invited to Dane's house for a New Year's Eve party to herald in the year 2007. The atmosphere was great, there was plenty of food and drink, and the music was good. I felt in a happy place and I started on the vodka. When Lee turned up, I smoked some of his weed. The party just kept getting better and better, at least it did until I saw a bottle of white rum, which was three-quarters full. It turned out that nobody else liked it, so I polished it off on my own. I then went up to use the toilet, where I passed out.

The following morning, I woke up in the foetal position on the toilet floor, which was no bigger than a car boot. I had taken off my jumper the night before and folded it neatly into the shape of a pillow. I had also managed to take my trainers off and put them to one side.

I eventually came round and went downstairs, where everyone was in hysterics over my antics at the party, although they had probably been a bit less pleased that I had locked the bathroom door from the inside. Because I never really took myself too seriously, I was able to laugh along with the jokes they were all having at my expense. In a way, it made me feel more accepted by them.

My friendship with Dane, Jay and Lee became stronger. We had similar interests, including cars, women and going out to bars. We began to meet up every few weekends, and that developed into going to Dane's house every weekend. Our typical weekend involved drinking until we passed out. I was always the first to fall asleep, because I was naturally tired after all my workouts at the gym during the week. The following morning, we would have a massive fry-up for breakfast and have a lot more laughs before going our separate ways. It was a great way to balance my busy week with a relaxed weekend around three guys who were totally on my wavelength.

I was only one semester away now from finishing my degree course, so I began applying for IT jobs. After a few weeks, I got invited to an interview with an IT company in Grosvenor Gardens in Central London. I bought myself a suit and began to prepare for my most important interview yet.

On the day of the interview, I took the Tube from Seven Sisters to Victoria. It was a very new experience for me, feeling at one with all those smart people on their way into the city. At the interview, the manager,

Mark, talked about the company and asked me about myself. It went pretty well, I thought, but they were looking for someone to start fairly immediately. I explained that I had to finish my degree course first, but that I would be available as soon as I had done so. I emphasised the work experience I already had at my old college and that was definitely accepted as a very positive point in my favour. Mark agreed to contact me in June, when I had finished at university, and we shook hands as I left. I was excited beyond belief, because I had almost certainly lined up a full-time job well before finishing at university.

My final semester flew by, but not without the considerable pressures of my final exams and the completion of my dissertation. I stopped working at the university gym and cut back on my social life in order to cram for my exams. I was almost at the finish line.

Uncle Ricardo began to isolate himself for long periods of time in order to avoid contact with my grandmother and me, although occasionally, out of the blue, he would start a conversation as if everything in his life was perfectly normal. While I was cramming for my final exams, though, things took a decided turn for the worse. He started banging on the very thin wall that separated our bedrooms, his bone of contention being that I was keeping him awake by studying into the small hours of the morning, even though I took great pains to do so quietly. Every night my studies were punctuated with his banging, and sometimes it carried on long after I had turned in for the night. He probably just forgot to stop, or perhaps he could hear noises inside his head that we couldn't.

I raised the issue with my grandmother, who was as unsympathetic as ever. She took Uncle Ricardo's side, as per usual, and told me that I had to stop studying by midnight in order to keep him calm. I think she was just too scared to say anything to him, just in case it set him off.

As my three years at university came to a close, I had mixed emotions. I felt that I had done all that I could, and I couldn't wait to graduate. I even thought I might have done enough to get a first-class degree. On the other hand, I had felt pretty exhausted at the time I took my final exams and I started to worry that the interruptions and sleep deprivation caused by Uncle Ricardo's shenanigans might have cost me in some way.

I had continued to work part-time at B&Q throughout my final semester, and one morning on my way to work a guy on the bus recognised me and said hello. I didn't immediately register who he was, but I soon twigged that it was Tre's cousin. He gave me Tre's number and the following day I called him. I hadn't seen Tre for a very long time and I was so happy to make contact with him. We both thought it would be great to catch up and arranged to meet the following week. When we did so, we swapped stories for hours. I told him all about my IT aspirations, but he wasn't working and he had nothing in the pipeline either. He was living at his mother's house near Alexandra Palace.

A few weeks into the holidays, I got a call from Mark to come in for another meeting at Grosvenor Gardens. He said he wanted to take me on full time as an IT Support Engineer, with a starting salary of £17,000. As it was my first professional job offer in the IT industry, I immediately accepted the position. I agreed to start in two weeks' time and I was very excited to be getting such a great opportunity. I decided that I would also continue to work Saturdays at B&Q and that I would continue to buy and sell stuff on eBay whenever I could.

When I started at Grosvenor Gardens, I was one of twelve engineers and my main task was to swap over all of our clients' data back-up tapes. As the clients were dotted around Central London, I spent my mornings doing the tape collection and my afternoons being trained in other areas of work by some of the other engineers. I brought my own lunch in, because I was still into my protein shakes, which I consumed along with huge tuna and sweetcorn sandwiches. After work, I went to the gym and pumped iron.

City life seemed to agree with me and I got along with all the engineers, and with Mark. It was expected that all the engineers should take Microsoft exams to become fully qualified, so I ordered a Microsoft exam book and began to study.

The only problem I had during those early summer months was that Uncle Ricardo continued to bang on my wall, even though I was no longer studying into the small hours.

Chapter 24:
It's Cardboard City for you

Some words cut so deep that they can scar you forever.

After three weeks of doing the tape rounds, I was completing them by 11 a.m. and my manager was happy to move me on to work projects. I began going to different client sites to carry out IT tasks, including fixing, maintaining or replacing computers, printers, servers and software. I got real satisfaction from finding solutions that helped clients and I tried to emulate the interpersonal skills of the senior engineers in doing so. I also began drinking coffee, which I didn't really like, to fit in with everyone around me.

At the end of July, though, I suffered a setback when I got the results of my university exams. I hadn't passed two of the modules I needed to obtain my degree, which meant I would have to go back and repeat them. I was really upset, especially because I felt justified in laying at least part of the blame on Uncle Ricardo and my grandmother. In any event, I enrolled for one more semester to complete my degree and went into work to explain the situation to Mark. He was really cool about it and he allowed me to continue working for him whilst also having the time off I needed to finish my degree.

On the plus side, I was still saving money and I felt that the time had come to buy a car by myself. I started to look in *AutoTrader* to see what I could get for my budget of £2,000. At the time, the VW Golf was a very popular car, but, because everyone seemed to have one, I wanted something different. I began looking at the VW Bora, which I liked the shape of.

A week later, I was waiting at a bus stop when my Dad popped out of nowhere. I hadn't seen him for a few years and he seemed happy to see me. As he gave me a lift home in his car, I told him I was looking for a VW Bora. That same evening, he went online and found a green one for sale in Bradford for £2,500. He told me to check it out on my PC and, if I liked it, to get the money ready and he would take me to buy it. I thought the colour was a bit different from the norm, and it also had sport suspension, so I made arrangements to withdraw £2,000, having agreed with the seller in the meantime that I would make an offer if the car seemed okay after a test drive. The following weekend, my Dad took me all to way to Bradford to test it out and I was more than happy with it. My Dad negotiated the price down to £2,000 and that was it, I was on the road again, more excited than ever at the prospect of the freedom and independence that come from having your own wheels.

I had big plans for my car, including a louder stereo system, bigger wheels, new suspension, some performance upgrades and a detailed clean. I felt as if I needed a project and it was great to have something to show for some of the money I had worked for and saved. I still had plenty in the bank, which I wanted to somehow invest in property, but I had to save some more first and also finish funding my Microsoft exams.

One Saturday afternoon, I was in my bedroom talking to some friends online when I heard shouting. Uncle Ricardo had run out the house to confront the boys in the street. My grandmother called me, and I went outside to find my uncle fighting one of the boys. All of a sudden, another boy came out of nowhere and joined in the fight. I tried to break it up, but Uncle Ricardo wouldn't listen. Eventually they stopped, and my uncle went back to his room, clearly resentful that I hadn't helped him in his attempt to beat the boys up. The tension between us increased and my grandmother didn't help by saying that it would now be my fault if the boys on the street took revenge by killing my uncle.

I put it to the back of my mind and instead focussed on my pride and joy. I had already bought a new set of wheels, replaced the suspension and fitted an induction kit to improve the air flow. I began running it on premium fuel to get the most out of the engine, and I took it to late-night car meets around London on weekends. It was looking and sounding great and I used to spend at least five hours on a Saturday cleaning it on my grandmother Lorna's driveway. I had reconciled with grandmother Lorna by this time (with my family, you never knew who was going to be for or against you from one week to the next) and I was pleased to be able to work on my car away from the madness of Uncle Ricardo and my grandmother Ann.

When I wasn't messing about with my car, it was business and studies as usual. I handed in my notice at B&Q, because it wasn't necessary to work there now that I had a full-time job. On the social front, I introduced Tre to my distant cousins and we began going to Dane's house together every Saturday for a drink-up and all the antics that went with it. On New Year's Eve (2007 into 2008), I once again got more drunk that the rest of the boys at a party at my mother's house and Dane had to take my keys away to prevent me from driving my car home. Someone dropped me and Tre back at my grandmother Ann's house and the next thing I remember was waking up the following morning to find Tre still unconscious on the floor.

While I was making some breakfast for Tre and me, I suddenly heard my uncle shout out: 'Who touched my poster?' I opened my door and saw that a poster on the landing wall had fallen off. Uncle Ricardo had a collection of Rastafarian posters from Africa and Jamaica dotted around the place.

'I didn't touch your poster,' I told him.

'Well, maybe your friend did!' he screamed.

'Listen, Uncle Ricardo, my friend hasn't touched your poster, he's not even awake.'

The argument carried on like this on the stairway and my grandmother came to the bottom of the stairs to see what was going on. Uncle Ricardo started to drag up other stuff, like me not defending him against the street boys that day. Exasperated, I suggested burying the hatchets and just trying to have peace between us.

'There will never be peace between us,' he shouted, and stormed back into his room.

It was clear that he remained intent on making my life a living hell, so I went downstairs to talk once more to my grandmother about the situation. I broke down in tears, which was very unusual for me. Grandmother Ann, however, remained in denial about Uncle Ricardo's mental health issues and pretty much told me to pull myself together.

I called my mother and spoke to her about the situation, and she at least agreed that what was going on at my grandmother's wasn't right. When I went over to collect my car from her house, she said she was going to arrange a family meeting to thrash things out once and for all. This was duly set up for the following weekend at Uncle Stewart's house.

When I arrived for the family pow-wow, Uncle Ricardo was sitting in the corner. Before I could say anything to him, though, he just got up and left. Uncle Stewart tried to call him back, but it was no use. The rest of the family had already gathered, including my mother and Tommy. The only person missing was Uncle Byron, who was due to arrive at any moment with his family.

My mother started the ball rolling, but this just served to ignite a massive argument with her mother (my grandmother Ann), who made out that I was a liar and that I was just making all the problems up. She was clearly so desperate to keep Uncle Ricardo living with her that by now she didn't much care what I thought or did. My grandfather Desmond was there and had clearly been primed on what to say, so he added that I should have beaten up the boys who attacked Uncle Ricardo in the street. Uncle Byron then turned up and within five minutes he had told me in no uncertain terms that Uncle Ricardo was going nowhere and that it would be 'Cardboard City' for me if I caused any more problems. This was the most significant threat of all, because it turned out that Uncle Byron was in fact the owner of my grandmother Ann's house. She had already signed it over to him to avoid inheritance tax when she died.

I was feeling pretty victimised by now, unable to make sense of what it was I was meant to have done wrong. Unlike Uncle Ricardo, I had not done hard drugs or engaged in any form of violence, and I certainly hadn't been to prison for beating up an old, defenceless man. What I was still far too naïve to realise, of course, is that families generally close ranks when one of them comes under attack. My mother was on my side, but it was clear that her standing within the family didn't amount to much either, presumably because of what she had done all those years ago to my Dad and to me and Laura.

In shock, I went back to my mother's house to try and make sense of the situation and figure out what to do next. Although she was being supportive of me, I still couldn't forgive her for what went before, and I certainly couldn't ever consider living under the same roof as the man who had bullied and hit me as a small child. She suggested then that I should try to buy my own place, which she thought made more sense than renting somewhere. But I didn't have enough money to buy my own place, and what I did have saved I wanted to one day put towards buying a property or properties that I could let out to others.

My mother then called Laura, who said I could stay at her house (where she lived with her boyfriend Mike) until I could sort something else out. I went back to my grandmother Ann's house and began to pack, staying well out of her and Uncle Ricardo's way. The following morning, I went down to pack my kitchen things and my grandmother was sitting there, looking very sorry for herself. I didn't say a word, just carried on packing my stuff. She handed me a piece of paper and told me it was a letter she had written for me to take to the council as proof of my eviction from her house. I told her I didn't need it.

I called Tre and told him what was happening. At the time, he was seeing a girl called Faye, who had a daughter from a previous relationship, and he asked me if I could take him and his stuff to move in with her while I was in removal mode anyway. I agreed to pick him up and take him to Palmers Green, where Faye lived. I had met her a few times and she seemed cool enough.

Chapter 25:
Getting a mortgage at the wrong time

You should only ever get on the property ladder if you understand what you're doing.

Laura called me on my mobile while I was dropping Tre off. She said she was concerned about all the stuff I was going to bring to her flat and that I couldn't bring my bed. I asked her where I was meant to sleep, and she told me that I would have to sleep on the floor. I hung up on her. As there seemed little point in ringing my mother at this point, I called my Dad to explain the predicament I now found myself in. He wasn't exactly supportive, though, suggesting only that I might as well go back to my grandmother Lorna's house. I knew that would be a mistake, as I couldn't rely on grandmother Lorna remaining stable long enough for me to settle in, never mind stay there for any length of time, especially if she was still under the influence of the even-less-stable Beth. I was being passed from pillar to post, and I felt welcome nowhere.

I just stood outside Faye's house in disbelief, my anxiety level now going through the roof. My memories of contemplating suicide as a child to escape Tommy's abuse came flooding back to me and I thought about purchasing several boxes of sleeping pills from different chemists to avoid suspicion. Luckily, though, Tre had overheard the conversations with Laura and my Dad.

'I just spoke to Faye,' he said. 'We want you to stay here with us.'

His words sounded like divine intervention and may just have saved my life that day. I was lost for words. I felt awkward, though, because Faye lived in a two-bedroom council house, with one of the bedrooms set up for her daughter Tamia.

'I can't take Tamia's room,' I said. 'It wouldn't be right.'

'It's okay,' he said. 'She doesn't sleep in there anyway.'

Tre took me into the house, where Faye confirmed that Tamia usually slept with her in any event, and that Tre would have to get used to that for a while. I made the decision there and then to accept their kind offer and move in over the weekend.

By Sunday, I had all my stuff at Faye's house. It meant an additional thirty to forty minutes on my commute to work, but it was a small price to pay to feel the support of the people around me.

On the Monday morning, I drove as close as I could get to the nearest Tube station and took a train to the client's office I was now stationed at in Holborn. By the time I got there, I was shattered, not only because of the longer commute, but also because I was utterly drained by the events of the previous week. After a while, Alfred, one of the staff members who sat next to me, noticed my gloomy mood and asked me if I was okay. He had worked for the company for three years and I got along with him pretty well, so I explained what had happened. It made him feel awkward and he didn't say much by way of reply. I tried to get on with my work as best as I could.

The following few days involved several conversations with my mother as she tried to convince me to put in a housing application to the council, whether to rent or buy. After submitting an application a week later, I was at least in the system. Shared ownership schemes were popping up at that time, but I didn't know much about them. My mother looked into them and told me I should apply for one to see what happened. The scheme allowed council tenants to part-buy and part-rent the same property. You paid a mortgage for the percentage you purchased and paid rent for the percentage that remained owned by the housing association. I viewed a number of properties in the weeks that followed, including a new-build, shared-ownership development on Tottenham High Road near the football stadium. They were still being built, so I only had access to the showroom flat on the second floor.

It had an open-plan kitchen and living area, and an unusually large bedroom and bathroom. The developers had done a good job in making the most of the available floor space. My mother also went to view it, following which she told me to go for it right away. I still wanted to view other flats, but once I had seen three others I decided to take my mother's advice and go for the new-build in Tottenham.

I met a guy called Peter, who worked for the managing agent, including as their mortgage advisor. He went through the criteria I needed to meet to apply for one of the flats. Initially, only key workers such as teachers, nurses and police personnel could apply, but once that demand had been satisfied then someone on the housing waiting list such as myself could also apply. I gave Peter all my relevant details and within a week he left me a message asking me to come into his office again. My application had been approved in principle, but we now needed to go over the financial side of things, which is when things really got complicated.

The flat was valued at £150,000 and the percentage available to purchase was 30 per cent, which meant I needed a £45,000 mortgage. As I was only earning

£17,000, Peter advised me to request a raise from my employers to support my mortgage application. It was all becoming a bit serious and, as much as I liked the flat, I felt very unsure about the whole thing. I was still traumatised by what had happened with the family and I wasn't really able to fully take on board what has happening. My mother kept going on about it, though, constantly encouraging me to sign my life away for something I didn't fully understand.

I took a couple of days to think things through, with the task of asking for a raise hanging over me like a dead weight, not least because I was already getting a day off work each week to finish my degree. I finally sent Mark (who was still my manager) an email to explain the situation, including some personal information about what had happened with my family and my potential homelessness.

We sat down to discuss my email the following day and, when we got to the bit about me needing a raise, I asked for £22,000. I thought that was fair, because I had been performing well and the average salary for IT support roles was a good bit more than I was earning at the time. Mark countered with an offer of £19,000, which I thought was a bit ungenerous considering how many lucrative contracts the company had. I made that very point, but he wouldn't budge, so I accepted his offer of £19,000. He confirmed it quickly in writing, so that I could use it for my mortgage application.

When I next went to see Peter, things became even more confusing. He explained that the interest rate would be fixed at 7.6 per cent for the first five years of my 25-year mortgage with the Halifax. My mother was with me and, as she already had a mortgage, I assumed she had a good idea about such financial matters. However, she pointed out none of the risks involved and failed to mention that 7.6 per cent was a high percentage rate for a mortgage. Peter also explained that my rent was going to be £370 per month for the percentage of the property I didn't own. I didn't understand much of the financial jargon, or even how a mortgage really worked, but my mother spurred me on and I authorised Peter to apply on my behalf for the mortgage. It was now a waiting game.

I got on with work in the meantime and very much enjoyed living with Tre and Faye. I tried to keep up with my workouts at the gym and began taking a high-calorie, high-protein weight gainer to build some extra muscle. I asked Tre if he wanted to come and train with me and he said he would, which worked well because I now had company at the gym. My social life was on the up again and I was once more seeing a few girls at the same time, which helped to balance much of the stress I was feeling as a result of my family issues and the whole property thing.

My energy levels began to dip quite drastically with so much going on, though, and I even began getting into work late. After a while, the client I was supporting sent a complaint to Mark about my timekeeping. When Mark pulled me up about it, I didn't say much, so he just emphasised the need for me to get myself together because I was a 'good kid' and had plenty of potential. I was, however, becoming bored just sitting around all day doing nothing very much. I wasn't finding the work nearly as challenging as I had when I first started. It had all become too easy and my mind was far from stimulated.

Things came to a head when I went into the client's office one morning only to be told that I should instead go to Soho Square to meet Mark at a different client's premises. I took the Tube to Tottenham Court Road and met Mark at the office of a publishing company. Mark explained that I needed to change locations in an attempt to prevent further issues with the client who was unhappy with me. I didn't know what to say, but I knew I was treading a very thin line and that at any moment I could find myself unemployed.

I was to work with another engineer called Rajj, who had been with the company for a few years and had already passed his Microsoft exams. He was a few years older than I was, but we clicked straight away. He had a very laid-back approach to work and within a couple of weeks we were having a lot of fun working together. In fact, we had a lot more fun than we should have had and spent more time out of the office than in it. Our typical day involved speaking about the jobs we needed to do and then, before actually doing anything, taking a walk towards Oxford Street to admire hordes of girls as they arrived to work in the area. We then went back to our client's office and did a couple of jobs before heading back out again for a mid-morning stroll. We went out to eat lunch, had another walk in the afternoon and then just chilled for a couple of hours before heading home at least forty-five minutes before we were meant to. When I told Tre about it, he said that my manager's plan to punish me by placing me in Soho had clearly backfired and he was right.

A few weeks later, I got word from Peter that my mortgage had been approved and that he was now ready to process my application for the flat. I gave him the go-ahead.

A couple of months after that, Mark came to the office in Soho to check how things were going and to tell me that he had once more received complaints about my performance. That surprised me, because I had done nothing but follow Rajj's lead the whole time I had been there. He then asked me to write a description of my role there, with a list of the benefits I brought to the client. He explained that there was some restructuring going on, and that all the company's engineers were being required to do the same thing. I didn't know what it all meant, but I wrote what he asked me to, feeling all the while that my days at the company were numbered. I tried to figure out who had made the complaints against me, but I simply had no idea.

At this point it finally began to sink in that I had allowed the turmoil of my personal life to affect my career and my work ethic, something that I had taken great pride in at college and university in particular. It had all been falling to pieces around me, and I had been unable to recognise, far less arrest, my downward spiral.

The company I worked for had generously allowed me time to finish my degree and had even agreed to a salary increase to help with my mortgage application. I had repaid them with a lack of respect and a poor work ethic. I was on the verge of losing my job and I decided to do what I could to keep it, but I also knew that it was probably too late.

Tre suggested to me that Rajj might have set me up because he was the one who would have reported back to Mark, but I didn't want to believe that. If the complaint had come from the client, Tre reckoned, it would surely have been levelled at both Rajj and myself.

Chapter 26:
Out of the frying pan and into the fire

The challenges of life are forever reshaping themselves. We must learn to expect that and deal with it.

I began to turn up to work on time, complete all my jobs and back away from Rajj's influence in order to show that I had turned over a new leaf. I liaised directly with Mark in the hope of re-establishing some rapport with him. After three weeks of pushing myself as hard as I could, though, he stopped by the office in Soho on a Thursday morning and asked if he could have a word with me in one of the meeting rooms. I was in the middle of fixing a PC, so I put that to one side and followed him. He pulled out a letter and put it on the table.

'Dean, after careful consideration, we have to let you go,' he said.

'Can you tell me why?' I asked, as if I didn't know already.

'We no longer have confidence in your performance or your ability to get on with other staff members,' he said.

His words led me to believe right away that Rajj had in fact had something to do with my dismissal, and I had to accept that I had placed my trust in the wrong person after all.

'I will give you a good reference,' he continued, 'and I wish you all the luck in your future career.'

He escorted me out of the office and led me outside the building, where he shook my hand. Although I was in shock, the first thing I thought to do was speak to Rajj, so I called him. When he answered, he acted as if my dismissal had also come as a shock to him and he was quick to point the finger at other engineers within the company, claiming that they had accused me of giving them wrong information whenever they called me. I knew he was bullshitting me and that he had set me up, and I felt like a complete idiot for having allowed that to happen.

I stood outside the office for fully thirty minutes, unable to shake off the thought that I had just lost a job at the very point of taking on a mortgage. I finally started to walk and after a while I called my mother and told her what happened. She tried to reassure me, but I nonetheless suggested that we pull the application for the flat. She was completely against the idea and tried to convince me that it was too late to do so. She even said she would help me out financially if needs be.

I headed back to Faye's house and was so drained when I got there that I fell asleep and didn't wake up until the following day. The sleep helped a bit, and when I woke up I began looking to see what other jobs might be out there for me. I had, after all, been promised a good reference, even though I had only been with the company for just under a year.

I channelled what remained of my energy into the gym and within two weeks of losing my job I received a letter from my university saying that I had passed all of my modules and that I would receive my degree in the post shortly, along with confirmation of when my graduation ceremony would take place. I was still in shock over the loss of my job, but I rang my mother and told her about getting my degree and not to book any holidays around the time the graduation ceremony should take place. I continued to liaise with her on a daily basis until we had appointed a solicitor to act on my behalf on the purchase of the flat, which I had decided to go ahead with. I would be able to furnish it from my savings and I was determined to get another job by the time the mortgage payments kicked in.

This constant communication with my mother started to annoy Tommy, who called to accuse me of only visiting my mother whenever I needed her for something, and never just to see how she was. A few days later, I went to their house to go over the legal stuff with my mother. Tommy sat at their dining table, mumbling away to himself. He then started going on again about me only visiting when I needed something, at which point I snapped.

After all the years of silence, I told my mother about the abuse I had suffered at his hands, and I told him straight that he had no right to offer me advice about anything. Time seemed to stand still for a while, and you could have cut the atmosphere with a knife.

'Did you hit him like he says,' my mother finally said.

'Yeah, I beat his arse, because it's what he deserved,' Tommy replied, sounding proud of his actions.

My mother thought it over for a while but said nothing much as Tommy and I continued to trade insults.

'So, you want me to leave Tommy, is that it?' she said after a long time.

'Why would I want that?' I said. 'You two are a perfect match. You belong together.'

It was clear that she was going to let Tommy's confession fly over her head, just as she had done with the years of abuse she must surely have known something about. She was going to remain in denial, and she would continue to defend him. She was still so blinded by her love for him that she was prepared to brush aside the fact that her husband had physically abused her son for a very long time, even after hearing him finally confess to the fact. I left without saying another word.

I was finally given a completion date of Monday, 18 August 2008 to take possession of my flat. I got dressed in a suit for the occasion and I got my keys at 6 p.m. A guy from the agency called Edward met me by the access gates on the ground floor and showed me where my allocated parking space was. He explained that the parking area was covered by CCTV and then led me up to my new home. When I walked in, I could immediately smell the fresh magnolia paint on the walls and the brand-new carpet.

I finally had a set of keys to my own private property, a place where I could build a life for myself with no family to hassle me. I walked around the empty space after the agent had left, as excited as I had ever been about anything. I didn't stay there on the first night because I had no bedding, so I went back to Faye's for one more night.

The following day I brought my duvet and a pillow, so that I could spend the night at the flat in total isolation. It felt like some sort of flat-blessing ceremony. I spent the night thinking about all the things I needed for the flat, which was pretty much everything. I decided that I wanted the flat to have a very modern yet comfortable feel to it, so I went with earthy greens and browns.

I soon set about buying furniture, cookware, crockery and cutlery. I wanted matching electrical appliances, so I chose Philips for everything: a 42-inch LCD television, a DVD player with surround sound and even an alarm clock. I got matching brushed-aluminium Russell Hobbs kitchenware to match the cooker. I got a king-size bed, because I had always slept in either a single or double and I wanted something huge. I got a dining table with four chairs and a half-leather, half-fabric corner sofa. It cost me a lot of money, but I felt as if I was due a break after all I had been through, even if a lot of what I had been through had been self-inflicted.

I was determined to keep my flat in pristine condition, so I spent countless hours making sure it was always clean from top to bottom. Everything was placed as neatly as it had been in the showroom flat. Whenever I had visitors, they accused me of having OCD, which I took as a compliment. I hadn't been formally diagnosed with it, but I sure liked the sound of it.

I eventually settled in and started to face the reality of dealing with the mortgage, rent, council tax and utilities, as well as my ongoing car expenses. I began applying for IT jobs and within a few weeks I had an interview for an IT support role in Hatton Garden. It was a web hosting company that supported clients remotely, which meant working in an office with other engineers and helping clients over the phone. For some strange reason, the manager didn't take much convincing to hire me and I was offered the job the very next day.

I arrived the following Monday morning to find that the office was the smallest workspace I had ever come across, but beggars could not be choosers, I thought. There was much banter within the office and I felt that the sense of humour was on my level. As there were only men in the office, sexist jokes were by no means off limits. On the Thursday, I met the director, who was from Northern Ireland. I clicked with him straight away, because he was very easy-going. On the Friday, the whole team agreed to meet after work for a drink in the pub around the corner from the office.

I went along in the hope of getting to know the guys better. Most of them started on beer and I had Guinness. They knocked their drinks back very quickly and, like an idiot, I tried to keep up, in spite of the fact that I had not drunk in quite a while. I was soon very drunk on vodka and after a few hours I made another mistake by following the director and one of the engineers to another pub, where they ordered Jaeger bombs, which I had never tried. All I could remember later was that I had a big glass filled with Red Bull and a shot glass filled with the darkest spirit I had ever seen. They said to me to drop the shot glass into the Red Bull and knock it all back after a count of three. So I did.

From then onwards, the evening was a total blur and we ended up at the director's flat in Farringdon, where, it turned out, he lived with the engineer who was with us. He warmed up some pizza for us and said that we would go on to Fabric, a popular nightclub in Farringdon. With all that I had consumed, though, I went straight to the bathroom, threw up and slumped down on the floor. When they came in looking for me, I told them to go without me. Everything after that was complete blackness and later reminded me very much of my worst teenage drinking days.

When I woke up the next morning, any slight movement of my head was painful. After about quarter of an hour, I realised that I was sleeping in the spare room of the flat. I got myself together and went to look for the other two, only to find nobody in the living area. I knocked on a bedroom door and heard 'come in' being uttered by a very groggy voice. I entered to find the director laid out on his bed like he didn't have a care in the world. I apologised for my actions, in particular for throwing up in his bathroom, but he just laughed it off, like it was a perfectly normal thing that had happened. I thanked him for letting me stay and said that I needed to get back home, so we agreed to catch up on the Monday.

When I got outside, the fresh air hit me so hard that it made my hangover ten times worse and I was soon sweating like a pig. I just wanted to be back in my flat as soon as possible, so I struggled to the nearest Tube station and eventually made it home.

On the Monday morning, the mood in the office was upbeat and comical in the aftermath of the night out. I started to wonder if I might even be entering a period of stability. Day by day, however, I started to realise that I wasn't as technically advanced as the other engineers and I started to worry whether I would be good enough for the role, especially given that I was on probation. I kept my head down and did my best, but my confidence had been knocked by the recent problems in my personal life and I knew that my interpersonal skills were probably not at their best either.

One Saturday morning I headed out to GSF (German, Swedish and French) Car Parts, a popular chain for people who drive European cars in the UK. I had just come out after buying a set of Brembo brakes and pads for my car, when I got a call from my manager.

'Hi Dean,' he said, 'I'm just ringing to let you know that, after careful consideration, we'll have to let you go as we don't feel confident in your ability to take on the position.'

I thought it was a bit cowardly of him to ring me on a Saturday morning to deliver the bad news, and I was unhappy that I had just spent money on car parts that I probably wouldn't have bought if I'd known that I was about to lose my job. Would I ever get my timing right, I began to wonder?

Chapter 27:
Graduation Day and taking tips from Britain's most violent prisoner

A graduation ceremony is the celebration of a milestone reached, and it should be shared with loved ones.

Unemployed once more and with the cost of the flat to worry about, I felt as if I was right back to square one. I tightened my belt, but I was already using the overdraft allowed within my current bank account and I had no way of clearing it. My confidence was also well and truly dented, which would not be helpful in finding new work, and I now had the additional problem of having been let go by two previous employers, one of which had only kept me for two weeks. I was going to have to be creative with my CV.

I got notification from the university that my graduation date was set for December 2008. That raised my spirits and I felt much happier having something to look forward to. In spite of the ongoing issues I had with my mother's relationship with Tommy, I wanted her to be there. I rang to tell her about the ceremony, but she had already booked a holiday to Cuba, even though I had asked her well in advance to keep the time free. Her excuse was that she had found a cheap deal which she couldn't let pass.

Five minutes later, she called to say that she could cancel her holiday to come to the ceremony. I told her not to bother, because I didn't want her coming out of guilt. I had wanted her to come because she was proud that I had earned a degree, but that clearly wasn't the case. I invited Tre and Harry instead, and they accepted

(I had kept in touch with Harry after he dropped out of the same course I was about to graduate from).

Faye was rehoused to Seven Sisters, which meant Tre was only a twenty-minute walk from my flat. When my graduation day arrived, I met Harry and Tre at the Barbican Centre, where the ceremony was to take place. I was measured for my graduation gown while Harry and Tre went to sit down in the theatre.

I was nervous about going on stage in front of so many people. When my group was ushered forward, I positioned myself in the middle. I watched as each graduate ahead of me received applause primarily from their own families, and I suddenly realised that my two friends would not be inclined to cheer in that way. Sure enough, when it was my turn to walk on stage, I received the polite clapping that all the graduates got from the assembled throng, but not a single cheer. I had rarely felt more alone.

I collected my certificate and photos and said goodbye to Tre and Harry, who had other things to do after the ceremony. I headed home, where I sat staring at my certificate for a long time. So, this is it, I thought. This is what four years of hard study and jobs on the side gets you. I found a nice place on my living-room wall to hang it on and stared at it for a while longer, trying to let my achievement sink in.

***

As 2009 began, I was still looking for work in the face of mounting pressure to pay my bills. In desperation, I turned to my mother for help, because she had promised she would support me if it became necessary to do so – it was one of the ways in which she had convinced me to complete the purchase of the flat just after I had lost my job. When I called her, though, her long sigh suggested that my request was the most unreasonable thing she had ever heard. I hung up without waiting to hear her reasons for being unable to help.

I decided to claim Jobseeker's Allowance while I continued to look for work. I should really have done this sooner, but I'd always regarded benefits as a last resort. I struggled through to March, with my visits to the gym the only outlet for the stress of having so many bills hanging over my head. I then began to get responses from potential employers. On a single day, I had two separate interviews in the same area of Chelsea, one at midday with an energy company and the other at 3 p.m. with a gas and oil company.

Both interviews felt pretty straightforward, although I was a bit taken aback during the second one when the HR Manager, Claire, asked me how I liked to be managed. I said something about being adaptable and wanting to have a good working relationship with those around me. A week later I got an email from the oil and gas company saying that they would like to offer me the position of PC Technician and that they wanted me to start the following week. I was overjoyed, and I prayed that my financial worries would soon go away. I envisaged good career prospects and a stable income for many years to come.

On my first day, I met the IT team, which consisted solely of the manager Jim and two engineers, Tom and Edward. Jim had been with the company for ten years, Tom and Edward for three. Jim took me round to meet everyone in the main building, where we were located, and in a smaller recently developed building five minutes away on foot. The company was owned by an Italian family and had been passed down from the father who founded it after he had died in a skiing accident in the French Alps.

The company located oil with the help of its own geoscientists and then drilled it in order to make massive amounts of money. My job as a PC technician was to manage the laptops that were available to staff going on business trips, and to build, install or fix new PCs. There were also software updates that needed to be pushed out from the central server, which we carried out on a shift basis. The job gave me the chance to get to know everyone in the company quickly, and I soon became known as the go-to man in the IT department. Tom and Edward were more involved on the server and programming side of things and allocated additional jobs to me via a ticketing system that we used to prioritise outstanding tasks.

The job went smoothly for a few months and it was good to have money coming in. I still couldn't clear my overdraft, though, and I had to make the really hard decision to sell my car. The pride and joy I had spent so much time and money on was the only thing that could resolve my financial shortfall, and I had to admit that it was something of a luxury in any event. It just sat in my allocated parking space during the working week, so I only ever used it at weekends. I gave it a final clean and advertised it on a few websites. Within four hours of listing it, I got a call from a man who was interested. I agreed to meet him after work that Thursday at a local shopping car park. He took it for a test drive and tried to haggle the price down, but I stuck to the price I advertised it for and he finally handed the money over. After counting it very carefully, I handed him the paperwork and off went my beloved VW Bora. My heart sunk to the bottom of my stomach as I watched it disappear into the distance.

With the car gone, my bank balance was out of the red and, without the ongoing costs of running the car, I was able to save some of my salary. I began focussing a lot more on my gym training, basing my regime as far as possible on that of Charles Bronson, Britain's most violent prisoner. Not because I admired his propensity for violence, you understand, but because he had written books on individual fitness programmes whilst in solitary confinement, which is where he spent most of his prison life. His real-life story was told in the film *Bronson*, which had just been released at the time I was getting into my personal fitness in a serious way. I got so obsessed with this that I began going to the shower area at my workplace whenever I could in an attempt to hit my target of 2,000 push-ups a day, just as Bronson had. I also took an energy supplement called N.O.-XPLODE, which helped to pump the blood around my body much faster. I got much fitter and stronger, but it also made me hyperactive.

In my heightened state, I spent many a late evening on MSN Messenger, conversing with a cousin in Canada (most people in the UK would have gone to bed by then anyway). One such evening, a surprise message popped up on my screen:

Isn't it a bit late for you to be up at this time?

I looked at the sender and saw that it was Stephanie. I had not been in touch with her for a couple of years, so we began catching up, which led to us also exchanging phone numbers. My mind raced ahead, thinking that we could enjoy full privacy in my flat, a level of privacy that had previously been denied us.

A few days later, we met up not far from where she lived. She looked happy to see me, so we hugged and I kissed her on the cheek. She took an instant liking to my new bulked-up shape and we were soon back at my flat.

I showed her round, but it was immediately apparent that a guided tour of my flat wasn't really what she had in mind. Within no time at all, we were having sex in my bedroom and it was even better than it used to be. Afterwards, she said she needed to go home, but I convinced her to send a text message to her mother with some excuse instead. It was the first time we spent a whole night together.

In the morning, we took up where we had left off the night before and it was afternoon before she finally headed back home. Over the next few weeks we saw each other more and more. I soon realised that she hadn't changed much, that she still liked to go out clubbing and hang around with what I considered to be the wrong crowd for her, on account of their drug-taking and general antisocial behaviour. I told her that I was only interested in a more stable relationship than the one we had before, which I guess was a bit of an ultimatum. She was cornered, forced into a decision to either carry on partying or spend most of her free time with me. She decided to give us a go, and she began to stay over even during the week. This meant I had to go home straight after work, which meant less time at the gym.

The mixture of coming off such intensive exercise and getting more sex than sleep at night began to take its toll and led to me feeling exhausted at work. One day, I made the mistake of sending out a wrong email, which caught Jim's attention. I sent him an email to apologise, but his response was terse. From that point on, he kept a close eye on me, which wasn't exactly difficult as we sat in the same office. The way he addressed me was now different to how he spoke to Tim and Edward, and I knew that my next anxiety attack probably wasn't far away.

Chapter 28:
Finally finding out what was wrong with me

The hardest thing about depression is recognising it, because only then can you begin to handle it.

Stephanie continued to feel constricted by our relationship, and in particular by the amount of control I needed to have over it. I tried to rein myself in, but I became insanely jealous every time the party girl in her came to the surface. We argued a lot, which put strain on us both. My performance at work was once more on a slippery slope, to the point where Jim was forever pulling me up about it. The combined worries of running the flat, managing a relationship with someone who seemed to me to act like a child half the time, and trying not to screw up in front of my manager at work practically had me at screaming point.

I stopped going to the gym, I began sleeping more and I watched countless films as an escape from the reality I had come to dread. I ate just one main meal a day, but I consumed huge amounts of junk food at that one sitting. My sole meal might consist of fried chicken, sweets, doughnuts, pizzas and crisps washed down with hot chocolate.

Jim began demanding that I discuss my workload with him first thing in the morning and last thing before leaving work, and that I report to him either side of my lunch break. He had no idea what was wrong with me, of course (neither did I), but it was also clear that he didn't have the management skills to handle it, whatever it was. His behaviour became erratic, he treated me differently from Tim or Edward, he spoke to me as if I was a child. He kept me behind to work on projects after hours, but without pay. I felt victimised, to the point where I declined to stay behind. This escalated to us both attending a meeting with the HR manager, during which I explained that I felt as if I was being bullied.

To my surprise, the HR manager effectively agreed with me. She pointed out that the occasional fifteen minutes of overtime would be appreciated by the company but was by no means obligatory. I had never felt so relieved.

Things improved slightly for a while and I managed to finish my jobs on time without Jim breathing down my neck the whole time. He even praised some of my work and I began to think that maybe we could get back to the working relationship we had started off with.

One ongoing issue was that, every Thursday, he went off with most of the male staff to play football for two hours over the lunch period. As I didn't play football, I asked if it was okay that I have a two-hour lunch break on my own, which he declined. I didn't say anything, I just decided to go the shower area and sleep while the rest of them played football. I certainly needed the rest, being so tired all the time, so as soon as they left I scoffed down my lunch (usually soup and cheese twists that I bought across the road from the office) and then headed off for my nap. The shower area was huge and there were always clean towels rolled up for staff. I laid one towel out on the floor, rolled another one up like a pillow, and slept soundly for an hour and half. On days when I only had a regular one-hour lunch break, I started going there to sleep for thirty minutes.

Luckily for me, shift patterns were introduced around that time to balance out workloads and provide cover over a longer period, which meant no more unpaid overtime. I was allowed to choose an 8–4.30 shift, which allowed me to get back to my flat earlier, where I promptly went back to sleep.

The improvements in my working environment lasted until March 2010, when I was required to configure a PC for the geoscientist team. There were issues with the software, due to imperfections in the image that Jim had built for the machine. Something that should have taken an hour went on for two days and Jim became increasingly frustrated over the long delay. He was sitting next to me while I was on the phone to Hewlett Packard trying to rectify the issue, when one of the senior directors overheard the tone he was using to speak to me.

'Is there a problem?' the director asked.

'No, but there will be,' Jim said.

I had had enough, given that he himself had caused the problem I was trying to resolve. I waited for him to go back to his office and sent him an email to book the following day off. That way, I would be able to calm down without us having another bust-up, I reasoned. I had also decided around this time that I needed to speak to my GP, because my feelings of depression simply wouldn't go away. When he declined my request, I went to the HR manager, who told him to authorise my day off without delay.

On the relationship front, things were going no better. I was so down all the time that I even found it difficult to get aroused near Stephanie. My confidence was at an all-time low.

I finally went to see my GP, who diagnosed me with clinical depression and signed me off work for three whole months. She explained that the common symptoms of this most serious form of depression included feelings of hopelessness, disrupted sleep patterns, food cravings, loss of libido, suicidal thoughts and anger or frustration over even small matters. In other words, she described the life I had been living on and off for years, and every single symptom I had been suffering full time for several months. I felt horrified that I had sunk so low, but also relieved to know what was wrong with me. It helped just to be able to give it a name, this thing that had debilitated me so much for so long. She prescribed me a course of antidepressants and put me forward for psychological therapy.

I sent the HR manager an email with a photocopy of my medical certificate. She replied with much empathy, and said she was going to pass the message on to my manager and also to the IT director in Italy. Luckily, I had been employed there for over a year, which meant I was entitled to full pay for three months before being transferred to statutory sick pay, which would be minimal in comparison.

I started my course of antidepressants, but within days of taking them I was left feeling absolutely lifeless. I had no energy for basic tasks, even for cleaning my flat. I just wanted to sit down and do nothing. I put it down to the initial side effects of the antidepressants, but over a week later I was showing no signs of revival. I asked my GP about reducing the dosage, but she told me I would need to be on the same medication for at least six months.

Feeling frustrated, I decided to research the side effects of my antidepressants. When I read the horrifying list of the complications they might cause, I decided to stop taking them. If I wanted to get back on my feet again, I thought, I was going to have to do it myself.

I received emails from the HR manager telling me that the IT director wanted to mediate between me and Jim to find a way that would allow us to work together when I was better. The more I thought about it, the more I considered that to be an impossibility. I thought of him as a control freak and a bully; he found me impossible to manage and wanted nothing more than to see the back of me. I knew that I could never return to work there.

As I was at home more, I often escorted Stephanie to her workplace in Finchley, where she worked for a holiday company. Her mother knew about our relationship by this time and was giving her grief over it. I still couldn't bear the thought of her talking to other men, especially ex-boyfriends, so I checked the messages on her phone when she wasn't looking. Once, when she left her laptop at the flat to be fixed, I searched through her files and photos and found photographs of some male friends she had in Greece. I went ballistic, but after simmering down, I agreed to try relationship counselling. I began to wonder if there was anything I didn't need counselling for. Between the grief she was getting from her mother and myself, it is unlikely that Stephanie was getting anything at all out of the relationship and I have no idea why she stuck with it as long as she did.

When we sent to see the relationship counsellor, we were advised to draw a line under everything that had gone before so that we could move on without all the emotional baggage that was dragging us down. I knew it made sense, but I didn't think I could trust Stephanie either.

Two weeks later, Stephanie told me that me that she was going on a family holiday to Greece. I instantly disapproved of the idea, but there was, of course, absolutely nothing I could do about it. I also began to see it as an opportunity, though. A week into her holiday, I plucked up the courage to send her an email to say that it was over between us, that I had come to the conclusion that neither of us could move forward while living in an atmosphere of distrust. I missed her terribly and it was weeks before I could think of anything else, but I eventually decided to go back to the gym and to look for work again.

I had dropped from over 14 to just 10 stone in the previous six months, but I now began to eat properly again and to train regularly at the gym. Within a few weeks, I started to return to my old self, without the aid of antidepressants. I took back control of my life, and I felt able to make decisions accordingly, the first of which was to hand in my notice (my three months on statutory sick pay was up by now) and apply for new jobs.

Within two months, I got invited to an interview with a government technology outfit in Vauxhall about an IT controller job. After walking along the side of the Thames from Vauxhall station, I was met on the ground floor of the building by a lady called Marie, who escorted me to the office itself. I was surprised that it wasn't much bigger than my flat, and that there were only nine members of staff. Having passed a technical test on the spot, I replied to their interview questions confidently and asked a lot of questions about the company to show that I had done my homework and that I was genuinely interested in the position. They explained that the successful applicant would be taking over management of the IT infrastructure from Mathew, who was transitioning into statistics, and that the job required working with little supervision, something which really appealed to me given my previous brushes with authority in the workplace.

The following day, I received an email offering me the job. I signed and returned the contract immediately and started work the following week. Samantha, the office manager, was not technically minded so I looked forward to working with a large degree of autonomy.

I settled in quickly, delighted to be back on a decent salary and working at such a nice location by the Thames. After a few weeks, it suddenly occurred to me that I hadn't had a holiday for as long as I could remember and that I should maybe do something about that.

Chapter 29:
Heaven on earth

Travelling to another country by yourself can be the most liberating experience.

My new routine was work, consuming calories and going to the gym five to seven days a week. I wanted to put on as much mass as possible, so I began eating between five and eight times a day, plus I was taking protein energy drinks. In the gym I spent anything from two to four hours working with the heaviest weights I could manage. I knew I was becoming obsessive again, but I also knew from experience that channelling my energy like that was the only way I knew to ward off the evil spirits of depression. I was conscious of the fact that they were waiting for me, so I had to keep one step ahead of them at all times.

I began training my cousin Lee in the gym, as he wanted to get in shape as well. While we were working out one day, I suggested that we do a guys' holiday abroad somewhere, which he also thought was a good idea. I began looking at different places and settled on Fuerteventura in the Canary Islands, which seemed to have a nice balance of beautiful beaches and a decent nightlife. I researched the internet for deals and found what I thought was the perfect package holiday. I didn't tell any of my other cousins or friends about it because I knew they either couldn't afford it or wouldn't be interested. I went ahead and booked, and waited for Lee to do likewise, but he had gone cold on the idea and he never did make the booking. I decided to go alone.

Within three months of starting my new fitness regime I shot up from 13 to over 16 stone. I got so big that I couldn't reach my back to scratch it, my clothes no longer fitted me, and I could hear myself snoring at night. I was so pumped up I could get by on three to five hours sleep a day, but I couldn't bring myself to stop taking the energy supplements because they were what enabled me to work out at my now fanatical level.

Two weeks before my holiday, I woke up in the middle of the night unable to breathe. I felt like I was suffocating and that my whole life was flashing before my eyes. I actually felt like I was going to die. I eventually managed to jump out of bed and run around to get some oxygen into my lungs, which had clearly been struggling during my sleep to expand sufficiently to pump oxygen in and out of my airways. When I finally calmed down, I was in tears.

That frightening experience told me that I had reached my physical limit with my weight training. Common sense dictated that I should ease off a little, including with the energy supplements, but I didn't. That's the thing about fanaticism, it replaces logic. Instead, I remained determined to get as fit and strong as I could for my holiday, so I carried on right up until the day before I was due to fly to Fuerteventura.

Once on board the plane at Gatwick, I was excited, but I also sensed an immediate relief from the stress that I had been putting myself under with the weight training. Maybe it would in fact be good to have a break from all that, I thought. Although I felt let down by Lee, I was also curious to know how I would cope on my own in a foreign country.

After we landed, my fellow holidaymakers and I boarded a shuttle coach to take us to our respective hotels. It was dark, so I didn't see much of the island on the way to the hotel. I was greeted by friendly receptionists and I immediately asked them about their gym. They told me that I just had to ask them for the key whenever I wanted to use it.

My room was well furnished, with Spanish floor tiles throughout, I had my own kitchen, dining area, living area with television, huge bedroom with super-king-size bed and massive bathroom. Although I had booked half board, it was too late for dinner that evening, but I had been left a sandwich and a bottle of water in the fridge. I sat down to chill, but instead I had a bit of an anxiety attack. I felt lonely and I began to think I'd made a big mistake. I even contemplated catching a flight back to London in the morning. I didn't know what I was going to do by myself in this strange place where I didn't know a single soul. I cheered up a little when I found a map of the island outlining the things you could do there, and I noticed in particular that the beach was not far away and that it only cost two euros to catch the hotel shuttle bus there and back.

The following morning, I woke up to bright skies and beautifully hot weather. I went to the dining area and discovered a huge breakfast buffet that included various types of fruit, pancakes, Spanish omelettes, cereals, tea, coffee and fruit juices. Within my package deal I could eat as much as I wanted, so I piled my plate high, twice. I went back up to my room, did some push-ups and packed a beach bag. I went down past reception and boarded the shuttle bus. Like a typical tourist, I immediately started taking photographs out of the window.

The beach was the cleanest I'd ever seen, and it stretched for miles. I kicked off my trainers and began walking in the sand, only to find that the sheer weight of my body mass made me sink down to the extent that it was difficult to walk in it. I wanted to get into the water, but only once I had found somewhere safe to put my bag. I paid two euros for one of the many sun loungers that were laid out in a row and chilled there for a while, looking around for suspicious-looking characters who might take my belongings while I was in the water. Having spotted none, I waded into the crystal-clear water, while still keeping a constant eye on my belongings. I swam a bit, but it was a struggle on account of my weight. After about forty-five minutes, I went back to my lounger, and I spent the rest of the morning alternating between it and the Atlantic Ocean.

When I got hungry at about two o'clock in the afternoon, I got changed and walked to a restaurant just three minutes from the beach. I ordered grilled chicken with salad and chips and after about ten minutes a waitress came out of the kitchen with it. When I saw her, I was taken back, because she looked just like Stephanie, but with a gentler demeanour about her. She smiled at me when she put my food down. I smiled back, resisting the urge to say something to her, but only because I was too shy to do so. I had already decided that I would be going back to that restaurant, though.

I boarded the shuttle bus back to the hotel and spent the rest of the afternoon in the gym. As far as I knew, I was the only person in the entire hotel to use it during my stay there. After showering and watching some Spanish TV, I headed down to the dining area, where I found another huge selection of different dishes to choose from. I had two main courses and two desserts. I did feel a bit awkward, though, because everyone else sat in couples or whole families and I felt the whole time that they were giving me funny looks. Perhaps some of the parents were worried that I might eat their children after single-handedly polishing off the buffet.

Still feeling energetic, I strolled the fifteen minutes into the town centre later in the evening. I checked out the bars and restaurants, but I didn't go into any of them. After an hour of so, I went back to my room and fell asleep.

The following day followed the same pattern, but I began to relax a lot more. Lying on my sun lounger looking up at the bluest sky I had ever seen, I thought I might have died and gone to heaven. I felt like a teenager again as I lay there contemplating the meaning of life. Maybe happiness was as simple as this, I thought. Perhaps having a job, and the money and possessions that came with it, were not so important after all. Surely all I needed was a beautiful woman to spend the rest of my life with on a holiday island like this. It felt like a million miles away from depression and self-doubt, from abuse and neglect, from difficult personal or work relationships. On holiday, nobody can get to you, I thought.

I became content doing the same thing every day, and I even plucked up the courage to talk a bit more to the waitress at the restaurant by the beach. The day before I left, I asked for her number, but she explained to me as well as she could in English that she was living there with her family and couldn't really give out her number to anyone. I gave her my email address instead and left it at that, happy that I had at least come out of my shell enough to give it a shot.

The week had flown by so quickly that at the end of it I felt an overwhelming sadness to be flying back to London, to be leaving my heaven on earth. I could have carried on living there forever, I thought. Sitting on the coach going back to the airport, I witnessed one final sunset beyond the shoreline and felt as if I was leaving a big part of me behind. I vowed to return.

On the flight home, I tried to focus on the thoughts that I had surely recharged my batteries, that I was in a better place emotionally following my break, that I was going home a less-broken man. When I got back to my flat, I did feel the comfort of home in the air, and I went to sleep feeling more assured than I had done for a long time. That night, I slept one of my best sleeps ever.

After just a few hours back at work on the Monday morning, though, I felt a heaviness drop right back on top of me. What I am doing here, I wondered, working nine to five in this tiny office to pay for a flat that is far too expensive to run? I put it down to post-holiday blues, and I tried to keep myself as busy as I could to avoid dwelling on that.

I started to talk to a woman called Wendy, who worked in the office for one of our subsidiaries. We somehow clicked, and we started taking our breaks together every day. Wendy would have a smoke and I would just enjoy the break away from my desk. She was in her early forties and lived in South London with her son from a previous relationship. Her manager was giving her a hard time and for some strange reason she felt that she could confide in me.

To relieve my increasing boredom at work, I had started reading everyone's emails (as the IT controller, I had full access to them). One day, I came across one which mentioned me by name. It was from the director to the accountant, asking how long I had been working for the company and how much I was earning. I didn't like the sound of that and Wendy and I soon came to the conclusion that the company wanted to get rid of me. I began applying for other jobs straight away, because the last thing I needed was to be unemployed again.

Within two weeks, I was summoned to a meeting with the director and senior manager, who explained to me that for cost reasons they had decided to outsource the IT function. I was to be made redundant. Due to the short length of my employment, I had no real rights to speak of, so I simply shook their hands and collected my things. I was unemployed for the fourth time in three years, and I was worried about how to explain another short period of work on my CV. Once more, the timing seemed cruel, because I might not have gone on holiday had I known what was about to happen. It was difficult to regret the holiday, though, as it had turned out to be one of the best weeks of my life.

Chapter 30:
Sinking back into the black hole of depression

You need the right help and 'life tools' to recognise life for what it really is and to reap the benefits it has to offer.

Being made redundant left me feeling hollow inside. In the space of three weeks, I had gone from the all-time high of my holiday to being dumped once more on the scrapheap. I began to doubt whether I would ever have a normal life, as I always seemed to take one step forward followed by two steps back.

Within a month, I had become totally introverted. I stopped looking for jobs, because I knew I couldn't face being interviewed or, even worse, having to learn a new job in a new environment with people I didn't know, and who would probably let me go in no time at all anyway.

I began to feel as if the walls of my flat were closing in on me. The place I had considered home became a battleground for me, and I was losing the battle. I went back to comfort food and I only went out outside when I ran out of it. I was soon back on benefits, which did little to improve my self-esteem. When my mother heard that I was depressed again, she didn't reach out to help. Instead, she took it upon herself to broadcast my mental health issues to everyone she knew, and more and more people distanced themselves from me as a result.

In March 2011, my referral for counselling services finally came through, a whole year after my GP had put me forward. I was to see a CBT (cognitive behavioural therapy) specialist just fifteen minutes' walk from my flat. I put a lot of hope into this, praying that I might gain a different perspective on my life or find solutions to at least some of my problems.

My therapist was called Emily, who started by explaining the structure that our sessions together would take. They were to be an hour long once a week on an agreed day, and there would be up to twenty sessions depending on how severe my mental health issues turned out to be. The first few sessions would allow me to explain my history and my feelings, in order for Emily to assess the best way forward.

I told her that I felt very low, that I couldn't seem to hold on to a job, and that the financial strain of living in my flat was getting me down. The more I told her, the more questions she asked and the more she wrote down in her notepad. By the fourth session I had gone as far back as my childhood, which is when Emily said that she had enough information from me to make an assessment.

She started to explain how I could shift the focus of my childhood away from me as the victim and on to those who had done me harm. When someone like Tommy abuses a child, she said, it may be because they themselves were similarly abused. Even though it doesn't excuse their actions, it can nonetheless help a victim to see their tormentor in the context of that bigger picture, because it at least allows the victim to understand the reasons behind their own suffering.

Emily also made it clear to me that I didn't have to speak to individual family members ever again if I didn't want to. It may have been an obvious thing to say, but to me it was more like a revelation. I had always felt 100 per cent obliged to remain within the body of the family, however uncomfortable it made me feel to do so. It was such a relief to hear that it's actually perfectly fine to distance yourself to the extent necessary from people who make you suffer. I left that session feeling as if a weight had been lifted from me. I began to pity people like Tommy and my mother, to see them with their faults laid bare, to realise that they were no better than me. I had known for a long time, of course, that they were capable of cruelty, but I had never before considered their own inadequacies, the fault lines within their characters that somehow rendered them incapable of better behaviour.

In my next session, Emily went over mindfulness meditation techniques, which she described as a tool to help alleviate the effects of trauma and prevent frequent relapses into depression. On the surface, it sounded perfectly simple: I should sit upright in a quiet space with my eyes closed and focus on my breathing. The challenging part was <u>not</u> focussing on my problems while I was sitting there doing nothing. I carried so many frustrations within me, however, that it was almost impossible to let them go even for a moment. I needed practice, but I wasn't sure I had the patience for it just yet.

As the weeks went by, I felt that I was steadily shifting the negativity of my family away from me, but my financial stress was going nowhere. I began applying for jobs and I tried to stay positive about that, but I felt the weight of my bills pushing down on me as I slipped back into depression. I wasn't getting a single reply from my job applications.

When I woke up in the morning, I went straight back to sleep, unable to face the day ahead. My savings were almost depleted when I received a letter from the housing association telling me that they were going to increase my rent by £35 a month. My eating habits were once more less than healthy, and I was losing weight again. I sank deeper and deeper into what felt increasingly like a black hole. On the one hand, I loved my flat so much. On the other hand, it was the sole cause of my financial worries. My thoughts turned once more to suicide, this time as a means of preventing the bailiffs from taking my flat away from me once I stopped paying my mortgage, which wouldn't be far off now.

A whole year went by like this. I had cut myself off from pretty much everyone I knew, which meant, of course, that I had nobody to talk to. I had become paranoid about leaving the flat, because I felt sure that people were watching me whenever I did. My self-confidence was at an all-time low and I became self-conscious about my appearance. My hair had started to thin out and I even developed some bald patches. Some days I couldn't look at myself in the mirror because I didn't want to see what I had become, physically or otherwise.

My only window on the world by now was television, which I used increasingly as a means to escape my dark thoughts. One evening, my cousin Allen texted me about a documentary film called *The Secret*, which was a condensed version of a best-selling book which claimed that everything you need can be satisfied by believing in an outcome. I have since learned that New Thought, the religious movement behind its beliefs, attracted celebrity endorsement and controversy in equal measure, but I was soon hooked. It gave me much-needed hope and I was soon adopting its positive thought processes into my life. I became goal-orientated and put together a list of things I wanted to achieve in my life. As I had always wanted to invest in property, I decided it would be a good idea to work in the mortgage industry to give me a better perspective on it, so I paid out for a crash course on mortgage advice.

I finally had something to look forward to, and I also met new people for the first time in a long time. My course was only three weeks long and there was an exam to take at the end of it. It was challenging, to say the least, because I had no financial background, which meant I didn't understand even the basic framework of the course. All the other students were either already working in the banking sector or had some other experience within the financial services industry, so straight away I had a disadvantage. I told myself not to get anxious and to stay focussed on the work and the benefits it would bring me, as per the teachings of New Thought.

The time soon came for our mock exams, which we had to take in class and which we therefore got the results of straight away. I gave it my all, but I scored eight marks below the pass mark. I was hugely disappointed, but I remained determined. I went over the course materials again and again, spending a whole week non-stop trying to get to grips with the content. I then headed to the test centre in Southgate, the same place I'd taken the theory test for my driver's licence in. This time I failed by seven marks. Undaunted, I rebooked for another test a few days later. I failed that one by four marks, but I refused to be disappointed. In my new, enlightened state of mind, I simply accepted that the financial sector wasn't for me and I went back to applying for IT jobs.

I applied for dozens of IT jobs every day until, in November 2012, I finally got two responses inviting me to interview. The first was for a job with a charity based in West London, the second to work at a major construction site in Farringdon in Central London.

The first interview, with the charity, was conducted by two very stern managers who would probably have put anyone off wanting a position within their company. The second interview, with the construction company, was held in Ascot so I took a train out there to meet the IT director, Paul, who had been with the company for twenty years. Right off the bat, we clicked. We had an informal conversation about the company and its social culture, and Paul went over the employment package and explained what would be required of me. I would be the sole IT support on a construction site with around 300 workers, with back-up as required from the technical team back at head office in Ascot.

I had only been on the train back to London for fifteen minutes when the recruitment manager sent me a job offer and the employment contract that went with it. I was taken back by the speed at which it happened, and I was overjoyed. I decided, however, to wait for the response from the charity before making my final decision. The following day, the charity took the decision for me when they told me that my application had been unsuccessful.

I started two weeks later and spent my first week commuting to Ascot for training at head office before moving to the Farringdon site, where I was employed as the ICT engineer on a large joint-venture contract. The worst part of my first week was a two-and-a-half-hour commute each way to and from Ascot, which meant getting up at 5 a.m. and getting home well into the evening. However, as it was only for one week, I got through it just fine.

On site at Farringdon, the workforce consisted of architects, directors, engineers and labourers. My initial impression was that I had never witnessed such uncivilized behaviour in the workplace, with shouting and swearing the default means of communication. It couldn't have been more different to the office environment I had experienced in the past. I was set up in an open office right bang in the middle of the testosterone-filled circus, with no privacy whatsoever and the devil's own job to try and concentrate on my job. I was beginning to realise why I had got the job so easily, but my new positive approach to life and the universe allowed me to settle into the job and adapt to the more casual approach required.

I also managed to regain some composure in my personal life and soon found myself back in the gym, but not before doing home workouts for six weeks to ease myself back in gently. Within two months, I was in the best shape of my life. I stuck to a healthy diet this time round, not the protein-filled, muscle fuel that I used to consume as part and parcel of my previous fitness regimes. Instead of going for a bulky physique by pumping iron, I focussed on properly conditioning my whole body. One benefit of my new job was that I walked to so many sites in a day that it pretty much covered my cardio needs, so all I needed to do was hit the gym in the evening for an hour and a half to top that up.

I made some friends at work and, with my confidence back where it needed to be and my finances improving, I even signed up on a few dating sites.

Chapter 31:
Another crazy relationship

Volatile relationships are like ticking time bombs, and you never know the moment they'll next explode.

In early 2013, I remained in a very good place, emotionally and psychologically. Even my work-life balance felt about right. As I was about to find out, though, the one thing I didn't seem able to shake off was my attraction to crazy women, although I never found out about their craziness until it was too late and I had once more fallen madly in love with them. I wasn't getting much better at managing these relationships either.

I had been sending messages to countless women on dating sites, but I hadn't received any promising replies. One evening, I saw the profile of someone I recognised from university, the friend of a girl I used to date. Her name was Katia and I remembered meeting her at least once, so I said 'hello' on the dating app. At first, she didn't remember who I was, but we began talking and eventually flirting. She agreed to come to my flat for a drink on a Saturday evening. She turned up looking even better than I remembered, and she was wearing a tight-fitting dress to accentuate her impressive figure. She had an unusual mix of Irish and Indian ancestry, which gave her very fair skin and long dark hair. She was a bit nervous at first, but we had a few vodkas to take the edge off.

The vodkas must have got to her before they got to me, because when she saw the pull-up bar that I had hanging over my door frame, she insisted on giving it a try. As she was only 5 feet 3 inches tall, she couldn't reach so I lifted her up by her sides so that she could grab the bar. She couldn't pull herself up, but when she dropped to the floor, she began to play fight with me. At least I thought she was play-fighting, until she started to punch me really hard. I had to tackle her to the ground to stop her.

'What's this?' I asked. 'A wrestling match?'

She was laughing all the time but, although I didn't mind the idea of playing a little rough, I was wary of my strength. I pulled her to me and we kissed intensely, which allowed us to focus on something a bit more interesting than wrestling. There was now no doubt that we had the hots for each other and we were soon in my bedroom having sex.

The weirdest thing was that we were so comfortable around each other in a physical sense, as if we had known each other for a long time. I had enjoyed strong connections with women before, but with Katia it felt almost as if we communicated first and foremost through our intimacy and that we didn't need to talk that much when we were around each other. The following day I needed to get my things ready for work on the Monday morning, but I told her she was welcome to stay over and leave for work at the same time as me in the morning.

She didn't need asking twice, and I was excited at the idea of an extra night with her. The following morning, we were pretty much glued to one other on the Tube, hugging and kissing until she got off at her usual stop, which was near where she worked as a nursery teacher. That day I replayed the weekend over and over again in my mind and realised that it was the best time I had had in a very long time. I felt such a strong connection with Katia that I had already dispensed with the idea of keeping my cards close to my chest, which is what I was usually inclined to do in the early stages of a relationship, especially given the wide experience I had of relationships going wrong after a while. That same evening, therefore, I called her and said that I didn't want us to just have a casual affair, and that I didn't want her to see anyone else. She said that was fine with her and we agreed to see each other again the following weekend.

On the Saturday, I met her at Seven Sisters station and immediately smelled alcohol on her breath. I teased her about drinking so early in the afternoon, but to my surprise she denied having had a drink at all. When we got back to the flat, she immediately came on to me, but I couldn't get the lie out of my mind and we ended up having our first argument over it. She started crying and told me that she did have a drink with her friends earlier, but that she didn't want me to know that she needed a drop of Dutch courage not be nervous around me. The mood eventually settled, and we got on with our weekend.

The following week, we had a phone conversation about when we first met and ended up arguing about the details of that. We were both too stubborn to back down, until after a while Katia explained that she sometimes had difficulty processing information on account of her dyslexia. As I thought dyslexia was a reading disorder, this didn't make much sense to me, but the revelation nonetheless rang alarm bells, whatever her actual condition might have been. I suggested in any event that we should be able to overcome it if we pulled together, which she readily agreed was the way to go.

We had about two good weeks until our next explosive arguments over ridiculously petty issues. I tried to make allowances on account of her condition, but she just kept on pushing the wrong buttons. So I told her that we needed to call it a day. She immediately stopped arguing and instead became as affectionate as she had ever been. It was all becoming a bit silly and, unless we could both grow up a bit, we were going to remain in trouble. It wasn't as if we were even young. I was twenty-eight years old and Katia wasn't far behind me, yet here we were behaving with the maturity level of teenagers. Katia did have an excuse, up to a point, which became clearer as time went on. It turned out that she had real problems at home. Her mother was disabled, but aggressive with it. Her father had mental health issues and didn't go out much. Both of her brothers argued constantly with her mother and the whole house was apparently like a war zone most of the time. I had a lot of sympathy for that situation, given my own troubled upbringing and subsequent mental health issues. I also loved Katia and I still hoped somehow that things would work out between us.

When things between us were good, they were very good. We were a loving couple and we helped each other out in our own ways. When she had problems at work, I helped her to update her CV, which resulted in her getting a job at another nursery, where she was much happier. That took some stress off both of us for a while.

When it was her birthday, I laid on lots of surprises for her. I booked us in for ten-pin bowling and dinner at All Star Lanes in Holborn. I bought her a chocolate cake and decorated it with the appropriate number of candles. When we got home, I changed into a Chippendales dancer outfit I had secretly ordered to keep the mood going, which she thought was hilarious, but which also had the desired effect that evening. She had smiled continuously for the whole day, which was very encouraging. Being out and about together seemed to be a lot easier than being holed up in the flat together.

When things were bad between us, on the other hand, they were very bad. She tried to physically fight me a lot, which probably wasn't the cleverest tactic with someone twice your size, and I ended up throwing things at the wall out of frustration. One day, I told her to leave the flat because she was doing my head in, but she just sat down by the front door and rambled on and on. I went into the kitchen, filled a jug with water and poured it over her head. On she rambled, the only difference being that she had started to cry by now. I told her to go back to her mother's house because I just couldn't cope with her any longer at that moment in time. Eventually, she left.

As with all my previous relationships, this one had ended up affecting other areas of my life. I had stopped training and my eating habits had become positively unhealthy again. I lasted a few more weeks in the forlorn hope that things might improve between us, but in the end, I accepted that it would always be this volatile with Katia and I broke off the relationship for the sake of my mental and physical health.

On the work front, we had just relocated to a different site, where an external IT company seemed suddenly to be crawling all over our infrastructure and systems. I spoke to their team leader, who told me that they were bringing in new equipment for some of the staff on site. When I raised this with my own management, they claimed to have no knowledge of it, although they had heard some rumours about an external company possibly taking over the IT service. Obviously, this raised questions in my mind about the security of my own position. On the plus side, my contract was permanent, so I thought maybe if I had to leave the present site I might just be relocated elsewhere. On the other hand, it wouldn't be the first time I got dumped on the scrapheap of the unemployed.

Chapter 32:
Enough is enough

No matter how much you think you need to hold on to your prized asset, it may just be that you're better off without it.

In my case, the prized asset was, of course, my flat, and I was beginning to wonder how long I could realistically hold on to it if I was once more made redundant. The external IT company was coming on site regularly and their staff had even been given their own desks.

A manager finally came down from head office to drop the bombshell. He explained that the external company was definitely going to take over the infrastructure and that if I couldn't be found another position within the company they would have to make me redundant. He gave me six weeks' notice and strongly advised me to look for alternative employment during that period. He promised to give me a good reference, which was clearly very important. I had a few good references on my CV by now, so the fact that this was my fifth IT job already was bad in terms of continuity but quite good in terms of my employability.

Many of my work friends, the people I had been supporting during my time with the company I was now about to leave behind, tried to help me look for alternative work, which gave me some heart.

The six weeks came and went, and I hadn't found anything else, so that was me out of a job for the fifth time. I got some redundancy pay and I was soon back on benefits, but I wasn't going to last long with the outgoings I had on my flat. By October of 2013, I was incurring rent and mortgage arrears and I took the decision I had been dreading for a very long time, which was to sell the flat and rid myself of the financial strain that came with it. I contacted the housing association to tell them I was interested in selling, and they advised me that I first needed to offer the flat to potential buyers looking for a shared-ownership property within their scheme. Only if that proved unsuccessful could I put the flat on the open market. Before I could do anything, though, I needed to get it valued.

The valuation came in at £170,000. I thought this was excellent, because in my naivety I thought I would make a profit of £20,000, enough to start the next phase of my life with. When I took the valuation certificate to the housing association, though, they explained that the way the structure of shared ownership worked was a 30/70 split in their favour on the selling price, i.e. the exact same split that I had bought in with in the first place. I don't know why I hadn't grasped this basic fact before, but my heart sank when I finally did, and I rued the day I let my mother talk me into it.

The housing association arranged an open day for potential buyers on their books to view the flat. Six people came to view on a Saturday and by the following Monday three of them had put an offer in. I didn't accept any of them, because I wasn't about to let the flat go without making a reasonable profit. I was annoyed that I couldn't advertise the flat on the open market, where I believed I stood to gain more from the sale.

I waited a while and got another valuation carried out by a different company. This came in at £190,000, but I wanted to ultimately aim for the £220,000 mark, so I decided to leave it for a while longer.

I badly needed a distraction, so I got back in the dating saddle. When I started to search the online sites, I found myself being attracted to very curvy women on the plus side. I had no idea why, I just was. After a while, I started talking to a single mother called Kim, of mixed Asian and English background. She was a size 18, which fitted perfectly the profile I had sought. When we met, I was taken aback to be so close to someone that size in the flesh, but I looked past it and we were soon enjoying the casual sex that we had both signed up for.

In March 2014, I arranged another valuation on the flat and the good news that came back was that it had been valued at £200,000. I was happy with that, but I needed to find a way around the housing association to get the flat on the open market. They insisted on arranging another open day, but on this occasion nobody turned up. My chance had come, and by the very next day I had authorisation to sell it on the open market.

I tried to contact a family friend who worked for an estate agency in Enfield, but when I got through to their offices he wasn't around, so another agent, called Sanjay, took down my details and arranged to visit. When he came round, he told me that we could go for an asking price of £210,000, and that the agency would only take a 1 per cent commission due to the ownership scheme I belonged to. He went through the challenges we would face trying to sell a property under a shared ownership scheme, but he agreed to go ahead with putting it on the market.

The following day, I cleared a lot of stuff out of the flat so that Sanjay could get the best photos possible for advertising the property. I even boxed up my TV set. Within a week, the flat was listed and the inevitable waiting game could begin.

Whenever I went to sign on for Jobseeker's Allowance, I spoke to other people in the same boat as me and learned about the retraining courses some of them were doing. I was particularly interested to find out that there was a course for fitness instructors, which I thought might be an opportunity to open a career path in an area which I already loved as a way of life. I spoke to an advisor, who said there were a few spaces left on the next course, which would begin the following month. I snapped one of them up.

The classes were held above a fitness studio at London Bridge, and the group consisted mostly of males, with only two female members. They were both nice, but I quickly reminded myself that I was there to pass a course, and that I couldn't afford distractions if I was to gain the qualification I so desperately wanted. I made friends with a guy called Dwayne and we agreed to be training partners all the way through to the final exam. Over the following three weeks, we learned so many new things about the human body and the way it works. Then we took the first theory exam, following which we were given a few days off while we waited for our results.

Sanjay called me out of the blue one day and told me that he had lined up a viewing for the coming weekend, so I spent the Friday evening cleaning the flat to my usual high standard. Sanjay arrived at 2 p.m. on the Saturday with a guy called Matthew, who was looking for an affordable flat in the area. He had seen a few already, but none that were kept to the standard that I kept mine to. Matthew seemed pleased with what he saw, and Sanjay said he would be in touch if there were any developments.

Sanjay called a couple of days later to tell me that he had managed to alleviate Matthew's concerns about the shared-ownership scheme, and that Matthew had accordingly put in an offer of £207,000. I agreed without hesitation, and Sanjay said he would put the wheels in motion.

With a buyer secured for the flat, I just needed to get through my course to hopefully pave the way for the fresh start I craved. The following week, we got the results of our theory exam and I was delighted to see that I had passed, as had Dwayne. Now we needed to prepare for the practical exam, which I hoped would come quite naturally to me because I had already spent years in various gyms helping other people with their fitness regimes. We practised every day up to the final exam and we gave it our all. We went through an entire fitness programme together while an examiner assessed us for two and a half hours. When we had finished, we were drained but also relieved. We thought it had gone well, but I didn't want to get too excited before receiving my results, which wouldn't happen for up to two weeks. I had long experience of doing worse in exams than I thought I had.

Dwayne and I congratulated each other on a job well done, regardless of the outcome, and went our separate ways. Just over a week later, I found out that I had passed. I called Dwayne and he told me that he had also passed, which was fantastic news. We had been equally driven, we had worked well together, and we had pulled each other through.

On the property front, I was at the conveyancing phase, which required me to hire a solicitor. I found a law firm near Edmonton Green and booked an appointment. The solicitor who saw me was a stunning-looking woman called Tulin, and it took quite a lot of effort to concentrate on what she had to tell me about the conveyancing process. I was brought back to earth, though, when she explained what their fees would be and when they had to be paid. I suggested the idea of deducting all my fees once the sale of the flat had been completed, but she made it clear that wasn't going to happen.

I left the meeting in a slight panic and went straight back to the flat to start applying for IT jobs. It had become clear to me that I wouldn't be able to wait for the start of my new career as a fitness instructor, and the salary attached to that particular job probably wouldn't cover the sort of money I had to raise in a hurry anyway. Not for the first time in my life, my abject naivety had left me in awkward position I would have foreseen if I had only done my homework. I remained determined to get the flat sold, though.

Two weeks into my job search, I got an interview with a company in Knightsbridge, opposite Harrods department store. I was greeted by an American woman called Alice, who was the executive PA. She explained that the company had been set up by two directors from South Africa, who needed ten UK members of staff to qualify for their entrepreneur visas. They wanted one of the ten to be an IT manager, who would be expected to look after their office and residential premises. Alice explained that the successful applicant would work alongside five PAs as well as supporting the two directors.

In order to gain some control over what was a very unstructured interview, I asked her about any existing issues with the IT systems. This resulted in Alice showing me around the office, where I was able to ask more questions about the kind of software the PAs were using. They didn't understand very much about it, which gave me an opportunity to look at one of their PCs and explain to them what they had. I hoped to have gained some trust and Alice said she would be in touch soon.

Chapter 33:
Working with the she-wolves

Working in the wrong environment with the wrong people is like being a fish out of water.

I got a call from Alice a few days after my interview to tell me that I had the job and that I could start any time I wanted within the following six weeks. As I was in desperate need of money, I said I would start the following week. I wasn't even bothered what the job might entail, because by this time I had lost faith in the IT industry and I was hardly looking to further my career within it.

On my first day, only one of the PAs (Annie) was at work. The office overlooked most of Knightsbridge, including Harrods itself, but I was no longer impressed by the sights of Central London or the money-driven, metropolitan lifestyle of the people who lived or worked there. I felt little connection with any of it.

The two South African-born directors were millionaires who had made their money through private investments. They had properties in Central London, but they travelled globally, so they were not in the office that often. The rest of the staff were young women in their early twenties. The four other PAs were Mandy, Helen, Julie and Samantha, with Alice as executive PA. Sitting at the desk next to me was the accountant, Zeeba, who was from Croatia and therefore the only non-British girl in the office. They were all attractive girls and I thought maybe it would make a nice change to work with just young women, far from the testosterone-driven sexism of some other places I had worked.

I couldn't have been more wrong. There was more greed and sexism in that office than I had ever seen, with what I could only describe as tantrums thrown in for good measure. The girls used the directors' company cards to buy sushi for their lunch, disrespected every man they had ever been with, and ruled out potential boyfriends with a financial status below that of an investment banker. I was shocked, not least because they clearly found me so insignificant that they thought it was okay to have these conversations in my presence. They didn't seem to have much work to do, so they were never short of time for gossip. Perhaps the directors, who had hired them only to qualify for their entrepreneurial visas after all, thought if they had to hire a few British workers, they might as well have some pretty ones.

I tried to keep my head down and remain focussed on my sole reason for being there, which was to pay my solicitors' fees. Tulin had dropped another bombshell when she told me that I would need to pay for transactions linked to stamp duty at the point of sale. I had assumed that stamp duty was only payable by buyers, not sellers, but she explained that it was because most of the stamp duty from the buyer had to go through my account on the way to the housing association and ultimately HMRC. I don't understand that any more now than I did then.

Another problem I had was that I had to deal with three sets of solicitors: mine, Matthew's, and those of the housing association. Because this level of bureaucracy was all new to me, I got more and more stressed and even started to worry that I might come out of the whole thing having made a loss in spite of the fact that the value of my flat had increased considerably while I was living in it.

Back at work, the girls in the office increasingly talked down to me and expected me to fix whatever their issues were on the spot. Julie snapped when I told her I needed her Apple ID to synchronise her iPad, iPhone and MacBook as she had just requested me to do. They all expected to be spoon-fed and, in Julie's case, I suspected it had much to do with her upbringing and the position she considered herself to hold within society (she was the sister of a famous actor, a fact which she mentioned on a regular basis). I explained to her that we could carry on once she had remembered her Apple ID and dropped Alice an email explaining what had happened, just to cover my back. On my way home that day, I kept looking over my shoulder lest I should suddenly be accosted by the famous actor in question.

I got a call from my cousin Elle that evening to tell me that my grandmother Ann was on her death bed in hospital again and had been asking to see me. I didn't know whether to buy the story, given grandmother Ann's miraculous recovery the last time we had all been summoned to the hospital, and I wasn't in any event prepared to forgive her for siding with mad Uncle Ricardo and almost rendering me homeless as a result. I told Elle that I wouldn't be going to the hospital.

I then received a text from Uncle Byron saying that I needed to go and see my grandmother. This was the same man who had threatened me with Cardboard City and I was annoyed that he even had my number. I knew that Elle must have given it to him.

I was being made to feel guilty by my family again, so I sat down and tried to use the tools that Emily had given to me during our counselling sessions. I started with Elle, recalling that she had a very bad relationship with her own father and had grown up as a tomboy while denying her attraction towards women. Two years into her marriage, she had started seeing women behind her husband's back, which he found out after checking her internet dating profile. When he left her, she lied that he had treated her badly and that he had seen other women behind her back. I had given her the benefit of the doubt for a long time because she was my cousin after all, but now she had crossed the line by telling me what I should do and involving Uncle Byron. I remembered Emily's advice and focussed on feeling sorry for Elle, given her troubled background. I also decided to cut her out of my life once and for all.

The phone calls from various people about my grandmother didn't stop, so I decided to go to the hospital in the end, but only late in the evening when nobody else was around. When I entered her private room, she burst into tears, but I was completely unaffected. I just wanted to show my face so that the phone calls would stop. We had a catch-up chat and I wished her a speedy recovery before heading back home. A few weeks later, I heard from some other cousins that my grandmother had gone back home and was making good progress.

At work, the circus remained in full swing. Helen demanded immediate help with a PC issue while I was helping Annie in full view of her. I explained calmly that I would be right over when I had finished what I was doing for Annie, but she screamed that she was going to get me fired if I didn't attend to her straight away. I just ignored her and carried on helping Annie until lunchtime. I then walked out of the office and pretty much stayed out for the rest of the day. I sent another email to Alice to cover my back should anything more come of the latest office tantrum.

I needed to do something to relieve the stress that was once more starting to drag me down. For reasons I still don't understand, it occurred to me that smoking some weed would be as good an outlet as any. I called a cousin of mine who sold drugs and asked to buy some. He was taken aback, because he knew how much I was usually into my health and fitness, but of course he agreed to sell some to me anyway. I had never been much of a drug taker, just having had the odd spliff, and I certainly didn't want to make a habit of it, but it did help me get through that difficult spell.

In October my solicitor said that the exchange of contracts on the flat should take place within a month, which was a great relief because my mortgage and rent arrears were racking up. I called every week after that for an update, but with three sets of solicitors involved the process inevitably dragged on. Finally, contracts were exchanged, and the completion date was set for 18 December 2014, the day after my thirtieth birthday. I began selling my furniture and kept the flat as clear as possible. I started to look at rooms to rent and viewed a few that were local to me in and around Tottenham. I found one that was ten minutes from where I lived, just off Lordship Lane, and arranged to go and meet the landlady, Vicky, who lived on site. She was very welcoming as she showed me around the house and, specifically, the room that was for rent. It all seemed a bit untidy at first glance, but I wanted to keep my costs down, so I agreed to take it.

I had to move all my stuff out of the flat on my birthday and I called Dane to ask him if he could help me transport my things to Vicky's house. Thankfully, he said yes. I managed to sell all my furniture on eBay and I packed everything else up ready for the big day. My emotions were all over the place, of course. I knew it made perfect financial sense to sell the flat, but I had been strongly attached to it for over seven years.

On moving day, I had no time to celebrate my landmark birthday as I removed ten bags of rubbish and cleaned the flat from top to bottom. Dane arrived early evening with his wife Alison and his Dad's Nissan Qashqai. Even with the benefit of the Qashqai, we needed to make three trips. It turned out that I couldn't fit anything like all my remaining stuff into the room at Vicky's, so Dane kindly agreed to store some of it for me.

My mood was sombre by the time we finished and I had to say goodbye to my flat. I cheered up for a while when Dane and Alison pulled out a birthday cake and some drinks for us to have at Vicky's. I was grateful and even a bit humbled, because it had been many years since I had celebrated any birthday.

Once Dane and Alison had left, the reality of what I had done began to set in. I no longer had my own place with my own furniture and other possessions. I had a room in a house that felt dated in comparison, and which was decorated in very dark colours. I had turned thirty years old and I had given over the last seven of those thirty years to pay for and maintain my flat. I had only been on one short holiday in that time and I had been out of work several times between jobs. The jobs themselves had brought highs and lows, mostly lows.

When I went to use the shower that evening, the smell in the bathroom was disgusting. I eventually realised it was because Vicky's cat had pooped on the floor right by the bathtub. An appropriate end to a shitty day, I thought.

Chapter 34:
A fresh start

Sometimes we have to make big changes in order to let go of the past.

When I mentioned the cat poop to Vicky, she didn't seem that bothered. When I spoke to the other housemates, they told me that Vicky freely admitted to being a messy individual. They told me of situations where she had used the same hoover that was in daily use around the house in order to scoop up poo from her carpets. I didn't just feel sick, I wondered if I might actually become ill living in such unhygienic conditions. I reminded myself that it was only temporary accommodation.

I was also suffering somewhat from the 'post-thirty blues' at the time. I hadn't covered myself in glory for the first thirty years of my life, and I wanted the next period to be better in so many ways. I took a long, hard look at my past relationship and work-related failings. I thought about my career path, my health and fitness levels, my self-esteem, even where I should live. I concluded that my attitude and my outlook on life needed to change, although I was under no illusions about how difficult that would be and how long it might take. I needed to be more honest with myself and try to accept who I was. I had to stop trying to fit in with the latest crowd. I knew I was at a crossroads, that I had an opportunity to move forward without the financial stress of the flat, and without the negative influences of those family members who seemed intent on dragging me back into their unhelpful way of life.

I treated Christmas day that year like any other. Having spent the previous seven Christmases alone, I was by now desensitised to its meaning and to the commercial madness that surrounded it. I did likewise on New Year's Eve, ordering an Indian takeaway and spending the time alone in my room trying to more firmly establish the improved mindset I wanted to move forward with. Being the obsessive-compulsive type, I loved to make lists, and there was no better time to make lists than on New Year's Eve. I made lists of the kinds of accommodation that would suit me as soon as I was able to escape my current unhygienic surroundings; of the career options open to me, especially those that related to fitness instruction; of the kinds of people I wanted in my social circle (there weren't many family members on that list, although the odd cousin, aunt and uncle did survive the cull); and of the traits that had to be present in the sort of woman I wanted in my life (these traits were now more to do with the romantic nature of a relationship, because I was finally starting to realise that it wasn't all about the sex).

Into the new year, I desperately wanted to enrol on a Personal Training Level 3 course, so I began looking up weekend courses that would allow me to study while still working with the she-wolves for the time being, but the timeframe of the practical exam made it impossible.

In the second week of January, I received full payment of the profit I had made from the sale of the flat, and a letter from the mortgage company confirming that I now owed them not a penny. I sat and stared at those letters for ages, feeling as if a huge weight had been lifted from me. Not many people my age took the decision to get off the property ladder, and even fewer would probably have considered it a good idea, but I was proud of that decision. It felt right for me. I hadn't made that much of a profit once all the fees had been deducted, but I was out of arrears and at least temporarily back in the black.

Towards the end of January, the directors booked the whole team on a business communications course, which I thought was a brilliant idea. I even hoped that, once trained, the girls would start to treat me with a bit more respect. Throughout the course, they were totally professional, giving the impression the whole time that they already knew about and agreed with everything the instructor said. I knew better, of course, and my hopes already seemed destined to be dashed on the rocks.

Armed with the list of traits that my ideal woman should have, I arranged to have dinner with a girl whose online dating profile suggested she might just fit the bill. Her name was Sharon and we met one Saturday evening when she picked me up from Broxbourne station and drove us to a country pub in Cheshunt. She was a single mother and had her own house in Stevenage, where she worked as a nursery teacher. The date went well, and I sensed a mutual attraction. We ended the evening with a kiss and agreed to meet again the following Saturday.

On the Thursday prior to the second date, I got a stomach virus and felt very ill indeed. I struggled into work on the Friday but had to leave halfway through the day. If I had any sense at all, I would have postponed my second date with Sharon, but I mustered what little energy I had on the Saturday and took a train to Stevenage, where she picked me up at the station. We drove to her house just to chill and get to know each other better. I was not intent on having sex in any event, because the new me was more about building a longer-term connection. There were pictures all over the wall of Sharon's family, particularly of her three-year-old daughter, who was spending the day at her grandmother's house.

After a while I sensed that Sharon was being a bit offish with me for some reason. I didn't want to cause a scene, so I tried to ignore it. I really wanted to go home, because I was still feeling ill from the stomach bug. I struggled on, though, and in an attempt to lighten the atmosphere I suggested heading out to eat dinner somewhere. We went to a Harvester in Hatfield, where we sat facing one another, so I could tell that something still wasn't right with her. We got through the dinner and she seemed upset as we were leaving. I asked her what was wrong, but she didn't want to say. As she drove me back to the station, she apologized for her behaviour. I asked her again what was wrong, but she said she couldn't tell me because she didn't want to cry. By this time, I did.

On the way home on the train, I thought her one of the most miserable people I had ever met. The promise of the first date had turned into the worst second date imaginable. I spent the next couple of days in bed trying to recover from my stomach bug, and on the Sunday evening I received a text from Sharon which finally solved the mystery of her abject misery. She explained that she was upset because I had mentioned online before we even met for the first time that I didn't want any children of my own. She had been too cowardly to bring the subject up again, so she just went ahead and wasted both our time. I amended my list to ensure that all future dates confirmed before we met that me not wanting children wasn't an issue. The reason I didn't want children, of course, was that I couldn't ever trust their mother not to abandon them and me.

I was at last feeling better by the Tuesday morning, so I went back to work. Within an hour of my arrival,

Alice sent me an abrupt email to say she wanted to have a meeting with me. When we sat down, she asked me for an update on a job I was given just before I took ill. Every time I went to explain that I had been ill, she interrupted me. I expected that tone from the other girls, but not from Alice, because our working relationship had always been good. She kept going on without really saying anything at all, so in the end I just went back to my desk, packed up my stuff and left.

I was distraught, but I also knew that I now had the time and the money to enrol for the Level 3 fitness instruction course. The change of career that I so desperately wanted might be about to happen, I thought. I found a course provider in Southgate and arranged to meet the course leader a couple of days later. It was a five-week intensive course, the same as the Level 2 course I had passed the year before. I booked in for the end of March and spent the intervening period brushing up on my old Level 2 material.

As with the Level 2 course, the Level 3 group was predominantly male, with just the one girl enrolling. I sat next to Mohammed, who, along with the rest of the class, had just finished their Level 2 course. The teacher told me I might be at a slight disadvantage due to the length of time since I completed my own Level 2 course, but I knew that I had determination on my side, as I always had when it came to education or self-improvement. I paired up with Mohammed and got on with it. Our first (theory) exam was on the second week of the course, so I had to study day and night just to get up to the pace of the rest of the class.

I thought the Level 2 course had been tough, but Level 3 was on a different scale altogether. Luckily, our teacher Simon was excellent at explaining the course content and pointing out what was required for our exams. I managed to pass the first exam with a reasonable mark, so the next hurdle was the practical, which was more intricate than Level 2 had been, not least because we were now being assessed in terms of how we would actually perform as personal trainers within the fitness industry.

Mohammed and I went through the delivery, health and safety, communication and instructional aspects of a personal training session as preparation for the final exam. Just as I had done the year before with Dwayne, we practised every day up to the day before the exam. A lot was riding on that final exam for me, because I was by now putting my hopes into a complete career change, into an area that I was truly passionate about. Failure was not an option, because that would mean going back down the dreaded IT path.

On the day of the exam, Mohammed and I were up last. I was so pumped up that I found that frustrating, but it did give us a chance to ask the rest of the class what to expect when they returned from their assessments. Mohammed 'mock-trained' me first and then it was finally my turn to show what I could do. I found myself getting into the most natural flow I had ever been in any work environment and it must have looked like I had been training people for a very long time. I actually enjoyed the exam, because it felt just like the previous training sessions I had delivered for real in my local gym. I thought I reached the end of the exam with no faults, but we then had to wait an hour for our results. As the tension mounted, I started to doubt my performance and couldn't help dwelling on past failures.

Finally, once each and every name and result had been read out, we knew that we had all passed. I felt like I wanted to cry. I had a qualification proving that I was fully competent in an area of my life that I was passionate about. It also meant that I was qualified in two very different types of work, which I hoped would be taken as a sign of versatility by potential employers.

The whole group was ecstatic and took an immediate decision to celebrate together by having some drinks and weed in the park near the college. I joined them, but I didn't drink or smoke with them. Instead, I enjoyed my own road to Damascus moment in that park. I thought if I could be on this level of high without drink or drugs, why not just embody the very essence of health and fitness from that day forward? I watched those grown adults in their tracksuits and hoodies acting out what looked for all the world like a scene from one of the teen dramas that are never off our TV screens.

With my qualification secured, and a change of career path in the offing, I thought maybe it made sense to change my environment by moving out of London, but not so far that I couldn't move back easily if I chose to do so. Hertfordshire seemed to fit the bill nicely. I set my sights on a job with First Gym, because their trainers were renowned within the industry, and they had a gym not far from Watford.

Unlike the lengthy recruitment process within the IT industry, gyms mostly required that you had your Level 3 instructor qualification and that your face looked as if it would fit. I agreed to meet with the manager at First Gym and took a train to the area the following day. Steve, the manager, took me through the simple recruitment process and explained that I just had to attend a three-day training course before I could work for First Gym.

Chapter 35:
Moving on (sort of)

Getting out of rented accommodation can be a lot harder than getting into it.

I turned up at my course in Central London, eager to learn and keen to help First Gym customers improve their health and fitness levels. I was somewhat brought back down to earth, however, when the instructors began to explain that the company was driven by sales targets more than anything else, and that we would have to pay 'rent' for the privilege of training clients at their gyms. Steve had conveniently failed to mention any of this to me when I met him. I completed the course in any event and gave Steve a call about the 'rent'. He didn't want to discuss it over the phone and told me that he would go through all the details with me when I started work. I should have insisted, of course, but I didn't, because I was too intent on getting my new career up and running to let 'details' get in my way. I agreed to start within three weeks.

I set about looking for a room to rent in the Borehamwood area and decided that I had to get a car to allow me to train clients away from the gym as well as in it. As much as I would have liked another VW Bora, I opted instead for the cheaper VW Polo, albeit a high-performance 1.9tdi model. There were a few on *Autotrader*, including a nice red one in Coventry selling for £950. I called the seller and he gave me the rundown on it, adding that his brother had only owned it for two weeks but had decided that he couldn't afford to insure or maintain it. I decided to go and have a look at it, so two days later I took a train to Coventry. I was nervous, because I'd heard stories of people being robbed while buying cars privately, but I decided I should be fine if I just kept my wits about me.

The seller was waiting for me at the station and as soon as I saw the car my heart started racing. It was a beauty, alright. He let me take it for a test drive and, being smaller than the VW Bora but with a bigger engine, it felt really fast. I purchased it on the spot, so the real test was having to drive it back to London, especially as I had not driven a car for five years by this time. I filled up with petrol and set off. It felt great to be driving again, to once more have the freedom to go where I wanted, when I wanted. The car drove perfectly fine all the way back to London, where I parked it outside Vicky's house.

When Vicky got home that night, I told her I was moving to Hertfordshire. She was happy for me, because she knew how much effort I had put into becoming a personal fitness trainer. The following day, I began looking online for rooms in or near Borehamwood. The area was very pricey, and I came across only one room that was affordable. I called David, the live-in landlord, and agreed to drive up and see the room two days later.

The house was at the end of a cul-de-sac in a nice area with lots of open space and greenery, which made quite a change compared to London. David was a fifty-year-old Englishman and had owned the house for twenty years. He came across as perfectly pleasant and even quite humorous. I thought it would be interesting not to live with ethnic people in an ethic community for the first time in my life. He told me something of his background, including that he had served as a young man in the Royal Navy, before venturing into journalism and from that to snapping celebrities as a paparazzo. He had been sued for taking invasive photographs of members of the royal family, which had crippled his business. He now ran his own blogging website, still on the theme of celebrities.

He went over the rules of the house with me and added that he had a girlfriend called Marianna who sometimes visited, and that he was usually in bed by 9 p.m. so that he could be up early the next morning to feed the birds in his garden. He emphasised that I couldn't have visitors and that he didn't like to be disturbed while he was working from home.

The restrictions had mounted up thick and fast, so I told him I would have a think about it and call him the following day once I made up my mind. I shook his hand and headed back to Vicky's, where I went straight online to look for another room. I still couldn't find anything else in the area that I could afford, so I called David the following day and agreed to send him the required deposit for the room. I would have much less freedom than I had at Vicky's, but at least David's house would be a lot cleaner.

I had to make two trips to move all my stuff to David's. After unloading everything from the first trip, I got the keys from David. On the second trip, it hit me that I had never lived away from London and that, in spite of all the bad memories I had of growing up and working there, it was still my home. I felt as if I was leaving a big part of me behind as I drove off into the darkness of the evening. I got to David's house late and didn't want to disturb him, so I unloaded as quickly as I could and went straight to sleep.

The following day, I unpacked my stuff and managed to get my room set up nice and tidy, just the way I liked it. Whenever I saw David, he was as bright as ever, telling me jokes whenever he got the chance.

Borehamwood seemed to live up to its name, though, because everywhere seemed to have shut by 9 p.m.

I was due to start my new job in three weeks' time, but I was allowed to use the gym facilities in the meantime. I trained hard to be as fit as I could possibly be by the time I started training others. It was all a bit daunting, though, because the local people didn't seem to welcome strangers easily into their fold and it was a challenge to form any kind of chemistry with them. I also missed my friends in North London, but I just kept myself to myself and got on with my dull routine back and forth between the gym and David's house.

One morning at around 5 a.m. I heard someone walking around in the garden and my first instinct was that someone must have come over David's garden fence. I jumped out of bed and pulled the curtain back only to see David feeding the birds. I began to wonder if he was all there.

That morning, David told me stories about his previous tenants and their reasons for leaving. The one before me had been a single mother, who only saw her daughter on the odd occasion. David had let the daughter visit, but he also rhymed off a number of very trivial-sounding misdemeanours committed by the mother. One day, he simply asked her to leave by the end of that same day, which was worrying, because landlords are meant to give notice to a tenant to leave their property. He told me about other tenants he had clashed with and, again, it didn't really sound as if any of them had deserved to be sent packing. I knew there and then that it would only be a matter of time until he clashed with me over something or other.

Later that day, he told me that Marianna was coming to dinner, so I took the hint and went out for the evening, but not before hanging around to see what she was like, which turned out to be nothing like I expected. She had been born in Italy, was about the same age as David, had two children and was an aspiring artist. She had a lovely presence about her and she even took the edge off David's normally straight-laced personality.

I drove back to London that evening, just to be in familiar surroundings. On the way back, an engine warning light started to flash. I realised that I hadn't had the car checked over, never mind serviced, since I bought it. Early the next morning, I drove it to the mechanic who used to work on my previous car in Tottenham and left the car with him for a service while I went off to get some breakfast. As I was walking along, I saw my Dad coming towards me. My first thought was to avoid him, but he saw me, which meant I really didn't have any other option but to talk to him. We had a brief catch-up and he told me that my grandmother Lorna wasn't well. I said I would go and visit her in a few days' time. I took his number when he offered it and went off to have breakfast. It had been fine seeing him in the end, which I put down to me being in a better place emotionally. Maybe the longer-term relationship between us had some potential, I thought.

One evening a few days later, about 9 p.m., I was in my room talking perfectly normally on the phone to my friend Eugene, who had been on the Level 3 personal trainer course with me. Suddenly, I heard a knock on my door. I opened it to find David standing there, looking annoyed. He told me that he could hear me murmuring away from the next room and said in future I should take phone calls downstairs. This was a new rule that hadn't been mentioned before.

I wasn't going to pay for a room where I couldn't use my phone, so I got straight on the internet to search for other rooms in the area. There was still nothing else I could afford locally, so I widened my search. I found a room in Welwyn Garden City, which was a twenty-minute drive away but had the advantage of being even cheaper than David's room.

I called the following morning and arranged a viewing. When I arrived later that same day, I was greeted by the woman who had advertised the room on behalf of her elderly parents, who were on holiday at the time. She introduced herself as Maggie and said that she lived in the house just behind the one we were standing in with her husband and three boys. The family was of Greek origin and Maggie seemed like a very nice person.

She showed me the room, which was rightly advertised as a single, but it was very large for a single room. There was another housemate already living there, called Jim. He worked at the local hospital as a consultant and Maggie said that he was hardly ever at home. She also mentioned that a cleaner came to the house on a regular basis.

Prompted by my remark about a crystal cabinet owned by her mother, we talked for a while about spirituality, which I had been curious about for some time. She said her mother was a reiki healer and used to be a florist in Greece. Maggie was also a healer, and a nutritionist, and she practised out of an office in the town centre. She also ended up mentioning that her husband, who was a musician with a famous British rock band, had built his own music studio in their garden. I was intrigued by the entire set-up, so I told Maggie I would see about getting my deposit back from my present landlord and that I would let her know as soon as possible.

I had a bad feeling about telling David (I had only been there for a week, after all) and decided to wait for the right moment. Marianna was due to dinner the following day, so I thought he might be in a good mood while preparing dinner for them both. I plucked up courage and invited him to my room, where I told him that I needed to move because I didn't want to disturb him in the evenings with my phone calls. His face dropped, and he stormed out of the room. Three minutes later, he came back.

'You're trying to fuck me over,' he shouted, 'and I won't allow it. You can take your things and leave and I'll take your ass to court!'

'David, you didn't tell me that I couldn't use my phone in my room before I moved in,' I said. 'If you had done, I might not have agreed to rent the room. Please just let me have my deposit back and we can part as friends.'

He told me I wouldn't be getting any deposit back and stormed out once more. I just sat there in a state of panic for a while, wondering what to do next. On the one hand, I couldn't stay now, not after what has just happened. On the other hand, I couldn't move without getting my deposit back.

A while later, David came to my room to apologise. He didn't really look like he meant it, though, so Marianna must have talked him into it. As I was leaving to go for a drive while they had their dinner, Marianna asked me why I wanted to move. I said that I didn't want to disturb David of an evening, but I didn't want to spend my time whispering and sneaking about quietly either. I drove back to Tottenham for a while that evening, just to feel some kind of normality. On the way back, I decided that I would get up at five o'clock the following morning and pack my stuff, whether I got my deposit back or not.

Chapter 36:
What have I gone and done now?

Mistakes are part of life, but they often bring opportunities with them.

I moved to Welwyn the following morning and soon got settled into Maggie's parents' house. As her parents were still away on holiday, I had the house to myself at first. Luckily, David transferred my deposit money to my bank account that same day, so I was able to give Maggie a deposit without being out of pocket.

I met Jim a few days after I moved in. He was a few years younger than me and seemed pretty cool. I still had two weeks to go before I was due to start at the gym, so I continued to train as much as I could in the meantime.

You could tell that Maggie's parents were very old by the furniture they had and the amount of clutter around the house. There were books, plants, clothes and what just looked like junk everywhere you looked, so there wasn't much space for me to store anything. It was more hygienic than Vicky's house, but I could still see why they needed a regular cleaner.

On my first day of work at the gym, Steve took me through the systems and I was logged on to the database as an employer. I asked him about the 'rent', but he said the area manager was due to visit the next day and that I should discuss it with him. He also asked me to be in at the ungodly hour of 5 a.m. the following morning to help open up the gym, which was something else he had failed to mention before.

After going through the gym opening and cleaning procedures the next morning, I was asked to take the 9 a.m. abdominal circuit class because Steve was going to be too busy to take it himself. That caught me off guard, because I had never instructed a whole class before, let alone an abdominal circuit. I asked him how to structure it, but he just told me to set it up any way I wanted. I feared a disaster and prayed that nobody would show up for the class. Just one member did, a lady that looked like she was in her sixties. I scrapped the abdominal class and carried out a whole personal training session with her. I was watched the whole time by the other trainers at the gym, probably checking to see if I was going to provide serious competition for them. When we had finished, the lady said she was very pleased with the session and that she would let me know if she wanted further sessions.

The area manager arrived and talked me through the rent structure. He explained that I wouldn't be liable for any 'rent' for the first month, but also that I wouldn't be paid anything over that period. My hours on general duties at the gym would reduce over the following three months, while the 'rent' I had to pay would increase. My only income after the first month would come from clients who booked individual sessions with me. He then asked me about my business model, but I had no idea what he was talking about. I finally admitted to myself that I had made a huge mistake joining that particular company, and by the following day I had sent an email to explain that I wouldn't be back because I couldn't afford to work for them.

I had to take stock quickly. I was in a rented room in a new area and I also had a car to run. I had allowed myself to be duped into the wrong job, but I knew I still wanted to forge a career in personal training. I needed a regular job in a regular gym, one which focussed on its members as opposed to the 'business models' of its trainers. That would give me a basic wage, which I could supplement by training my own clients outside the gym.

I began looking locally for gym instructor vacancies and found one at a leisure centre in Hitchin, which was a thirty-minute drive from Welwyn. I sent off my application and within three days the manager of the leisure centre, Martin, invited me in for an interview.

When I went there, Martin showed me around the centre. The gym itself was tiny in comparison to the one I had decided not to 'rent' space in, and the free weights area was basic at best. I was then invited to carry out a training session on one of their personal trainers, a girl called Emma. I tried to keep it all as relaxed as possible, but Emma and Martin remained dispassionate throughout. If it was a deliberate interview technique, it was a strange one. I then had a one-to-one interview with Martin, but I couldn't tell from his emotionless expression whether he liked my answers or not. I was quite relieved when it all came to an end. The staff notice board suggested a total absence of ethnicity, just like the previous one had, and I was beginning to wonder if that was an issue around these parts. It would certainly explain the lack of welcome I felt wherever I went, I thought to myself.

I went home with zero expectations and felt my anxiety level shooting up. I even had some junk food for the first time in a long time. When Martin called me two days later, I braced myself for rejection, even though I wasn't sure that I wanted to work in such a miserable atmosphere anyway. Rejection was still rejection, though. When he told me that he felt I was the right match for the role after interviewing all the candidates, you could have knocked me down with a feather.

Two days later, the elderly owners of the house came back from their holiday in Greece. The old lady was called Kirsty, her husband Saul. Kirsty had such a hunched back that she couldn't walk upright, but she had a strong spirit and seemed very polite. Saul was a bit more of a mystery, coming across as polite enough, but somehow guarded. I could see now why the house was in a bit of a state, because they weren't physically fit enough to do much about it. It also now made sense that Maggie had bought a house right next door to them. We spoke at length and I told them I would be happy to help out around the house or go to the shops for them.

While talking to Kirsty, my grandmother Lorna popped back into my head. I called my Dad to say that I would come to visit her the following day. When I got there, she looked very frail and had lost a lot of weight since I last saw her. She had undergone heart surgery and was having complications with her diabetes. I tried to suggest healthy alternatives to improve her diet, but she wasn't interested.

My Dad was living with her at the time in Edmonton, where she had moved after selling the house in Stamford Hill. The house in Edmonton was mortgage-free and she had invested some of the profit she made on the Stamford Hill house into other properties, along with Olivia, one of her three daughters. There were ongoing issues with one of the other daughters, Mariam, who had caused so many problems while living with her that my Dad had thrown her out in the end. Mariam's son, my cousin Warren, had also lived with grandmother Lorna the previous year, until he got thrown out for selling my Dad's laptop to help feed his drug addiction. I left feeling relieved that I had very little to do with my family these days.

I arrived for my first day at the leisure centre with a degree of trepidation. Martin explained that there was a shift pattern and that I would cover four days each week on a rotation basis with the other instructors. He also said that whoever worked the late shift had to clean the whole gym, including the toilets and shower areas, before leaving. That was an unwelcome revelation, and it was becoming apparent that the leisure-centre budget was set pretty low. My main role, though, was to induct new members into the gym by showing them how to use the equipment safely and by designing their fitness program based on their body stats, which I would then help to monitor on a regular basis. I also had to manage the gym by myself if I was the only instructor on duty at the beginning or end of the working day.

The other instructors were Bryan, Leia, Dawn and, of course, Emma. Bryan played for the local rugby team and had been working at the leisure centre for ten years. Emma had been there for four years and also carried out personal training aligned to recreational power lifting. Leia had been at the centre for about a year and, still in her early twenties, was just setting out on her fitness career. She was utterly gorgeous, so I reminded myself that it was never a good idea to date someone you worked with. She might have thought I was a bit old for her anyway. Dawn had also been there about a year. She had a son from a previous relationship and she and Bryan had become an item within a few months of her joining.

Because I wasn't from the area, and on account of my ethnic origins, I felt as if I stuck out like a sore thumb at first. It didn't help that most conversations in the gym were related to local places and events, which meant nothing to me. After about a month, though, I felt as if the others were warming to me a bit, so I began to find my feet at long last. The worst part of the job was the cleaning, but I just had to man up and get on with it.

Into my second month in the area, my life continued to consist almost solely of work and spending my spare time alone in my room. I needed an outlet of sorts, so I joined a bodybuilder gym in Cheshunt, called Mutant Gym, which I really enjoyed going to. Around this time, I also began looking into meditation a bit more. I remembered some of it from my counselling sessions with Emily back in 2011 and I began to practise it every day now. It helped to calm my mind and made me feel less anxious about living and working away from London. It also allowed me to detach myself more and more from the past that had haunted me for so long, and to make the transition from my previous life of suffering to one of empowerment.

My personality changed, and other people seemed to sense an aura around me. I was suddenly making new friends with many of the members of the leisure centre. Martin said he was happy with my work ethic and the other instructors were definitely taking a liking to me. The more at peace I became with myself through meditation, the more the staff opened up to me. The downside was that they told me their problems, to the point of bitching about members, each other and even Martin. I also became the go-to person whenever the team had issues that needed resolving. I wasn't used to that role in life, so it frightened me a little, but is also made me feel valued, something that I had very much lacked in my life to date.

The only thing missing from my life now was romance. I was on every dating site under the sun, but I wasn't getting much interest. I wondered if maybe I was getting on a bit, or even if my ethnicity was unhelpful in terms of the profile that attracted women in that part of the country.

Chapter 37:
Back to the Seventh Circle of Hell

Make the most of the good times, because you never know what's around the corner.

Apart from the lack of romance, my life remained on a fairly even keel until one morning in October 2015. I was busy making myself a green tea, when Kirsty walked into the kitchen.

'Do you brush your teeth in the shower?' she said.

'No, why do you ask?'

'Well, the cleaner said she found toothpaste on the shower curtain.'

'I use the bathroom sink to brush my teeth.'

'Are you sure, because there is a toothpaste stain high up on the curtain.'

Refusing to let go of her theme, she also asked me if I had been using Jim's toiletries. I went to my room and brought my leather toiletries bag down to show that I had a plentiful supply of my own toiletries, but I could see from her face that I was talking to a brick wall.

Here we go again, I thought. What is it about me that sooner or later attracts the wrath of others, however unwarranted? Maybe I was just too placid, which in turn made me look vulnerable to attack? I knew from personal bitter experience that bullies, whether within the home or in the workplace, will always seek out those who look as if they can't or won't defend themselves, but this was beyond the pale. There I stood, a muscle-bound, six-foot-tall man, being hounded by a three-foot-tall old woman with a hunchback. What message was I sending out that made me look such easy prey?

Dismayed and saddened by this unwelcome turn of events, I resigned myself to once more look for alternative accommodation. Working for the minimum wage over as many hours as I could get at a leisure centre, though, my problem remained one of affordability.

Around that time, I got an email from Wendy. We hadn't been in touch for five years, since the time we worked together in the same government office in Vauxhall. We had a good catch-up, at the end of which she invited me to stay for a weekend so that I could have some breathing space from my diminutive but unexpectedly fierce landlady.

The following week, I drove to her two-bedroom house in Dartford, where she had been living with her son and pet dog since selling the house she previously owned in Woolwich. It was lovely to see her again and we soon felt relaxed in each other's company, just as we had all those years ago.

She had been having an on-off relationship with her boyfriend and things remained a bit rocky between them, she said. As she didn't have a spare bedroom, she suggested that I could sleep in her bed with a duvet between us. I thought that was a bad idea, because I knew Wendy had a soft spot for me, whereas I had never really thought of her in that way – for one thing, I was in my early thirties and she was in her late forties. On the other hand, I also felt aroused at the idea of it, not least because I hadn't had sex in a very long time. I went along with the idea in any event, and felt very nervous getting into bed alongside her, albeit on the other side of the duvet that divided us. I made no moves, and neither did she. I sensed that she wanted to, but probably didn't want to make the first move for fear of rejection. I lay there telling myself that it would be a perfectly natural thing to have sex with Wendy, but that it would also be the end of a beautiful friendship if I did. I would never be able to look at her in the same way again, I thought, and tried to get some sleep.

We made it through to the morning without sexual contact of any description, but I had the feeling that Wendy was more than a bit annoyed about that. I decided not to stay another night, just in case it all got a bit awkward, so I drove back to Welwyn in the afternoon.

The following week, I had Wendy crying to me on the phone because she said she was being pressurised by her manager to leave her job, because of accusations of slander brought by another member of staff, which she said were false. On that same day, her boyfriend broke up with her, so by now she was in pieces. I felt very bad for her and tried to console her to the extent possible on the phone. I told her that it sounded to me like her manager's approach was unlawful and suggested the next steps she might take – Wendy had been in the same job for fourteen years, whereas I had been in and out of work to the point where I understood employment contracts better than most. I was happy to be her shoulder to cry on and listened sympathetically to her problems, no matter how long she needed to talk about them.

I had been avoiding Kirsty in the house for a while and she must have known that I was not best pleased with her. One morning, she came into the kitchen while I was again making some green tea and told me that she was sorry about her previous accusations. She said it was Jim who had been brushing his teeth in the shower, but she hadn't wanted to accept that fact. I had long since sensed a clear distinction between the way she and Saul spoke to me compared to the manner in which they spoke to Jim, and here she was pretty much admitting that she had not wanted to believe that her blue-eyed boy could possibly have been at fault, not when she had a less-than-blue-eyed boy to use as a scapegoat.

When I updated Wendy on this latest development with Kirsty, she immediately offered to let me move in with her and look for employment in gyms in her area. As generous as that was, I didn't really want to burden Wendy with my problems, and there was the 'other issue' to think of as well. I told her I'd see how things went before deciding what my next steps should be.

One morning in November, I was making breakfast when Saul walked into the kitchen.

'Good morning, Saul,' I said.

'Did you use the downstairs toilet last night?' he replied.

'No, why do you ask?'

'We know you used it last night, because we could hear the extractor fan and we saw the light on.'

'Well, I didn't use it, Saul. I came home from work, made dinner and went to sleep as usual. I don't need to use the downstairs toilet because I have one next to my bedroom.'

The conversation ended with Saul shouting at me to own up.

I had finally had enough. As a paying tenant, I really shouldn't be treated like this, I thought. I went to my room and called Wendy, who again offered me the opportunity to stay with her. I told her I'd get back to her.

Going to Wendy's would be a last resort, so I went on my laptop and looked online for a local room to rent. There was absolutely nothing available. Clutching at straws, I called my Dad, told him what had happened and asked him if I could stay at grandmother Lorna's until I could figure something out. He told me that would be okay because they had a spare room.

I went back downstairs and told Kirsty and Saul that I was giving them notice that I would leave in one months' time. Kirsty didn't know what to say, so she said nothing. Saul just ranted on about me using the downstairs toilet. Maggie came over to see what was going on, so I guessed that Kirsty must have called her while I was upstairs. I told Maggie I didn't appreciate being accused of trivial stuff I hadn't even done and had to move out for that reason. She defended her mother over the shower curtain episode, presumably unaware that Kirsty had already confessed on that one. I was clearly in a three-against-one argument that I couldn't hope to win, so I just offered to pay my final month's rent as long as they promised to return my deposit when I left. Maggie was a bit hesitant but said that, as long as the room was being left in good condition, I would get my deposit back, although she didn't say when.

The following day I explained my situation to Steve, who simply stated the obvious fact that it would be too difficult for me to commute from London to Hitchin, adding that January would be the busiest time of the year and that he would need staff to be one hundred per cent reliable over that demanding period. I soon enough told the other staff and many of the members that I would be leaving. It caused a bit of a stir and many of them were kind enough to remark that the gym would be losing a valuable asset because I had brought a positive energy to the place.

It was time for me and Hertfordshire to part company, just as soon as I had seen out my notice periods at home and at work. I managed to stay reasonably calm while I did so, thanks primarily to the soothing influence of my meditation techniques.

On my last day at the house, I packed up my car under the watchful gaze of Saul, Kirsty and Maggie, which made for an awkward atmosphere. We were civil enough to one another, though, and I asked Saul to check the room before I left to make sure he was happy with it, which he said he was. Maggie said she would sort out my deposit money the following day. I shook everyone's hand and left.

On the drive back to London, I felt hollow inside. I really didn't want to move in with my grandmother or face another round of family melodrama, but it was my only option other than Wendy's house. I got back around 11 p.m., after everyone was asleep, and got unpacked before turning in myself.

The following day, I called Maggie about the deposit money, but she didn't answer my calls. I sent her text messages and left her voicemails, but I didn't get as much as an acknowledgement back. The next day I drove all the way back up to Welwyn and surprised Kirsty when she opened the door to me. I told her I really needed my deposit back, so she called Maggie at work. Maggie spoke to me on the phone and once more said she would sort it out later. I gave her until the following day to do so. She continued to avoid my calls, so I called the house and told Kirsty, and then Saul after she handed the phone to him, that I meant business and would take action against them if they did not honour their commitment to me.

Later that day I got a text message from Maggie accusing me of harassing her parents. She added that I had left the rug in the bedroom muddy, along with the welcome mat by the front door. I reminded her that her father had said he was happy with the room and that the welcome mat was in a communal area and therefore not my responsibility. She said she was going to deduct the cost of the cleaning from my deposit and that's exactly what she did before transferring me 60 per cent of what was due to me.

My Dad told me they probably weren't paying tax on their rental income, so I reported them to HMRC, the local council and the site where they advertised the room for rent. I never heard from them after that, but I like to think that HMRC had them convicted and that they lived out their days in a rat-infested dungeon in the Tower of London. I still felt cheated, of course, but I managed to let it go after a couple of weeks.

Once I had gathered my senses, I started to think about what I was going to do for work. I had to face the fact that, as much as fitness was my passion, it wasn't going to pay me enough to have even a reasonable standard of living.

Although I was loath to admit it, I knew that IT was the only option I had to get back on my feet. Salaries were much higher in that industry and I remained well qualified to work in it. I therefore began applying for IT jobs once more. I also went back to my old gym in Tottenham.

Part of me was relieved to be back in familiar surroundings, but the congestion and general cost of living in London took some getting used to again. Because I could not afford to give my grandmother rent money, I helped her out in other ways. I took her to Tesco and the local market to do her shopping; I went with her to appointments at the doctor's surgery and hospital; and I picked up her prescriptions from the chemist. In the interest of family unity, I also patched things up with my cousin Elle.

I knew from experience, however, that it was never going to be a bed of roses living within the confines of my dysfunctional family. Before long, I would be proved horribly right.

Chapter 38:
Being boiled alive in the witches' cauldron

Dysfunctional families don't live together like normal people; they fight each other on psychological battlefields.

In February 2016, four months after returning to London, I still hadn't had any luck on the job front, so I had to go back on benefits again. This was not only demeaning, it also gave some members of the family the ammunition they needed to launch a fresh series of attacks.

My grandmother Lorna had a tendency to complain about every little thing, from the weather to each and every member of the family, so it came as no surprise that I had racked up a catalogue of misdemeanours by the end of those four months. They included things like taking too long to wash the dishes, not doing my laundry at the right time of day and cooking food that smelled (which is in fact the case when you adhere to the type of high-protein diet that goes hand in hand with a fitness regime). She got under my skin, but I knew it was just her miserable way and I could just about grin and bear it. I didn't have much choice, of course.

The real problems started when her daughters, my Dad's sisters, joined the fray. They were Olivia, Mariam and Beth, and I thought of them as the three witches from Shakespeare's *Macbeth*, always stirring things up in their cauldron deep in the forest in the dead of night.

Olivia was the first to boil up trouble that year, making snide remarks about me not applying myself hard enough in my attempts to find work. It wasn't just the things she said, though, it was the way in which she said them. For many years she had swanned around looking down on everyone around her, passing judgement on individual family members like some self-appointed oracle. Notwithstanding her condescending manner, I tried to make allowances for her because I knew her first marriage had fallen apart against her wishes and that she still loved her first husband even after taking up with a distant cousin, a flashy guy who made a small fortune selling replica watches on the street. I also thought that her haughty manner was largely a means of disguising her own failed marriage, of sending out a message to everyone that she was in fact above such tragedy.

She was not short of money either, which I think gave her a sense of superiority over those less well off than herself. Once, when I did manage to get an interview with an IT firm in Barnet, I came downstairs in my suit when she happened to be there. She immediately praised my smart appearance and wished me luck for my interview. It was a clear sign of just how much appearances mattered to her. Following that interview, I got a rejection letter within days and the look on Olivia's face when I told her reverted to one of disappointment and perhaps even disgust.

When my grandmother took ill with a cold – which can, of course, have serious consequences for an elderly person with diabetes and a heart condition – Aunt Mariam decided to enter the fray by turning up on a regular basis. She was still bitter with my Dad for telling her to leave my grandmother's house that time, so she took every opportunity she could to have a go at him. By way of example, she said my grandmother was ill because my Dad wasn't taking care of her enough – his going to Bristol every weekend to see Julia and his daughter remained a particular bone of contention with all three sisters.

One morning, we awoke to the sound of Mariam's voice downstairs. She had come to take my grandmother to the hospital. Unknown to us, my grandmother had an appointment at the North Middlesex Hospital that day, which she had failed to mention to my Dad or myself, the two people who had been accompanying her to hospital appointments for some months by then. In a clear attempt to undermine us, either Mariam or my grandmother had made alternative arrangements. This rang alarm bells, because, of the three witches, Mariam and Olivia were the two who most liked to mix potions together. The third of the witches, Beth, was not on potion-mixing terms with them, so she was more kindly disposed towards my Dad for that reason. I didn't trust her any more than the other two, of course, for it was she who had poisoned my grandmother to get me kicked out of the house in Stamford Hill when I was just a teenager.

My grandmother was kept in the hospital for observation and, in the absence of any communication from Mariam, all my Dad and I could do was sit tight and await news. After a few days, Beth finally managed to get an update from Olivia, which she passed on to us along with the name of the ward that my grandmother was in. I drove to the hospital the next day with my grandmother's glasses, medication and insulin, all of which she had left behind because she had gone with Mariam, who hadn't thought to check what she might need. When I got there, all three witches were huddled over my grandmother. When they saw me, they looked at me like I was a piece of dirt. Olivia asked what had kept me, and Mariam mumbled something about not having had any sleep waiting to be relieved. Beth just looked at me and said nothing, even though she knew how much help I had given my grandmother in recent months. I knew just looking at them that they were hatching a plot, or possibly even casting a spell, to get me out of my grandmother's house.

After a while, Mariam and Olivia slinked off, leaving me and Beth to it. Beth asked me why I let them talk to me like that, and I said that I wasn't prepared to sink to their level, because I knew I had been nothing but kind and tolerant to my grandmother while staying with her. My grandmother just lay there listening to all of this and showed no reaction, as if we were talking about some other family entirely.

My grandmother was kept in hospital for two more weeks, during which time I went to see her most days. When it was coming up to the time for her to be released, I wasn't aware that any travel arrangements had been made to get her home. I therefore gave one of the nurses my name and contact number so that they could call me if she needed to be collected. In the event, Mariam brought her home, and the blissful peace and quiet I had enjoyed for a couple of weeks came to an abrupt end.

A couple of days later, Olivia and Mariam came to visit her. I was on my laptop at the dining table, and I could hear every word they said. It consisted mainly of bitching about my Dad and Beth.

After a while, Mariam decided it was my turn:

'Why did you put your name down at the hospital as your grandmother's next of kin?' she asked.

'I didn't put my name down as her next of kin,' I replied.

'Yes, you did, I found out from the nurses.'

'No, I left my name and number and told the nurse to let me know if my grandmother needed to be collected.'

I knew it wasn't going to be left at that, so I surreptitiously started to record the remainder of the conversation on my phone. It paid off handsomely, as the two of them and my grandmother continued to bitch about this and that family member. As I listened to their diatribe, it occurred to me that the women in my Dad's family were truly hateful human beings.

As Beth at least continued to side with my Dad, I sent her the recording. Needless to say, it was not a happy coven for a while after that, but I was satisfied that they would at least have less time to attack other family members while they scratched and bit at one another.

I continued to update Wendy on the situation, and she continued to suggest that I go and stay with her. I resisted the temptation, explaining that securing employment remained my main concern and that having my own room at my grandmother's house was still the best base for going about that. I just had to sleep as late as possible and spend as much time in my room as I could to avoid the worst excesses of the conflict that raged below me.

My grandmother's house was not what many people would describe as a home, and her offspring were not what most people would wish for as a family. They lived out their lives on a battleground and the weapons they used against one another were hate, spite and negativity. My grandmother continued to pull their strings and very much enjoyed the results. I started to think of her as some kind of mad puppeteer.

Mariam, in particular, seemed to be followed everywhere by a dark cloud. Her parenting skills were on a par with my own mother's because, although she didn't desert her son Warren as my mother had deserted me, she used to tell him that he was worthless and that nobody liked him. After school, he often went home to an empty kitchen. Small wonder, perhaps, that he ended up on drugs.

One morning, I was making breakfast and my grandmother asked me if I could peel her a pineapple. I said I would, just as soon I had fired off an email that I almost had ready to go to a prospective employer. Just then, the doorbell rang, and I opened the front door to Mariam, who walked past me without as much as saying hello. I retreated to my room to stay out of her way. After I had sent off a few more job applications, I overheard my grandmother bitching about me not having peeled her pineapple yet, so I went downstairs to do so and to make myself some green tea.

'Didn't your grandmother tell you to peel a pineapple?' Mariam asked.

'Yes, I'm going to do it now,' I said, gritting my teeth.

She then went off on one of her tirades against me, probably fuelled by my recording of her previous bitching session with Olivia and my grandmother.

Something inside me snapped.

'Don't fucking talk to me like that!' I shouted, so loudly that I almost scared myself.

My grandmother looked as shocked as I had ever seen her, because it was probably the first time she had ever heard me shout, far less swear.

Chapter 39:
The original witch

Elderly relatives are often the most two-faced members of your family, presumably because they've had more time to perfect the art.

I was so infuriated following the pineapple episode that I called my Dad to tell him what happened. Talking to him calmed me down a bit, following which I went downstairs to apologise to my grandmother for shouting and swearing in her house. I also put a series of questions to her.

'Have I ever stolen from you?'
'Have I ever brought drugs into your house?'
'Have I ever brought any of my friends here?'
'Have I ever refused to take you food shopping, or take you to the hospital or the doctor, or pick up your prescriptions?'
'Have I ever asked you for money?'

I was of course comparing my own track record with that of Warren, and I was well aware that his mother Mariam was listening to me from the kitchen.

My grandmother answered no to each and every question, so I then asked her:

'In which case, what exactly have I done wrong?'
'You haven't done anything wrong,' she said, looking as if she had been caught off guard by my line of questioning.

Mariam returned and took up her previous points about me not pulling my weight, not trying hard enough to find a job, etc, etc. I decided to hit her where it would hurt the most.

'I don't remember stealing your laptop, at least', I said, in a direct comparison to Warren having stolen my Dad's laptop from my grandmother's house to fund his drug-taking. This clearly hit a nerve, because she was visibly taken aback.

I decided to keep the pressure on and asked her outright what her problem was with me, looking her very clearly in the eye as I did so. She hesitated, went to say something, changed her mind, and just down looked at the floor instead. After two full minutes of silence, she finally blurted out: 'You're living here rent-free! Should anything happen to your Nan, you can't be here!'

Both she and Warren had also lived at my grandmother's house rent-free, because my grandmother had never once asked any family member for rent. Mariam had been working at the time she stayed there, so she could easily have afforded to pay something. There would have been no point, of course, because my grandmother didn't need the money.

I hadn't ever given my grandmother money for rent either, so I had no right to get on my high horse over this, but I knew I had done more for my grandmother around the house than Warren ever had. Unlike other family members, I had also never asked my grandmother to pay for diesel when I drove her to the shops or hospital or doctor's surgery.

I gave up arguing in the end and left the house to go for a drive, just to get away from them. As I drove round, however, I couldn't help wondering what Mariam had meant about me not being able to be in the house should anything happen to my grandmother.

I called Wendy to tell her what happened and she explained to me that, because I was living in the house with my grandmother's permission, I would be classified as a sitting tenant should my grandmother die while I was still living there. The penny finally dropped. If the family couldn't get me out of the property, they wouldn't be able to sell the house on the open market to realise their inheritance.

Beth, after getting a call from my grandmother, turned up at the house later that same day in an attempt to help resolve the latest 'situation'. When I got home that evening, she was still there, drinking whisky and talking to my grandmother. She gave me some advice, but it wasn't exactly helpful. She said if I had problems with Mariam, I should take them up with Mariam herself, as if that hadn't already happened. My grandmother's advice was even worse. She suggested that I should stay in my room whenever Mariam called, as if I was some kind of dog to be hidden away when people who didn't like dogs came to visit. When I pointed out the idiocy of their suggestions, they suggested I move into Beth's house with her and her husband instead. Beth was clearly as desperate as Mariam for her inheritance, and I couldn't help wondering at the stupidity of my grandmother, who didn't seem to realise that they were pretty much wishing her dead. In fact, they were pretty much saying it in front of her.

I went to bed more anxious than I had been in a long time and feeling completely unwanted within my own family. Mariam and I avoided each other to the extent possible from that day on, and she completely ignored me even when we did find ourselves in the presence of other family members. It was a very uncomfortable time for me, but at least I still had the gym as an outlet for my frustrations.

As my grandmother regained some strength following her most recent spell in hospital, she began to bitch about everyone again with increasing levels of vitriol. My latest crime was to use the grill to cook some chicken breast to take to the gym to keep my protein levels up while working out. Apparently, it was particularly strong-smelling chicken.

I felt like I was walking a tightrope the whole time, and my mental health was taking a huge hit. I became paranoid about not being able to say or do anything right, and I started to doubt my ability to function in society more generally. I began spending more and more time in my room, unable to face going downstairs in the morning to take the latest barrage of criticism.

I applied for jobs like crazy and finally managed to get an interview for an IT job in Leeds in late 2016. I had anticipated the interview taking place over the phone, or maybe Skype, but the recruitment agency told me that I needed to go to the company's office in Leeds. I had never driven that far before, and I could barely scrape the money together for a tank of diesel, but I was so desperate that I agreed to travel up there for the interview.

When the day came, I got up at the crack of dawn and drove for four and a half hours to reach Leeds. I was exhausted when I got there, but in the hour I had left I managed to get something to eat while I went over my interview notes. I was impressed with the company's offices when I walked in, just as I had been when studying their track record while preparing for my interview. They had begun as a start-up company five years beforehand and had expanded quickly owing to the quality of their services.

The interview couldn't have gone better. They seemed impressed with my professional approach and said they would have no hesitation about putting me in front of their clients. The only thing I lacked, they said, was database software experience, so I pointed out that I would be confident of familiarising myself with their platforms within a short space of time.

I drove back to London on a high note, knowing that I had given a good impression. I really wanted the job, because it was a great opportunity and the salary on offer was more than enough for me to begin a new life in Leeds, far from the madness of my family. Two days later, I got a call from the agency. They told me that the company had been very impressed with me, but at the end of the day they wanted someone with the relevant database experience. I was crestfallen, and also angry that the agency hadn't established that before I trekked all the way to Leeds and back, especially given the cost involved.

With my job prospects and bank balance both dwindling by the day, I was facing major sacrifices. I considered selling my car to release some money, but I knew that I would be totally imprisoned within my grandmother's house without the freedom it provided. I therefore took the tough decision to cancel my gym membership.

Not having the gym as a means of escapism from my troubles hit me hard. I was by now reduced to applying for jobs and attending the job centre as required. That was it. I couldn't go to Wendy's house, because I still regarded the idea as a last resort, as a real sign that I had sunk to the bottom in accepting charity from a friend. My frustration and loneliness evolved into depression. I became so mentally drained that all my brain could process were very basic thoughts and actions. I felt like a child with little sense of the real world. I lay on my bed just looking around me. The thought of getting up or walking anywhere rendered me helpless. The thought of leaving the house terrified me. I started to think once more that death was the only realistic answer to my problems, and I started to consider the methods available to me. I thought about hanging myself, about taking an overdose of something or other, about leaping to my death from a high building or cliff.

That none of the available options appealed to me very much I took as a sign that maybe it would be better to find a way of snapping my way out of the dark place I found myself in. I forced myself to do little things, to set myself childlike goals. Like go to the toilet and wash my hands or go downstairs and make a cup of tea. After a couple of days of this I could feel my basic senses slowly returning. The hardest thing was pretending that my breakdown hadn't happened, because no one cared enough to have even noticed it.

In December that year my grandmother became ill again, and this time it was worse than ever before. She had apparently caught a virus from Laura's young son (my nephew) when they had visited us. Mariam, who hadn't been seen for a while, suddenly turned up to take her to the hospital again while my Dad and I were asleep. I again took to visiting my grandmother in hospital, always timing it so that I wouldn't run into any of my aunts. I usually went in the evening to just sit with her and assure her that everything was fine at home and that I was keeping the house clean while she was away.

Her heart was deteriorating, and she was very weak, but she continued to bitch about all her children to me. I tried desperately to feel compassion for her, because she was still my grandmother after all, but I also thought of her as an old fool. Everyone who tried to help her was criticised, which at least reminded me that I wasn't the only person she had been unkind to. We had originally anticipated that she would be in hospital for maybe two weeks, but Christmas was fast approaching and there was no indication from the doctors that she would be released anytime soon.

I made the most of having the house to myself, especially when my Dad went off to Bristol to be with his other family. I felt like a huge weight had been lifted from me, because the witch sisters never turned up while the mother witch was away.

With even more time to think, I decided to advertise my car for sale on the internet. It still felt wrong, but I had to look at the bigger picture. I also got back into meditating for the first time in a long time.

On New Year's Eve, I was alone in the house, so I ordered in a huge Indian takeaway dinner. The house felt lighter and I thoroughly enjoyed myself, happy to be going into the New Year with nobody negative around me.

My freedom from stress only lasted until the second week of January, though, when my grandmother was finally discharged from hospital. Mariam and Beth brought her home and swooned around as if they cared, but it was all for show because they stopped coming to see her again after just one week. They would have to wait a while longer for the inheritance they so desperately craved.

Chapter 40:
The return of the dark place

It's easy for other people to humiliate you if you're vulnerable and outnumbered, but there's no way of understanding why they want to do that to you in the first place.

One evening, my Dad asked me to go to the shops to buy a takeaway dinner for everyone, including the evil Mariam. I did as he asked and then found myself at the dinner table right opposite Mariam. She didn't look once in my direction, and she was the only one not to thank me for going out to get the food. I finished my dinner before everyone else and went straight to my room. Beth and Mariam stayed at the dinner table to talk to my grandmother after everyone had finished eating. What I didn't know at the time was that Mariam asked my grandmother why I was still living in her house, as if my grandmother had previously agreed to get rid of me by then, which was undoubtedly true.

It was Beth who rang to tell me what Mariam had said. She also told me that Mariam and Olivia had been talking my grandmother into kicking me out of the house for almost a year. I felt like I had just been stabbed in the guts, and it didn't help that Beth then took the opportunity to twist the knife while it was in there.

'Your Dad should have never told you that it was okay to move back into your Nan's house,' she said.
'Well, I asked him to ask her if I could move back in and she said yes, no problem.'
'Well, she shouldn't have said yes.'

I realised then that Beth had been plotting with the others all along. It hadn't always been obvious, because she was much better at being two-faced than the others. One minute she was claiming to be on your side, probably to gather information to take back to the coven. The next minute, it was clear that she was pulling the strings. It was hardly lost on me that this was the second time she had decided to orchestrate my removal from my grandmother Lorna's house. She had succeeded before, and I had no doubt that she was capable of pulling it off again.

Throughout all the turmoil between his sisters and me, my Dad remained on the fence at all times, never once sticking up for me. He was just too much of a coward to give me any backing because his sisters had a long track record of keeping him in his place. He knew that I looked after his mother while I lived in the house with them both, and that his sisters did very little except turn up from time to time to join in bitching sessions with her, but he would do anything for a quiet life during the week and looked forward only to getting away to Bristol at weekends.

My mental health suffered further under the pressure of this fresh onslaught and I felt myself being pulled back down into the darkness of depression. I went to see my doctor and was once more referred for CBT counselling. It had been six years since my previous programme and it depressed me even more to think that I was no further forward after all that time. My new therapist was Sarah and I gave her the complete rundown of everything that was going on in my life, highlighting my self-doubt because nothing I ever did seemed to be good enough for anyone, not even my own father. Based on that initial visit, Sarah said that she would book me in for ten sessions in total.

I returned to the house after my counselling session to find Olivia talking to my Dad and grandmother Lorna. She asked me if I had any luck finding a job. I said I hadn't but that I was still applying. 'Even asylum seekers coming into this country can get jobs straight away,' she pointed out.

It was particularly demeaning that she said that to me in the presence of my Dad, who of course said nothing to back me up, even though he and everybody else knew how hard I had been trying to find work.

I felt as if I made some progress with Sarah, who encouraged me to focus my attention on the good things in my life. There weren't that many good things at the time, of course, but I did what I could to remain positive. I still had a few sympathetic people in my life, like Wendy and my cousin Elle. Just as Emily had done six years previously, Sarah also advised me not to be drawn into family arguments, to just step away whenever anyone had a go at me.

Just as I started to relax a bit, though, I received the hammer blow I had been fearing. And it came from the worst possible source. The date was 5 February 2017, a Sunday, when I was in my room watching a film. My Dad called up to me to come downstairs. I walked into the dining area to find him sitting there with grandmother Lorna. He asked me to sit down because they needed to talk to me about something.

'I already know what you're going to say, but go on anyway,' I said.

'Well, as you know, Dean,' my Dad said, 'your Nan is not well, so Olivia has spoken to our cousin who owns a nursing home in Manchester and together they have managed to find a live-in carer to support her.'

'Okay, that's good,' I said.

'Well, it is, and it isn't, Dean. We will need to use your room for the carer. As she'll be coming this week, you'll have to find somewhere else to stay in a hurry.'

I just sat there, dumbstruck, even though I had known that this day would come. What I couldn't get to sink in was that it was my own Dad who was telling me to get out.

My grandmother then said: 'I'm sorry, Dean, I have to think about myself. Are there any friends you can stay with?'

'It's fine,' I said. 'I'll sort something out, but I'll need to have something in writing from you to show the council that I've been made homeless.'

They became uptight at this and my grandmother said: 'No, we can't give you anything in writing, Dean, because if the council find out you've been living here it might affect my carer's allowance.'

I didn't really understand what her last statement meant, but I just got up and went back to my room anyway. Any progress I had made with my counselling sessions went straight out the window as I went into complete panic mode. I called Wendy to tell her what had happened, and she insisted once more that I move in with her, but I was in shock and I just told her that I would let her know. I left the house a couple of hours later to go for a drive and after a while I stopped to ring Elle to tell her about this latest development as well. She told me to go to her mother's house for dinner so that we could talk properly about everything.

I arrived at my Aunt Jane's house and found Elle at the front door with her young son Sam, getting ready to go to the shops. I went in and explained the situation to Jane, whose brother used to be married to Olivia. She said she was surprised and disappointed at the family's behaviour and told me to stay in touch and to let her know what was going on. I had dinner there and finally drove back to my grandmother's at around 1 a.m. My Dad and Lorna were asleep so I went straight to bed and set my alarm for 7 a.m. I knew the days ahead were going to be busy, one way or another.

The following morning, I applied to the council's Homeless Section and contacted my GP and Sarah, just in case they tried to get in touch with me at my grandmother's house in future, and also to make emergency appointments with both of them. I called Dane and asked him if I could store my stuff in his garden shed, which he was fine with. I also spoke to Wendy to find out if it was still okay to finally stay at her place temporarily. She had no hesitation in agreeing and I felt the pressure ease just a little bit.

I didn't say anything to my grandmother straight away, as I didn't want anyone knowing exactly what day I would be leaving. I just wanted to make a quiet exit without any fuss or unpleasantness. She had allowed me to live in her house for a long time, and I would be forever grateful for that, but she had also caused me much trauma and grief, which I would never be able to erase from my mind.

I decided to leave on the Wednesday, three days after receiving the ultimatum to get out. I told my grandmother that I would be leaving on the Friday and that I would be going to stay with a friend she didn't know in West London. I was by now determined that the family should not be able to trace me once I'd gone.

That night, when I was in my room packing, the full trauma of my circumstances began to sink in and I realised that there was nothing I could do to stop myself having another breakdown. I sent a text message to Wendy to tell her not to phone me, which she was due to do, because I didn't think I would be stable enough to have a conversation. She texted me back to ask me to call her as soon as I could. I didn't want anyone to hear me, so I went out to my car to ring her. As soon as she picked up, I went quiet. She stayed on the line, not speaking, just being there for me. As my tears began to fall, I realised that I had not cried for as long as I could remember.

'Why are my family treating me like this?' I finally said. 'I haven't done anything wrong, and I've never done anything to harm any of them.' She tried her best to console me, but the more I talked, the more I felt myself breaking down.

After a heavy sleep, I woke up the next day ready for my latest in a very long series of moves. When I began to pack up my car, my grandmother asked me what was going on. I told her that I was just moving some stuff to store at another friend's house, and that I was not moving out just yet. Mariam turned up at noon, which was the last thing I needed. I could hear the two of them laughing and joking about me in the kitchen, and I never felt so humiliated in my entire life, which was really saying something, because I was not exactly a stranger to humiliation.

I couldn't fit everything into the car, which became so packed that I could hardly see out of it. Because I knew I wouldn't be able to face coming back, I left a few things in a kitchen cupboard and a desk fan and some old clothes in my room. I also left my keys in my room and looked around it one last time before leaving. I would be relieved to get out of the house, but I also recognised that quite a lot of my life had been spent in the privacy of that room, so I was also sad to be leaving it behind. On a number of occasions, it had served as a refuge from the troubles I experienced in the world outside, a world that I didn't seem to belong to.

I drove off for the last time, without bothering to say goodbye and without giving the two women inside a final chance to have a laugh at my expense. I didn't let my coward of a father know I'd gone either. On my phone, I blocked the numbers of that whole side of the family, except Elle, so that they could never contact me again.

I drove towards Dane's in Colchester, which should have taken about an hour. On the A12, though, a lorry had exploded and was causing tailbacks that limited my progress to about 5 miles per hour. I didn't have a phone charger in the car, but I needed my phone to find my way to Dane's house. I started to panic as my battery percentage dropped to single figures. Without the navigation app I was using, I was going to end up lost in a city I didn't know. It took me over three hours to get through the traffic and by the time I approached Colchester my phone battery was down to 2 per cent. I then took a wrong turn, which threw me into yet more panic. At any moment the phone could have died on me and that would have been that.

Luckily, the navigation app managed to get me through the town centre and on to Dane's house. When he came out, I said nothing. I just showed him my phone, which was displaying 1 per cent. As he looked at it, it went dead.

I got the car unloaded and had a twenty-minute chat with Dane about my situation. He told me that my life was like something out of a film and that the shit I had been through was just not normal. I hit the road once more and drove to my Aunt Jane's house, as Elle had told me I could go and stay the night there.

Chapter 41:
It's a West Indian thing

The psychological baggage that our grandparents bring to the UK can hamper the growth of their families for many generations to come.

The following day I woke up on the living-room sofa to the morning light shining through the huge patio doors of my Aunt Jane's house. She was in the kitchen making tea and it felt great to be in such a normal environment. Because of all of my appointments in the local area, Jane had said I could stay there for a while, so I once more stood Wendy down. It felt good not to fear getting up and not having to worry about being judged or criticised as soon as I opened my mouth. It was also a great opportunity to get on my laptop and apply for jobs.

I had long conversations with Jane and Elle about the trauma of being homeless and unemployed, and about what I had been through with both sides of the family. After only a short while, I was taken aback to discover that their views on life were remarkably similar to the other females in the family. They stuck up for family members in general, whatever their faults, which is not in itself a bad thing, but it made me wary about what I said to them. They were just about willing to accept that the male members of the family were not all they should be, but would broach no criticism when it came to female members of the family.

When the subject of my childhood came up, I told them about the abuse I had suffered at Tommy's hands, and about the fact that my mother had stood back and let it happen. Elle in particular seemed to have a soft spot for my mother and found ways to defend her, albeit from a totally uninformed position. As far as Tommy was concerned, I got the impression that they both felt that he had every right to discipline me in the ways that he had. It was just the West Indian way of bringing up boys, they inferred. When I asked them what they would do if their partner abused one of their children to that extent, they just went quiet. I liked to think they would at least take a dim view of a female child being abused in one way or another, but I stopped short of asking the question because it was clear that they had definite inbuilt prejudices that would not be broken down for generations to come. Even if it was normal behaviour for West Indian fathers or stepfathers to punch their children with force as a punishment for bedwetting, it never occurred to them that British society generally had long since moved on from such a Victorian view of discipline.

During that week I went to see my GP and when I entered the surgery I saw a cousin that I hadn't seen in years. It was Chrissy, who was working there as a receptionist. I arranged to meet her for lunch that same day to have a catch-up.

Over lunch, Chrissy and I spoke about everything that had happened to us since we last saw each other and, when we had finished, I agreed to pick her up after work and drop her home. When we got there, she told me to come in and say hello to her dad. I was hesitant, because the last time I was there was when he hosted the family pow-wow that got me kicked out of my grandmother Ann's house. I decided I had nothing to lose and went in. Uncle Stewart was lounging on his sofa and looked pleased to see me. I sat down and chatted with him for a while. I explained the predicament I was in at the time, but he didn't seem much interested in that. While I was there, my grandmother Ann happened to call their home phone and Uncle Stewart told her I was there. He then handed me the phone, so I spoke to her and answered her questions about my situation.

She seemed okay on the phone and I told her that, although I was on the verge of leaving to stay at my friend Wendy's house in Dartford temporarily until my housing situation was sorted out, I would visit her when I came back to Tottenham for a doctor's appointment the following week.

I felt that day that there might be a glimmer of hope as far as reconciling with that side of the family was concerned, but I had been there before and I had been disappointed and even cast out in the end. If it happened at all, it would be a long process, I thought.

Wendy had been in touch constantly since I left grandmother Lorna's house, pressuring me to go and stay with her. As I was also conscious of the fact that it probably wouldn't be long before I outstayed my welcome at Jane's house, I packed up my car and drove to Dartford that Sunday. Wendy literally welcomed me with open arms as she gave me a big hug. I don't think I had ever seen her so happy to see me and it felt nice to be wanted. I also knew, though, that she wanted much more from the relationship than I did, and that I probably couldn't stay too long before that became an issue. In the meantime, I was more than happy to be able to sleep on a blow-up bed on the living-room floor. She tried to make my stay as comfortable as possible, arranging my bedding and making sure I had fresh towels.

Wendy's son Tim worked for National Rail on different shifts, so she told me that he might come in late from work some days. She also mentioned that she was back with her boyfriend Mike, but that she very much resented his past mistakes and wasn't entirely opposed to having casual fun with other men. It wasn't exactly difficult to read between the lines of what she was saying, but the last thing I needed on top of my ongoing mental health issues at that time was a complicated relationship. I simply replied that I was grateful to have shelter in her home, that I would try to get in her way as little as possible, and that I would be doing everything in my power to get back on my feet as quickly as possible.

That week, before I drove back to North London for my doctor's appointment, I sent Chrissy a text asking if it was okay to stay at her dad's for the night as I was coming to see the doctor and then visit my grandmother Ann the following day before heading back to Wendy's. She texted back to say that her dad wouldn't allow it, so I asked her if I had done something wrong. She said I hadn't, that it was just his rules. I finished the exchange by saying that I hoped I hadn't offended him and that I would catch up with him another time. Perhaps any idea of reconciliation would have to wait, I thought.

I called my grandmother Ann to confirm my visit the next day and pointed out that I might have offended her son by asking to stay overnight at his house. She just laughed it off, saying that he was like that with everybody. She asked me some more about my current situation and I said that I had now moved into my friend Wendy's house for the time being. This must have touched a nerve, because she immediately went on the attack. 'You need to stand on your own two feet,' she shouted down the phone, 'you shouldn't be relying on anybody else and your friend shouldn't allow you to stay there. Why do you have to be such a burden to everybody?'

I was in shock at the suddenness of the attack, so I said nothing. I already knew how much of a burden I was to the people around me and I wanted nothing more than to be standing on my own two feet again.

'What happened to your flat?' she continued. 'Why didn't you work hard enough to keep it?'

Unable to cope with her onslaught, I simply said goodbye and ended the call, resigned to the fact that I remained every bit the outcast as far as she and Uncle Stewart were concerned.

A few days later, Wendy said that Mike was coming to stay the night and that I would therefore be able to meet him for the first time. I liked the idea of that, because it would be an opportunity to show him that, as far as I was concerned, Wendy and I were just good friends. It turned out that we got along very well, and I was especially interested in all the different countries he had been to and the stories he had to tell about them.

I carried on applying for jobs on my laptop while I was at Wendy's, even in the evenings, but she was forever asking me to sit next to her on the sofa so that we could watch a film together. In my situation at that time, I wasn't really in the mood for watching films, never mind anything else, but Wendy started to take offence at my refusals. I soon also discovered that she was a bit of a control freak, to the extent that she wouldn't even let me wash my own clothes.

I suddenly got a call from an agency about a fitness job in Dubai I had applied for the previous year. The recruiter, a girl called Jennifer, explained to me that the position had reopened, that my details matched the requirement for the role and that she would arrange a Skype interview with the manager within a few days if I was still interested. Without hesitation, I asked her to put me forward for the position. It was an opportunity that had the potential to transform my life and I certainly had no qualms about leaving the country, not having any real ties here anyway. When I told Wendy, she was very negative about the idea. She criticized Dubai for being a Muslim country and said that the laws would be too strict for me. It wasn't the first time I had heard Wendy make racist remarks, but it was more surprising at that time because Tim was seeing a Muslim girl. Thankfully, she was enough of a hypocrite to disguise her feelings whenever he brought his girlfriend to the house.

I knew that Wendy wasn't keen on me leaving the country for her own selfish reasons, but I nonetheless made it clear that I would be gone in a flash if they offered me the job. From that point on, things were not the same between us and the atmosphere in the house deteriorated somewhat.

I soon got another call from Jennifer to tell me that the manager liked my CV and to let me have a time slot for a Skype interview the following day. I was very excited at the prospect and I began going over my personal training coursework to brush up on my knowledge in that area.

The next day I got my laptop and notes set up on Wendy's dining table. As luck would have it, she had to go to the doctor's, which gave me some much-needed space. Because I was well prepared, I didn't feel nervous when the interview got underway and it all flowed nicely. I could see that the manager was pleased with the answers I gave to his questions and at the end he explained to me that, assuming I passed the first interview stage, there would be two more stages via Skype before any successful applicant could be offered the job. I called Jennifer to give her feedback and she said she would let me know whether I had succeeded in getting through to the next stage.

I told Wendy about the interview and she wasn't happy, but I was just pleased to have some hope back in my life. She also said that Mike was coming to stay with her again for a while, so I decided to give them some privacy and arranged to go back to my Aunt Jane's for a few nights following my next doctor's appointment the following day.

Chapter 42:
The end of the road

Sometimes there comes a point when you just have to accept that you're on your own.

While I was staying at Aunt Jane's, I received a copy of my counselling report via my GP. Everything I had said about my childhood was in there. For the time being, I kept it to myself.

I got a call from Jennifer to tell me that I was through to the second stage of the interview for the Dubai job and that I was booked in for the following day. My hopes grew, and I even felt a degree of self-confidence coming back while I prepared for the second stage.

In the second interview, one of the company's trainers took me through a technical test and I answered every single question correctly. He then sent me a case study and told me that I would have to go through it with the manager if I got through to the final stage. It then became another waiting game.

After a few days at Aunt Jane's, I drove back to Wendy's. I immediately noticed that she was acting differently towards me, playing it a bit cooler than before. She asked me how it had been at my aunt's house and I said it had been fine. I told her about the second interview and that I might get through to the third stage. She just smiled and told me that she and Mike were thinking about trying to make things work between them and that he might move back in with her. She even asked for a rough idea of when I might be moving out.

Having pretty much begged me to move in with her in the first place, it was clear that she couldn't cope with me being there if I wasn't going to give her what she wanted. I knew she was lying about Mike, because I knew she despised him. Every single day that I had spent in her house she had complained about him non-stop. It was clear that she didn't love him. I said I hoped to be gone within six weeks. The truth was I had no idea what was going to happen to me from that point on. I was very close to using the overdraft in my bank account and I had just one possibility on the job front. I became very anxious knowing that I was no longer wanted by Wendy, who had been my fall-back position for quite some time. I couldn't really blame her, of course, because I was the one who had time and again refused her the relationship she so desperately wanted us to have.

The following day I got an email from Jennifer confirming that I was through to the last stage of the interview process and that I was booked in for the Friday. I told Wendy about it, emphasising that I might not have to stay at her house for much longer. She gave me the fake smile I was used to seeing by now and the atmosphere in the house just got more and more awkward with each passing day. I spent most of my time that week at the local library to keep my mind clear for what could be the most important interview of my life. When Friday arrived, Wendy told me that Tim and his young daughter were coming over to stay for the weekend and hinted at the idea of me visiting my aunt so that they could have the house to themselves. I told her that I would leave as soon as I had finished my interview, which was set for 2 p.m.

As the time of my interview approached, Wendy began putting out colouring crayons and books for her granddaughter on the dining table where I was sitting, ready for the Skype interview on my laptop. She said that Tim and his daughter would need to use the table and that I would need to sit somewhere else to do my interview. I knew that they weren't coming until much later and that she was just messing me about to disrupt my interview preparation. I moved to the living area anyway. At 1.55 p.m., Wendy asked me if I could help her move some garden chairs up to the loft. By this time my blood was at boiling point, but I helped her with the chairs to keep the peace and came back downstairs just in time for the interview. The manager then sent me an email saying he was going to be ten minutes late, whereupon Wendy told me to go to the back of the house to do my interview so that I was out of the way in the living area. I quickly grabbed all of my notes and laptop and set up once more for the interview. As I waited, Wendy talked constantly about nothing very much. Even when the Skype call came through, she wouldn't leave me alone. I told her firmly that I really needed to do the interview at that point and, luckily, she ambled off upstairs.

I gave that final interview my all and the manager seemed happy throughout. When it was over, he told me that he would let the agency know about my application within a few days. I breathed a sigh of relief after signing off, but I was also furious with Wendy for trying to ruin it for me. She came downstairs smiling, as if nothing untoward had happened, and said she was off to pick up her granddaughter from school. It was my turn to offer up a fake smile. After she left, I quickly jumped in the shower, got dressed and packed my car, all within twenty minutes. I knew our friendship was finally over, but I didn't want to create a scene over it, so I just got in my car and drove to North London. I pulled up outside my aunt's house, but she wasn't in and her car wasn't there. I called her and asked if I could stay because of what happened at Wendy's.

She said that she was at her mother's house and was not coming back that evening, and that Elle was staying with her girlfriend. I called Elle, who suggested I call a mutual friend of ours, a tattoo artist called Eddie who lived in Cheshunt. I called him and he told me to come straight to his house. When I got there, the place was buzzing. Eddie had a lot of friends round watching a boxing match. The house was somewhat unique, in that the walls were painted black and there was a tattoo studio in the living room.

We went upstairs to his room, where I told him what had happened. He said I could stay for a while, but that he always had clients coming and going to get tattoos done and that he and his friends usually stayed up very late every night. He also didn't have a spare bedroom, so he could only offer me the sofa in the living area to sleep on. I was grateful for any shelter I could get, and I told him so.

As the evening went on, I spoke to a lot of the other guys there. It was good to have company for a change. They were all drinking spirits and having a good time, but then they started going to the back of the kitchen in small groups. I went in to make myself some tea and saw that they were snorting lines of coke. I had entered a house full of addicts, with little prospect of getting the sleep I now very badly needed. By four o'clock in the morning, they were all as high as a kite and there seemed no prospect of anyone leaving. I sat down on the sofa and closed my eyes, but I was jolted awake by the noise every time I fell asleep.

Finally, around eight o'clock in the morning, everyone left. Eddie told me he was going to get some sleep and advised me to do the same. I slept till around eleven, when a woman walked into the house, gave me a dirty look, and went into the kitchen to start cleaning.

My first impression was that she was Eddie's cleaner, so I thought I'd better get up just in case she wanted to clean anywhere near the sofa. I went upstairs and brushed my teeth, then came back downstairs to make some tea. I asked the woman if she was Eddie's girlfriend and she told me she was his mother.

I was embarrassed because she probably thought I was one of Eddie's druggy friends. When Eddie finally woke up, he explained my situation to her, but she was clearly not happy about me sleeping on the sofa. The following four days and nights were a real eye-opener for me. The cycle of night-time drugs and alcohol continued, limiting my sleep to two to four hours a night. I still applied for jobs, kept my appointments, and progressed my housing application, though. I also got the reply from Jennifer that I had been hoping for when she got in touch to tell me that I had got the job in Dubai. She sent me over the contract and told me to sign and return it if I was happy with it.

As I went through the detail of it, however, I saw bit by bit that the contract didn't in any way match the employment package that had been sent to me at the start of the application process. I assumed they had made a mistake and asked Jennifer to query it. An hour later, she got back to me to say that the package was correct and that the contract I had before me was what was on offer. It was one quarter of the original salary and came with no accommodation, which was meant to be included. I was devastated. I had so much riding on that opportunity and had gone through three interviews only to learn that it had all been a bit of a scam. When I told Jennifer that I wouldn't be signing the contract, she said she wasn't surprised and that she would speak to another company in the same region who were looking for fitness staff.

I was once again left wondering if my life just wasn't meant to be. It felt like one disappointment after another would follow me wherever I went. What was I doing so wrong? Could it be that I just wasn't equipped for the life I wanted to lead?

To top things off that day, Eddie explained to me that his mother wasn't happy about me sleeping on the sofa and that his aunt was going to be coming out of hospital, which meant I had to leave pretty much immediately. I thanked him for his hospitality and called Elle to ask if I could come over and she said I could.

I got my things together yet again and drove to my Aunt Jane's in Ponders End. Since I had last stayed there, she had arranged to have a lot of work done on the house, so the very next day she began to hint that I would very soon need somewhere else to stay. When she suggested I make peace with my mother, I gave her my counselling report to read. By the time she got to the second page she had begun to cry. That bought me some time as no mention was made of the need for me to leave for the next two weeks.

Having Aunt Jane read about my childhood reminded me that she was one of the women that Tommy had screwed when I was about eleven years old. My mother confronted her about it, following which they didn't talk for a very long time, and stayed with Tommy regardless. My mother had justified this to herself time after time by putting the blame for the relationships on all the other women. I wondered maybe if Jane's conscience over her affair with Tommy had led to her suggestion that I try to reconcile with my mother, but it was much more likely that she just wanted me gone from her house.

Jennifer called about another fitness job in Dubai and told me that the company in question was willing to cover all my expenses, including accommodation. I told her to put me forward for the position as it sounded promising, but I wasn't counting any chickens given the previous scam.

When the builders began work on my aunt's house, I volunteered to stay indoors and keep an eye on them so that she could go out during the day. I had received an email from Jennifer about an interview for the second company, so I needed the time to revise for that anyway. During that period, I managed to get into a bit of a routine. I caught up on my sleep, started to eat healthily again and went for walks to improve my fitness. I even began doing some bodyweight exercises in the house. All of this helped to rebuild my confidence a little. With the right job opportunity, I knew I could get back on my feet and regain a degree of stability in my life. I began to have some hope, to feel some balance.

I knew by now, however, to always expect two steps back after taking one step forward, and so it proved. I got a letter from the council telling me that I was considered a non-priority case and did not therefore qualify for housing, and my aunt told me that major internal works were about to start in the house and that the sooner I reconciled with my mother, the better. It was as if she'd forgotten the contents of my counselling report already. Everything was now riding once more on an interview with a company in Dubai. If that didn't pan out, I was very much at risk of becoming homeless. I had run out of places to stay.

On the morning of my interview, I woke up feeling a bit nervous as I had a lot hanging over my head and a lot depending on the outcome of the day ahead. When I walked into the kitchen, Elle was making breakfast for herself and her girlfriend. She didn't offer me any, which was unusual, and I could feel an uncomfortable vibe in the air. I made myself a cup of tea and cracked on with my revision for the interview.

The kitchen was a mess when they had finished their breakfast and I overheard Elle's girlfriend offering to wash the dishes, but Elle told her just to leave it and they left the house together. Elle was known for being lazy, a factor which contributed to her increasing obesity. About a quarter of an hour later, I got a call from her. She launched into a tirade about me not contributing financially to the household bills, not patching things up with my mother and not pulling my weight around the house. That final accusation was pretty rich, coming from Elle. She had plenty of weight to pull; she just chose not to pull it. I, on the other hand, had been doing my fair share of cleaning and even took Elle's young son to school and picked him up afterward. However, she belonged in that house and I didn't, and that was that. My Aunt Jane and Elle had dropped enough hints about me leaving and I hadn't taken them because I had nowhere else to go. Now it was getting nasty, and I knew I couldn't hang around there like a bad smell for much longer.

Elle could have chosen a better moment, of course, because her verbal onslaught wasn't great preparation for an important interview. I tried to calm myself using the meditative techniques I had learned from Emily during my original CBT sessions, but I hadn't got very far when the Skype call came through. Before we even got to the interview questions, though, the manager on the other end of the line raised the point that the job was for a group trainer with relevant qualifications, which I did not have. There was no point in having the interview, so we just ended the connection there and then. Jennifer had messed up for a second time and that's the thing about recruitment agencies – they're only as competent as the person you deal with. Jennifer simply wasn't competent, and I knew now that the Dubai option was over for me.

And so was everything else. I showered, got dressed and packed up my car. My aunt came back while I was doing so, but she went straight upstairs to her bedroom without saying hello, never mind goodbye. I closed the front door, got into my car, and drove off. Only this time, I had nowhere to go.

Chapter 43:
Working as a reluctant drug-runner

Even down-and-outs can have job prospects if they really want them.

After driving for less than ten minutes, I pulled the car over and just sat there at the side of the road. At first, my mind went totally blank, but after a while the blank feeling was replaced with panic, anxiety and general confusion. I couldn't stop the prospect of suicide creeping back into my mind, but I tried everything I knew to fight it off.

In desperation, I remembered a distant cousin that had once come to visit my Aunt Jane. He was a troubled soul with serious issues, but I had his number and I thought he might provide a temporary roof over my head. I called to tell him what had happened, and he told me to come over.

Rio's background was colourful, to say the least. Like me, he had experienced a life of ups and downs, but with fewer ups. He had hung around with the wrong crowd from an early age and had found himself in trouble with the police for all sorts of reasons, from driving cars with no insurance to selling drugs. He had three children with a long-term partner, but she had ended the relationship because he got aggressive whenever he took drugs, which was all the time. While living in a YMCA hostel, he was taken to hospital, where he was diagnosed with diabetes. That was a cloud with a silver lining, though, because he lost his place at the hostel while he was in hospital and that made him a priority case with the council. Therefore, when he was released from hospital, he was allocated the bedsit in Tottenham where he was staying now.

I knew I shouldn't be asking him for shelter, because he was in a small bedsit, which was really not practical for two grown men, but it was that or nothing for me that night. When I got there, I saw that his place was a complete mess. The floor had rotten food all over it, the whole place reeked of marijuana and tobacco, there were dirty clothes everywhere and all the ashtrays were overflowing. The whole bedsit comprised of two tiny rooms. One had a shower, toilet and sink in it. The other had a single bed, a small desk with his PlayStation on it, a single wardrobe, two kitchen units on the floor and two above the sink. In the kitchen area, there was also a small refrigerator and two-hob electric cooker. The entire place was 10 feet long by 7 feet wide. Given that I'm 6 feet tall, the only place I could possibly sleep was on the one narrow length of hardwood floor that wasn't already covered. Fortunately, I at least had a pillow and a picnic blanket with me (I also had a duvet in the boot of my car, but there was no room for it on Rio's floor anyway).

On the plus side, Rio was very intelligent and good to talk to. He had figured out that a strict vegan diet would help control his diabetes, so that's what he stuck to. On the downside, he sold marijuana and cocaine to fund what was a very expensive way to eat. He also had a fascination with the Rastafarian movement, which led him to believe in government-driven conspiracies and to conclude that he was very much a victim of those. The dynamic between us, though, was good, in spite of the fact that the only thing we had in common was that we were struggling to make our respective ways in life.

Apart from the benefits he claimed, dealing drugs had been his only form of income since he was a teenager.

As his clients sometimes came to his bedsit to collect their drugs, I soon realised how unsafe it was to be at Eddie's.

I continued to press the council for sheltered accommodation, look for work in either the IT or personal fitness industries, and attend doctor's appointments. As my mental health was back at a low point, I was referred by my GP to a social worker for support, but that didn't help much because I was a low-priority case there as well. I did my best to stay focussed, though, and, to my surprise, I managed to secure a job interview with an IT hosted solutions company based in Chancery Lane. The position was that of Media and IT Asset Manager and I was qualified enough to warrant proper consideration.

I researched the company in question on my laptop while Rio weighed crack on a set of digital scales beside me. It was difficult to imagine a greater contrast in two otherwise parallel lives. Rio was putting everything at risk dealing drugs, but he was at least earning money. I had practically exhausted my £750 overdraft at the bank, so I began to eat just once a day so that I could afford the paltry travel expenses I needed for my upcoming interview.

Rio kept asking me to drive him to different places every day so that he could deliver to his clients, and I did so for no other reason than he was letting me stay at his place. I didn't ask him for any money for diesel, although having to buy it was putting a terrible strain on my finances. After a while, it began to irritate me that he was making much more selling drugs in a day than I received in Jobseeker's Allowance in a fortnight, yet he still complained about never having any money.

I had just enough money to get my suit dry cleaned before my interview, and I kept it in its polythene cover at Rio's place to ward off the smell of marijuana, which I thought might not enhance my job prospects. On the day of the interview, I took the Tube to Chancery Lane and headed to the company's office in time for my 1 p.m. appointment.

The receptionist showed me to the boardroom, where the interview was to take place, and explained that the two managers who would interview me were running about twenty minutes late. I was glad, because it gave me more time to gauge my surroundings, read some of the company material that was lying around the boardroom and go through my interview notes.

An hour and ten minutes later, the managers finally arrived, full of apologies for having kept me waiting and looking a little stressed. I saw that as an opportunity, because I had had plenty of time to compose myself and I probably looked quite relaxed in comparison. I did my best to control the interview by asking every question I could think of about the job description, the company and the services they offered to their clients. I figured that the longer I kept them there, the more I would stick in their minds when they came to review applicants for the position. The chemistry felt good throughout and they ended the interview by explaining to me that I would be contracted out to a major bank if I was successful. I told them that I would be happy to start as soon as possible, but they pointed out that there would now be a lengthy vetting process which could take up to two months.

I left the office feeling positive but concerned about the length of time it would take even if I was successful. Given my recent track record, I also knew about the need to manage my expectations downwards. I headed back to Rio's and came back to earth with a bump when I saw him sitting on the floor preparing crack for his clients.

He asked me how the interview went and I replied that it had gone smoothly.

The following day, I got a call inviting me to another interview, this time with an IT company with a head office near Southampton, which is where I would need to go for the interview. I thought maybe my luck was changing, that I was going to be on a roll for a while even, but there was a problem. My car insurance, road tax and MOT were all due to be renewed that week and I really didn't have the money to pay for them.

I decided to call my bank, explain the hardship I was going through and inform them that I had interviews underway for potential jobs. When I made the call, I pretty much pleaded with them to extend my overdraft so I could keep my car on the road to attend interviews. They said they had to speak to the overdrafts team about my situation and that they would call me back shortly. While I waited, I went out to the communal passageway of Rio's building, where I meditated and prayed as hard as I could for the right answer. Five minutes later, I got a call back approving an additional £500 on my overdraft. I was so relieved, and barely unable to believe my luck. To keep costs down, I went to a few different garages to find the cheapest quote for an MOT and found a place not far from the bedsit. I soon had my MOT certificate, along with up-to-date tax and insurance.

I was very worried about using my car to take Rio round his clients, because by now it was my only safe place in the world and I couldn't afford to lose it or, worse still, get arrested for using it for illegal purposes. My health was also deteriorating rapidly due to the lack of nutrition caused by my very tight budget, but I tried to stay positive. I began to meditate and pray every morning to help me through this latest difficult period. I had never been one for praying, but it had worked to get my overdraft extended, so I thought I would stick with it for a while.

I revised hard for my second interview and drove to Southampton when the day arrived for my 12 p.m. appointment. However, I hit bad traffic on the journey down and reached the company's office at exactly twelve o'clock, which was cutting it too fine. I tried hard to settle my nerves and put on a brave face as I sat down with one of their directors to go over the job specification. I soon settled and adopted the same strategy as last time by taking control to the extent possible. I asked lots of questions, offered ideas about how I could contribute to the company and explained how my skill set matched the role perfectly. I sensed a positive mood and before I knew it the interview was over. The director escorted me back to the reception area, where he told me he would be in contact within a week to offer me feedback from the interview.

For the second time in two weeks, I left an interview on a high note. As the sun was shining, I drove back to London with my windows down, playing music and feeling as if I didn't have a care in the world. When I got back to Rio's, he was getting ready for his next delivery round and, after enquiring how my interview went, asked if I could take him round his various 'friends' in my car that evening. I reluctantly agreed, but I had just emptied my fuel tank on the long trip to Southampton and back, and I didn't fancy filling it up for the purposes of drug-running, so I asked him if he could at least give me some money for fuel if I drove him round. That annoyed him, presumably because he thought he was doing more than enough for me already, and he probably had a point at that. In the end, he handed me £2.50 and asked me to leave by the following day because he needed his space back. I agreed to do so, not that I had any choice in the matter.

I told Rio I was going out and that I'd be back in time for his evening run. I drove to Tottenham Marshes, where I parked up to try and think through what my next move should be. I now knew that I would be homeless by the following morning and that my car would be my only night-time shelter from that point on. I accepted my fate and tried to figure out how on earth I was going to cope with life as a homeless person.

Chapter 44:
My worst fear realised

It takes surprisingly little time to adapt to homelessness.

I spent the evening with Rio acting as if everything was fine, but, in reality, I was shattered and increasingly fearful of what lay ahead. I woke early the next morning and started packing my car for what felt like the hundredth time. Rio had gone to the shops and when he got back he saw me packing but asked me to drop him at his nan's house anyway. I agreed to do so, just to avoid any unpleasantness.

Once all my bags were packed, we headed out to the car. Rio didn't offer to carry a single bag. He just stood there until I had the last of them packed. I wanted nothing more than to be far away from him and I was relieved after dropping him off.

I needed to find a quiet place to get my head together, so I went back to the car park I had gone to the previous evening at Tottenham Marshes. As I sat there, the shock of my circumstances began to sink in. Unsurprisingly, I had never had to live in a car before, but that felt like the least of my worries. The car had covered 160,000 miles by then, the steering rack needed changing, the brakes were going and one of my tyres was looking a bit worse for wear, having only just scraped through the recent MOT.

I no longer had breakdown cover either, because I hadn't been able to afford it when I renewed the insurance with my enlarged bank overdraft. The idea of my new home breaking down at the side of the road at any moment frightened the hell out of me. I also didn't know how I was going to survive on my Jobseeker's Allowance alone, especially if I needed fuel to get to interviews, and I knew that keeping myself presentable enough to attend interviews was also going to be an issue.

My thoughts were interrupted by a call from Rio, who was ringing to tell me that his shower gel was missing. The shower gel he was referring too was actually one I had bought for both of us to use, so I explained to him that I had packed it in a bag with my other belongings. He launched into a manic diatribe about the shower gel belonged to him, accused me of stealing it and demanded to know when I was going to go back and replace it. I explained again that the shower gel technically belonged to me, given that I had paid for it, and that I had more to worry about than shower gel, like being homeless, for example. By now he was shouting and swearing, which led to direct threats about what he was going to do to me. At that point, I seriously considered going round there, just to have the pleasure of beating him senseless, but in the end I just hung up, too weary to go on. The last thing I needed right then was a prison sentence. It would be a roof over my head certainly, but it wouldn't look good on job applications, and I wasn't ready to give up hope of finding work just yet.

Rio continued to bombard me with threatening text messages, so he became the latest in a long line of family members to get blocked on my phone. As the day wore on, it slowly occurred to me that I needed to figure out where I was going to park up overnight in order to get some sleep. I needed a quiet road without many cars around, so I drove towards Waltham Abbey. Because my cousin Pete used to live there, I knew there were some secluded residential roads in the area. After forty minutes of driving around, I came upon Pick Hill. As I drove down it, I saw mostly detached houses. Too wealthy, I thought, probably not the sort of people who want a homeless guy outside in his car. As the road curved right, though, I saw a row of bungalows. Probably retired people, I concluded, and therefore unlikely to threaten me too much even if they did spot me sleeping in my car. I found a patch of grass just beyond a house with no side windows to overlook me. I parked up and sat quietly for thirty minutes, watching out for local residents and assessing how busy the road was going to be. I decided it was a safe haven for the night.

Without consciously knowing it, my only thoughts were now of survival, and my defences were accordingly on high alert. I suddenly realised that I hadn't eaten or been to the toilet all day, and I assumed my body had decided not to trouble me with such trivialities because my mind had sent it messages to let it know that the normal rules of engagement were in abeyance for the time being. I drove to Enfield to get a burger and go to the toilet, by which time it was eleven o'clock.

I was completely exhausted, so I drove back to my spot at Pick Hill, where I found everything to be perfectly still. I pulled up as quickly as I could to avoid drawing attention to myself and turned off the ignition.

I then tried to figure out how I was going to sleep in the car. Because I had a two-door Polo, I could only access the rear seats by moving one of the front seats forward. Even if I got in there, though, my six-feet-long body would have nowhere to stretch itself out. I also had to think about safety. If someone tried to break into the car or otherwise attack it, I might have to jump out quickly. As the front passenger seat had on it the personal belongings that I needed to keep handy (for example, my toiletries), my sole remaining option was to move and recline the driver's seat back as far as possible. This would also afford the advantage of being able to start the engine and make a quick getaway should the need arise.

Luckily, I still had my duvet and pillow, but finding a sleeping position remained the challenge. I had taken my trainers and socks off and my bare feet kept bashing the car pedals and my knee kept hitting the gear stick. I ended up putting my pillow on the highest part of the headrest, pulling the duvet up over me and bending my legs into the foetal position. I was now lying on my side at a 30-degree angle, which was really not comfortable.

Once I settled down as well as I could, I noticed that the streetlights had gone off and all I could see were the stars in the night sky. Because the Waltham Abbey area had much more open land than urban London, there was less light pollution than I was used to. In that moment, I looked at the stars with amazement for the very first time. I had never seen anything quite so beautiful, and for a little while I forgot about my problems.

From time to time, I drifted off to sleep, but I woke up every time I heard the slightest noise, thinking that there must be someone or something nearby, possibly even approaching the car. I was fully awakened by the noise of a large truck at five o'clock the next morning and couldn't get back to sleep afterwards. Daylight entered my car like water filling a bath, just washing over me. It warmed and comforted me, until I remembered that with daylight came visibility. People would soon see me as they went about their morning routine, so I needed to get going.

I reached into my leather toilet bag to get my toothbrush, toothpaste, tongue brush and mouthwash. I then brushed my teeth thoroughly, all the while looking around me in a state of vigilance. I gargled with my mouthwash to finish and spat it out the car window once I was sure nobody was looking. I then drove to the McDonalds near the town centre, which was open 24 hours a day, and went in to use the toilet and get something to eat.

I sat there planning my finances. I had £73.10 a week to live on, which isn't that much in London, especially if you need to run a car, pay for a mobile phone and service a bank overdraft. The priority had to be the car because it was my only form of shelter, so fuel was essential. I would just put a little diesel in at a time and try to coast as much as possible to conserve it. The next priority was food and the cheapest place to buy that was where I was now sitting, in McDonald's. Their Pound Saver menu had items from 99p, so I decided to purchase one item off that menu each day. I would be hungry, but I wouldn't starve either. I would only be able to afford to eat once a day, so I decided it would be best to eat my one item in the late afternoon. In order to maintain hydration, I would purchase the cheapest 2-litre bottle of water I could find.

To keep clean, I would use baby wipes in the car and use the showers at the leisure centre in Enfield whenever I could afford the entrance fee. I would take my clothes to a self-service launderette, not only because it would be cheap, but also because it would offer temporary shelter. Unfortunately, though, my trainers were so worn that there were holes in both of the soles. I had plastic bags I could put inside them to keep dirt out, but when it rained I just had to accept that my feet would get soaked and very dirty indeed. I would just have to change my socks on a regular basis and find somewhere to rinse the dirty ones through.

Once I had planned those essentials, I considered my need for a regular internet connection to apply for jobs. In addition to McDonalds free Wi-Fi, I decided to use the facilities at the Ridge Avenue Library in Winchmore Hill.

The final thing I needed to sort out was where to park my car at night. This was a tricky one, because I didn't want to be seen. For one thing, I was acutely embarrassed about being homeless. I was also paranoid about being robbed or attacked, or being hassled by the police. I would need a number of regular spots, I decided, in order to avoid undue attention.

To begin with, I took a drive around Enfield and found a country lane called Hadley Road, which went uphill to an area where there were no houses. It was just a single road surrounded by open fields and a couple of lay-bys where I could park my car. That road led in turn to Ferny Hill, where there were three lay-bys to choose from. I pulled into one of them and sat in my car to assess the area. The lay-by was long enough to take ten cars at a time and there didn't seem to be much traffic going by. There were no pavements alongside the road either, which meant there wouldn't be many passers-by on foot.

I stepped out into bright sunshine and looked up at a magnificent tree that seemed to stand guard over the area. I just stood there, immersing myself in my new surroundings and in the realisation of my new lifestyle, if homelessness can be called such a thing. On the one hand, I felt the pressure of my situation bearing down on me, but I also found myself counting what blessings I had left. I had transportation which doubled up as shelter from the elements. I was dependent upon no one. I had no one to answer to but myself. I was fortunate to become homeless with the winter months behind me and the warmer summer months to look forward to, which meant no freezing nights for the foreseeable future. And, most importantly, I had reached a point of no return. Surely, things could only get better from here on in. At the very least, I was prepared to give life one last chance.

Chapter 45:
The noose of death

If you can stop fearing death, you can stop fearing anything.

As I settled in for the night on Ferny Hill, I felt absolutely petrified to begin with. As had happened the previous night at Pick Hill, though, I became alive to the natural world about me. The sky was crystal clear, and the moon and stars were brighter than I had ever seen them. I began to wonder if life shouldn't be more about appreciating what was around us than worrying about the material things we were programmed to worry about from an early age. Sitting there, I found it difficult to place any importance on family conflict, relationship break-ups, job losses, poverty or any of the other things that can drag us down to the depths of despair under normal circumstances. I fell asleep with a surprising sense of calm.

Each time I woke up during the night my anxieties woke up with me, but I managed to suppress them on each occasion and fall back to sleep. Not long after five o'clock the following morning, the sun was already warming the inside of the car. The first thing I saw when I opened my eyes was a crow perched on the highest point of the tree right in front of me. In the absence of anything else to do, I decided to meditate. I finished by praying for a miracle that might turn my fortunes around and set about preparing myself for the day that lay ahead. I brushed my teeth, cleaned myself as best I could with baby wipes, got changed and drove into town.

I went to McDonalds to use their Wi-Fi and charge my phone and laptop. I spent the whole morning there over one tea, applying for jobs and begging the council to give me somewhere to stay, all to no avail. I couldn't sit in McDonalds all day, so around midday I drove to Enfield Town Library and sat down there with my laptop. I decided there were only so many jobs I could apply for in one day and after a while I just sat there looking around the library. There were so many books on so many different subjects that I suddenly had the idea of writing one myself. I could write about my own life, I thought. As well as giving me something useful to do with my time, it might help me to put my thoughts and experiences into some kind of overall context. Perhaps other men might even find it useful if they found themselves suffering in the ways I had. It would also have the undoubted advantage of providing me with regular shelter in the library, especially on those days when the weather outside wasn't ideally suited to the homeless way of life.

I stared at the screen for twenty minutes or so and took the decision to start at the very beginning, at my earliest memories of a brief but happy childhood while my parents were still together. The words were soon flowing, and for a while I felt full of purpose.

After a week or so of my new routine of applying for jobs in the morning in McDonalds and writing in the library in the afternoon, I hit another low point when I realised that I was still not really getting anywhere. I was sitting in my now regular lay-by on Ferny Hill around six o'clock one evening when I realised how hopeless my situation remained. I just wasn't sure how much more rejection I could take. The council still didn't view me as a priority case and my hard-earned CV wasn't even getting me interviews.

I looked up at the tree I had become accustomed to spending my nights beside and noticed a particularly long, thick branch. This is it, I thought, this is what my life has been leading up to. All I had to do to end my suffering was purchase a long rope, make a noose and hang myself on that branch. It was positioned in such a way that nobody would see me during the act itself, so death would have plenty of time to take me. I contemplated the pain I might suffer. I had read somewhere about people snapping their necks when they dropped, and about the agony that caused while waiting for their oxygen supply to run out. I knew I could prevent that from happening, though, because I had the upper body strength to ease myself down into the noose. I felt a strange calmness come over me, knowing that I had a way out, that my life didn't have to play out along the lines of what had gone before. I didn't feel the need to do it immediately, but I was happy knowing that once my other options had finally run out, I could put myself out of my misery at a time and place of my own choosing.

I was still waiting to hear from the IT hosted solutions company based in Chancery Lane (I assumed they were still running their checks on me as I hasn't heard anything from them for a while) and the thought of writing my book still excited me in my more positive moments. I could hear a voice in my head telling me that I could make it through, that it wasn't yet my time to give it all up, and that I should relax in the knowledge that I had a guaranteed way out if and when that time did come. By the time I had finished thinking all this through, I was mentally exhausted and fell into a deep sleep.

The following morning, I booked an emergency appointment with my GP and went to see her at the surgery. After I explained my latest situation and the decision I had taken the previous evening, she arranged for a psychiatrist and a social worker to come and see me at the surgery that same day. They assessed my mental state and offered me antidepressants, which I refused on the basis that I did not consider myself to have any hormonal imbalance. My suicide ideation was based purely on the logic that death was preferable to long-term homelessness. They wrote a letter for me to take to the emergency housing section of the local council to add to the housing application I had already made months ago. I took it straight there, only to be told that they would add it to my file and that they had no idea when I would next hear from them. I started to wonder if the mistake I was making was keeping myself clean and tidy. Was I being considered low priority because I refused to conform to most people's stereotypical idea of what a homeless person should look like? Perhaps I just didn't smell bad enough for the council's liking?

After an emotionally draining day, I drove to the lay-by that was now my home (I had given up on the idea of going to different places each night). With my new perspective on life and death, I began to think that if I had ultimate power over my very existence, then, surely, I also had the power to shape my life for as long as I was going to live it. I grabbed my notepad and drew a table with three columns. In the first column I wrote what was important to me; in the second I put down what I wanted out of life; and in the third I noted the actions I needed to take in order to achieve what I wanted. I opened my mind to endless possibility and refused to contemplate failure, choosing instead to believe for the time being that for every problem there must be a solution.

Armed with this positive energy, I went into a meditation routine, during which I gave thanks not just for the things that were in my life, but also for the possibilities that lay ahead of me. I gave thanks for the possibility of my own place, my own bed, a new job, perfect health and emotional stability. I also gave thanks for the opportunity to write my life story and I made it a priority to finish my book as soon as I possibly could.

The next morning, I headed over to the library and continued my search for a job before doing some work on the book. In the afternoon, my thoughts suddenly returned to my ongoing curiosity over spiritualism, so I ran a search on my laptop to see if there was a spiritualist church in the area where I might meet some like-minded people. I found one in Enfield called Beacon of Light. It was open a few times a week and they practised mediumship and healing, both of which had long since fascinated me, even though I didn't know a great deal about them. Healing was of particular interest to me, of course, because I felt as if I could do with some. Coincidentally, there was a healing service that very day, so I drove to the church in time for its 6 p.m. start.

I was greeted by a church member called Simon, who immediately made me feel welcome. He showed me over to an annex, where there were a few people already waiting to be seen by the healers. The atmosphere was wonderfully serene, with incense sticks burning and spiritual music playing in the background. I felt comfortable straight away and sat down to socialise with the others who were waiting. There was not a single moment in there when I thought about my homelessness and I certainly had no intention of mentioning it to anyone in any event. Whenever anyone asked where I lived, I simply replied that I lived in Enfield near Ferny Hill, which was not of course a lie.

Because I changed them every day, my clothes remained fairly clean, so on the surface you would never have guessed that I was homeless. That might have worked against me at the local council, but I felt very glad in that church not to look too out of place. It occurred to me that I could socialise in a place like that without anyone passing judgement on me or even knowing the first thing about me. Let's face it, I didn't have anything to lose and I certainly didn't belong anywhere else. Perhaps I could even get back on my feet before anyone realised my circumstances, I thought.

After about twenty minutes, I was approached by a lovely lady called Linda, who invited me into the main church for my healing session. There were three other healers in the middle of sessions when I entered, but the atmosphere was just as calm as it had been over in the annex. Linda began by asking me about myself and my reasons for needing to be healed. I explained that I had experienced a lot of trauma in my life to date, mainly with my family, and that it had taken its toll on me emotionally, psychologically and even physically. I said that I wanted to leave all that behind and move on to a better life. I mentioned nothing about my provisional decision to take my own life if things didn't take a turn for the better in the reasonably near future.

Linda said that she would do her best to heal me spiritually and that all I needed to do was remain seated with my eyes closed so that she could work on helping me. She said she didn't need to touch me because a healing energy could work its way from her mind to mine without any physical contact being necessary. I was immediately overwhelmed to receive so much care and attention, because I couldn't remember another time in my life when someone wanted to help me so unconditionally. I felt a loving energy and freely surrendered myself to it. After what felt like about fifteen minutes, I heard Linda gently telling me that she had finished. I was in such a deep meditative state that it took me a little while to regain my senses. When I did so, I thanked Linda for her help and went back to the annex to socialise some more before it was time for the church to close for the evening.

I left the church that night feeling as though an invisible weight had been lifted from me. Although my overriding mindset remained one of survival from one day to the next, I felt a bit more energised to deal with whatever was to come. I drove back to Ferny Hill and settled in for the night. As I looked up at the stars, I found myself wishing that I could try another planet for a while, because there must be one that suits me better than this, I thought.

As the weeks went by in that summer of 2017, I started to attend the church on a semi-regular basis and in doing so I made a few new friends. Sometimes I was just too weak to go, though, because money was sometimes tight to the point where I had to stop eating for a couple of days at a time. As if mental exhaustion wasn't enough, my body was no longer coping either. I guess it didn't help that it had to sleep in a very awkward position every night. The previous year, I had been able to put so much effort into improving my health and fitness, but now they were going in the completely opposite direction. In addition, my anxiety spiked whenever I drove anywhere, because the fuel indicator was always close to empty and my nerves jangled at the thought of breaking down. I knew that losing my car would be the final straw for me.

A strange regular occurrence was that I started to see crows everywhere I went. From the moment I woke up in the car, whenever I found myself outside the library or in the McDonalds car park, or just walking along the road, I would see crows. It became such a profound experience that I began to accept them as companions, or even, in my needier moments, as angels watching over me. I looked forward to their company each day and I was grateful for their friendship.

One day, out of the blue, I got a call from Michael, an old gym friend that I hadn't seen for years. He had heard from a mutual friend about my situation and suggested that I go and stay with him for a while. The only problem was that he lived nearly four hours away in Hull. I wasn't sure what to do, so I told him I'd call him back. There was much to consider, not least that my car was using more fuel than normal, had a slow leak in three of its tyres and was suffering from less-than-responsive brakes. On the other hand, I could apply for jobs and write my book pretty much anywhere, and there was still no sign of getting any shelter from the council. I decided to wait it out until I received my Jobseeker's Allowance payment the following week and called Michael back to tell him that I would drive to Hull then.

The journey to Hull was nerve-wracking, not least because I had no breakdown cover for my ailing Polo. When it had finally limped all the way there, I was greeted at the door by Michael's girlfriend, Fearne.

Michael had been dealing with attention deficit hyperactivity disorder (ADHD) all his life and the gym was his passion, because, like me, he had been able to use it as a means of letting off steam and escaping the problems that life threw his way. His thing was powerlifting, and he had clearly stuck at it since I last saw him, because he had ballooned from 17 stone when I last saw him to the 25 stone I saw before me now. He was obviously taking an awful lot of steroids.

He told me that he had moved to Hull just over a year ago, after inheriting some money from his grandmother when she passed away. He had spent his inheritance on the two-bedroom house he was living in now. Just before he purchased the house, he had met Fearne at a speed-dating event. They were the same age and they had hit it off in spite of Fearne having some issues due to medical complications in her past (I didn't know what that meant, and I didn't ask). They had moved to Hull together soon after meeting.

Michael had told me on the phone that he and Fearne had a few pets, but that hadn't prepared me for the awful state of their house. I had seen similar horrors on television, but never in real life. They had two dogs, four rabbits, two cats and four kittens, which would have been fine, except they were all living together in squalor.

The house was completely covered in animal faeces and urine, dried-up pet food mashed into the carpet, straw from the rabbit cages, dirty clothes and plates and much general rubbish. The scent was too vile to describe. After about ten minutes, I thought I was going to throw up, so I said I needed to use the toilet. That turned out to be a bad mistake. The rabbit cages were in the bathroom and the straw on the floor was covered in their faeces and urine. The toilet, sink, bath and shower were all covered in hairy grime.

When I ventured into the kitchen, it was similarly trashed, with rubbish and grease all over the floor, unwashed dishes and pots everywhere you looked and open pet-food tins providing a feast for a resident swarm of flies.

I truly appreciated Michael's offer to let me stay there, but I knew that I would soon fall ill in that house in my weakened state. It was an awkward predicament and I knew I had no choice but to stay at least one night.

I had been looking forward to my first shower in a while (I hadn't been able to afford to go the leisure centre for a while), but I certainly wouldn't be able to use their bathroom for anything other than absolute necessities.

As Michael worked as a bouncer at a nightclub in the town centre, I quickly offered to drive him to work, glad of the chance to get out of the house and get some fresh air into my lungs.

Chapter 46:
Hope returns

Things can only get so complicated until necessary change happens.

Once I headed back to Michael's house, I went in and had a conversation with Fearne about general life topics. While I was doing that, I saw that there were brand-new cleaning products in the kitchen, so I took them out and began to clean the kitchen worktops. While I did that, I taught Fearne how to clean the kitchen as she had never been shown when she was growing up. I also explained to her the risks of bad hygiene in the home, which could be dangerous to her and Michael's health. After four hours of cleaning, I had only finished one side of the kitchen, but it looked so clean that Fearne was surprised to see just how different it looked. I took a picture of the kitchen and sent it over to Michael. I was so tired that I decided to head to the bedroom and sleep.

Michael's bedroom was a mess, but not as bad as the rest of the house, so I grabbed my duvet and slept on the floor. Michael returned from work at 4 a.m. and woke me up in the process, so we talked about my plans for getting back on my feet. Eventually Michael went to sleep and I went downstairs around ten o'clock to make a cup of tea. But as soon as I walked into the living area, the stench of the house hit me and I had no choice but to pack my car so I could head back to Enfield. The house was too filthy to stay in and when Fearne came down for breakfast I just told her that I needed to get back to London for an appointment, which was a lie, but I didn't want to upset her with the truth about the house. I told her to let Michael know when he woke up and I set off at 2 p.m. to get back to London. The drive back was even scarier because I realised that no matter how hard I tried to move out of my car, I just ended up back in it. At least the inside of the car was cleaner than Michael's house, though.

I eventually made it back to Enfield. Trying to stay as positive as possible, I pulled up on a side road, grabbed my laptop and carried on writing my book until the laptop battery died. Later that evening I got a call from Michael, asking me why I left and if it was because of his house. I just told him the same thing that I'd told Fearne because I didn't want to upset him. I was in a tough spot financially because I had used some of my budget for fuel and it was a complete waste of a journey. Over the next week I carried on applying for jobs and writing my book inside the car. One afternoon Michael called me and told me that he had shown his mother the picture of the kitchen and said that she would pay me to clean the whole of the house and even book me into a hotel so I had somewhere clean to sleep. I could not pass up this opportunity, so Michael got his mother to transfer me fuel money to drive back to Hull. I felt as if this might be a chance to get back on my feet.

I made the arrangements with Michael and drove back to Hull on the very same day. The weather was hot and my car was driving reasonably well. When I arrived in Hull I stopped at Michael's and got the details for the hotel, which was on top of a pub, five minutes from where Michael lived. I drove there straight away. I dropped my things in the room of the hotel and went to the shops to buy a bottle of disinfectant, two bottles of shower gel, a bottle of shampoo and two flannels. I ran back to the room in the hotel, put the shower on, took my clothes off and jumped in. Considering I had not showered for almost five weeks and had not felt water on my body for such a long time, I almost felt nervous about it. This luxury that I had been used to every day in the past before it was taken away from me, I was now experiencing for the first time in a long time. I grabbed the bottle of disinfectant and the flannel and I cleaned myself twenty times. Once I was happy that I was disinfected, I stayed in the shower until I had used up both bottles of shower gel and the shampoo. I spent two and half hours in that shower.

I was so paranoid about being dirty that I had kept washing myself over and over again. I was so happy to have had the chance to clean myself that I got on my knees and gave thanks in prayer. The overwhelming excitement almost had me in shock, so I had to sit down and calm myself for a while. I then had a desperately needed shave and by the time I was finished I looked like a completely different person. Michael called me and told me to meet him in the local Greek restaurant two minutes from the hotel. I was starving by this point and was looking forward to the evening. I met Michael and Fearne in the restaurant and Michael said he would cover my bill and proceeded to order us a huge meze platter. By this time my stomach was used to eating one item from McDonald's and sometimes nothing at all. I wasn't sure how I was going to handle the large amounts of food that were about to be presented to us, but the food was amazing and I ate as much as my stomach could hold. After dinner I was so stuffed and exhausted that I headed straight back to my room and agreed to meet Michael in the morning to begin the cleaning. When I got back to the room, I was so excited at the idea of sleeping on a bed that I could not wait to get in. I felt a comfort over my body that I had not experienced for a long while. It had been one of the best days of my life.

The following morning, I headed over to Michael's and decided to begin cleaning the house from the first floor down to the ground floor. I started in Michael's room and it took me twelve hours to completely clean it due to all the rubbish that was in there. Once it was finished, it looked like a different room altogether. Over the following few days, I cleaned the whole of the upstairs and then it came time for me to clean the bathroom. This was to be the biggest challenge. What with all the rabbit faeces, urine, hay, food and hair, I had to wear rubber gloves at all times and even tied a T-shirt around my face to prevent myself breathing in all the airborne crap. I had never cleaned a bathroom so filthy and I was shocked that Michael could have allowed his house to become so uninhabitable.

After four days the whole of the upstairs was complete and the next challenge was the ground floor of the house. I began in the living room, which had the strongest smell of the whole house, due to the fact that the carpet contained dried-in animal urine, hay, faeces, pet food, human food and hair. It took sixty black bags to clear the living room of all the crap, however after three days it was done. The last challenge was the the kitchen and just the oven alone was going to take two days because it had never been cleaned of food stains, fungus, mould and dead slugs. I nearly vomited on many occasions. However, I had to see past all that and just concentrate on the job. My focus was strong and I knew that, in my then survival state of mind, anything went. The kitchen took four days and twenty more bags of rubbish.

When I had finished, Michael and Fearne were amazed. Michael got upset with himself because he had let the house fall into such a state. I tried my best to educate both of them on how to keep the house clean, but I knew that it would only be a matter of time before they would slip back into bad habits.

Michael sent photos of the house to his mother and she was very happy with the results and transferred me the money for the job. In my limited free time in Hull, I had been meditating and visualizing every morning. I also managed to get some more of my book written and I applied for a number of jobs. It was time for me to head back to Enfield.

I left Hull on a very high note, with a feeling of achievement and also the peace of mind that Fearne and Michael were going to live in a much cleaner and more hygienic home. I packed my car, said goodbye to Michael and Fearne and hit the road. The drive back was good, with the sun beating down on me, a sense of financial peace of mind and an increased level of determination.

Once I got back to Enfield, I settled in for a few days living in the car as I continued to work on my book and look for jobs and housing. A week had gone by when I received a call from an IT company near London Bridge and they invited me in for an interview two days later. The following day I took my formal suit to be dry cleaned, had a shave at the barber's and went to the local leisure centre to use the shower facilities. I spent the whole evening doing my research into the company and the job itself. The following morning, I woke up and meditated, visualised myself already having the job, brushed my teeth and drove to a secluded spot where I could get changed into my suit. It is challenging to get into a suit inside a car, given the lack of privacy and space.

Once I was fully suited, my mindset changed from that of a homeless person to that of a professional. I drove to the Tube station and made my way to London

Bridge, which gave me time to revise my notes on the train. I caught my reflection in a window and couldn't believe how far I had come on my journey, believing that I was very close to securing a job which would change my life completely.

I got to the company's office twenty minutes early and met with the sales director, who was friendly and welcoming. I did not feel nervous at all. In fact, I felt more confident than ever before. I had a 'nothing to lose, everything to gain' attitude. Throughout the interview my approach was professional to the point I was even surprising myself. I explained the many ways in which I could be beneficial to the company, talking as if the job was already mine. The manager seemed impressed and he explained the salary package, which offered a lot more money than I had anticipated. He then explained that the next stage would be a further interview, this time with the company director, and that they would be in touch within a couple of days. I left the interview feeling positive, because I already knew that they were going to call me back for the second interview and I also felt that the confidence I used to have was coming back to me.

The following day I called the local housing authority to check the status of my application, but they said the same thing to me as always. Unless I was a pregnant woman or had a serious health condition, I was not a priority. Being homeless with suicidal tendencies just didn't get enough points on the system, so the council simply referred me to charity groups and a housing association. I called the charity groups, who weren't keen to engage given my mental health issues. The housing association registered me on their system but explained that employed people would always get priority over the homeless. It just did not make sense to me how their systems worked. Even if I secured a job, I would still have to live in my car for an additional two months before I could afford to get a place of my own.

    I went back to church the following day and everyone was happy to see me, which lifted my spirits somewhat. When asked where I had been, I told them I had been visiting a friend in Hull. I had never mentioned my situation to anyone at the church, but Simon spoke to me after the evening service and the conversation turned to where I lived. I couldn't lie, so I pretty much told him about my circumstances. He was amazed that I was dealing with my situation in a such a calm and collected way and said that he couldn't cope if he had to go through what I was going through.

Chapter 47:
That one opportunity

Some miracles are so far beyond our hopes and expectations that we can't even begin to imagine them.

A few days later I was invited back for the second-stage interview with the company near London Bridge. The manager who had interviewed me the first time introduced me to the Sales Director and we sat down in the same meeting room as before. The Sales Director was a bit sterner in his interview style and harder to figure out, but I tried to give as many reasons as I could to convince him why I was the perfect fit for the position. The interview was not as long as the first one and I left the office with a degree of uncertainty in my mind.

The following day I got a call from another company, who invited me in for an interview for their IT Asset Manager position at Blackfriars. The company outsourced their IT services to a large portfolio of high-end clients. I got to work straight away on the necessary research and preparation for the interview, which was two days away. I was still mentally exhausted from the second interview with the other company, but I stayed strong and focussed. I had become used to getting ready in my car for interviews and I concentrated instead on what my life would be like once I had a job. I arrived outside the company office thirty minutes early so I revised my notes before heading in. The receptionist told me that the managers who would interview me were running thirty minutes late. I revised some more, only to be told that that the managers were going to be another forty-five minutes. I waited patiently, psyching myself up into thinking that the job was in the bag. By the time the managers arrived, I was more than ready, whereas they seemed a bit nervous and stressed, presumably because they had arrived so late. This all worked to my advantage and I pretty much dominated the interview.

As the interview progressed, they explained to me that, if successful, I would be sub-contracted to work for one of the largest private banks in the world. I felt excited at the prospect. As the interview was coming to a close, they told me that there would be a long vetting process beforehand. It could take up to two months to complete, because the company they used to vet prospective employees was based in America. At the end of the interview, I just knew that I had got the job. I headed back to Enfield and I was so drained that I ended up sleeping in the car with my interview suit on.

The following day I got a call from the first company, who told me that I had not been successful for their position as I was missing one of the skill sets required for the job. Although that was a disappointment, the possibility of the position at Blackfriars kept my spirits up. I got back to my book writing.

A few days later, I got an email from the IT Company saying that they would like to make me a conditional offer, dependent only on my vetting results. I was so excited that I was very close to having a job, but I had to bear in mind that the vetting process could take a long time and that the results could snatch the job offer away from me at any time.

As the weeks went by, I became anxious that the money I had from the cleaning job was reducing significantly. I was beginning to feel the pressure again. I stopped going to church. With no other job prospects on the horizon, I had no choice but to focus on my book, but I felt like I was slipping back into the fragile state of mind

I was in when I first moved into my car. I reduced my eating back to once a day and became weak, which made me sleep more in the car. I was finding it hard to stay awake in the library while I was writing the book on my laptop and applying for jobs. It got to a stage one day when I had to stop and have a break, so I found a field by Waltham Abbey, parked my car, and went for a walk. There were cows in a field, a small river, and lots of birds flying around. It was exactly what I needed to take my mind off things. I spent two hours walking around that field, clearing my mind and focussing on the present moment of the nature surrounding me. This relieved much of the negative energy that had been building up in previous weeks and I felt lighter as I walked back to the car.

I decided that if I didn't get the job my last hope was going to be my book. I had no other options. I still had in the back of my mind the idea of suicide. I knew if I became completely broke to the point that I would end up homeless on the street, then that would be it for me. There was no way I would survive on the street because I was barely managing as it was in my car.

After three more weeks, I finished writing my book. I was so relieved and so happy to have reached a milestone in my life, to have created something so profound that it might not change just my life, but possibly even the lives of others. As much as I wanted to celebrate the completion of my book, I could not afford to do anything but go for a long walk in the field by Waltham Abbey. The weather was perfect and I felt that a huge weight had been shifted from me, into the form of a book no less. I somehow felt that I was free to live my life the way that I wanted to, because I could now see life for what it really was.

As I walked, I contemplated and meditated, my path feeling lighter than it had ever done, with no more obstacles in front of me. The book had become symbolic of my life's journey and I somehow realised that my decisions from that point on needed to best serve me, instead of serving those who sought to keep me down. I looked up at the clear blue sky and felt sombre, yet at peace.

One Tuesday afternoon, while I was in the library, I thought about the conditional offer the company had sent me for the IT Asset Manager job. I decided to send it to the housing association to see if it would make any difference. The following week, while I was in the library applying for jobs, I got a call from them saying that they had processed my application further in light of the conditional job offer and that they would like me to view a room in Ponders End on the following day. I was so overwhelmed I had to get them to repeat what they said three times until it sunk in. I was beyond excited but still unable to accept the reality of it, because by this time I was very used to a lack of support from public services.

On Friday 18 August, I woke up very early and got myself ready for my appointment with the housing association. I drove to Ponders End and met with a housing officer called Richard, who explained that we were going to look at the room straight away. Richard drove me in his car to the house on Alma Road, near Ponders End train station, and we pulled up into a communal parking area. I followed him to a row of three terraced houses that looked like ex-council properties, but they were in good condition. He took me to the middle property and, as we entered, Richard explained to me that there were four bedrooms in the house, three of which were already occupied by male tenants, and that we were going to look at the fourth room available. As I looked around the ground floor, I saw that the house was very clean and I couldn't help smiling. We then headed up to the first floor to check out the room and, before we entered, Richard explained that it was a single room. He told me to let him know whether I thought it was going to be big enough for me to live in. When he opened the door, I saw that the room had been decorated. There was a new carpet, new curtains, a new chest of drawers, a built-in wardrobe and a new single bed. The size of the room was more than perfect for me and I could not believe my luck. 'Where do I sign?' I asked him, as there was no way I was going to pass up this opportunity. We went back to the office and I signed all the documents and the tenancy agreement and Richard said I could move in straight away. I waited for the key to arrive as the contractors who decorated the room still had it. After twenty minutes, they arrived and handed me the key. I wasted no time, quickly walking to my car and driving straight to the house. As soon as I got there, I parked my car, walked towards the house feeling very nervous, put the key in the front door and walked in. I dropped to my knees and gave thanks for this unexpected miracle.

Once I got myself together, I went straight upstairs to the bedroom. It did not feel real, because I had been homeless for seven months by then. After thirty minutes of trying to let everything sink in, I unpacked my car and took my belongings to my room. It struck me that my basic needs, such as having a shower, sleeping on a bed, eating food, having access to clean water, washing my clothes and even something as small as making a cup of tea, had been absent for such a long time that it felt like I had just won the lottery. The things we take for granted had become luxuries during my homelessness, but now I would be able to enjoy these basic but very meaningful things again. My perspective on life was suddenly and completely different, and it felt like much of the resentment I had been holding in my heart was washing away.

My first night sleeping in my own room was one of the best sleeps I ever had in my life. It felt like the first time in my life I'd slept without an invisible weight hanging over my head, that I might somehow be capable of stripping away all the things that were not good for me. I could dispense with bad friends, unhelpful family, financial hardship, bad health, depression, poor relationships, and a Dean that no longer existed. Almost thirty-three years of my life had been a struggle, but that struggle was now coming to an end. I might always resent the lost years up to a point, but I was proud of what I had achieved in spite of everything.

After a few days of settling into the new house and meeting my housemates, I wanted to go back to church to see the friends I had made there. I went for the healing service on the following Monday. Everyone was surprised to see me as they had been worried about my whereabouts. Simon must have told them my story.

They had been shocked by it, because no one knew until then that I had been living in my car while turning up to church with a smile on my face and an apparently positive attitude. Everyone looked at me a lot differently after that. They showed me an overwhelming compassion as I explained that I had considered my situation to be my responsibility and that perhaps I had needed to go through that experience to be the person I now felt I could be. A strong bond formed between us over the ensuing period. They realised that things are not always what they seem. I realised that my spirit had not been broken and that I was strong enough to be one of them in my transformed state.

Life began to settle down and the only uncertainty hanging over me now was the vetting process for the IT

Asset Manager job. I contacted the HR department at the company and they confirmed to me over the phone that the results had just come through. They would be sending me the employment contract, with a start date in two weeks' time. When I got off the phone, I sat down on my bed and felt myself shaking in disbelief.

Up until this point, the year had involved the loss of my flat, homelessness, a decline in my mental and physical health, a loss of hair, unemployment, a breakdown in my relationships with family and friends, financial debt, loneliness, starvation, and a breaking point that nearly drove me to take my own life. On the other hand, I had managed to write an entire book while being homeless, earn money by carrying out the most disgusting job ever, find my inner self, make new friends at church, find accommodation, and secure a job working at one of the largest private banks in the world.

I understand that many bad things happen for the right reasons, and that fate will play whatever part it chooses to play for each and everyone for us. But it was not my time to die. It was my time to live life the way I had always wanted to. Losing everything had made me realise who I was and what was important to me. It took the idea of suicide to teach me that if you don't fear death there is absolutely no reason to fear life.

My life had led me along a path that was very rough at times, but I'd had the strength to hold on. It had been a roller coaster of a ride, even if it felt like there were far more lows than highs. But I now realise that no matter how low the lows go, the highs must surely follow. The advantage of rock bottom is that you have nothing left to fear, and all that is left for me now is to enjoy my life as the real man I was always destined to be.

Dean Roberts, 2018

Epilogue

It is now five years since I finished writing the story I told in this book. I'm not going to pretend that it has all been plain sailing since then, but I do remain in a much better place than I was in the earlier years of my life.

I did continue to suffer from depression at times. I had some panic attacks which resulted in a hospital visit to in the middle of the night and some further treatment to manage my ongoing symptoms at the time.

I ended up getting through two more IT jobs, which did nothing for my general well-being and which confirmed that it really isn't a healthy profession for me or anyone else who has skin less thick than that of an elephant.

I had to say goodbye to an old friend after 8 years and 189,000 miles. I like to think that my beloved VW Polo is still going strong in that great scrapheap in the sky.

But some very positive things have happened as well. I found Ray Hamilton, an accomplished writer, editor and tutor who believed in me and my story enough to want to edit my manuscript.

By the start of 2020, things were also looking up on some other fronts. I had just completed three months of a six-month diploma course in coaching and mentoring, and I was averaging 95% on my grades.

And then Covid struck. Given my history, I probably wasn't ideally suited to a prolonged lockdown and the flatmates I had at the time were not ones I would have chosen to be locked down with. But I got through it. I survived. Many people didn't, of course, and that in itself is a humbling thought.

During that difficult time, I used an outdoor gym to keep fit. The roof I had over my head was a godsend and

I still shudder to think what lockdown would have been like still living in my car.

As for the here and now, I am happy. And I feel blessed for all the following reasons:

- My book is being published.
- My health and fitness levels are high, but not excessively so. I train smarter, eat healthier and understand the need for balance in my life.
- I can manage my finances properly, partly because I have bitter experience of wrong advice and wrong decisions. I compartmentalise my income and expenditure and I pay my bills on time.
- I have coached a number of people in my new career, always receiving feedback which suggests I am very good at what I now do.
- I can apply my coaching methods to myself, in the full knowledge that my earlier life would have been so much better if I knew then what I know now.
- I continue to learn and to grow.
- I accept that threats, challenges, and conflicts are a part of life from time to time, and that not everyone is necessarily out to get me.
- I can live with my scars.
- I can look back without hatred and I can leave the past where it belongs. In the past. I want nothing from it. I need nothing from it.
- I allow determination and optimism through curiosity to lead me rather than suicide.
- I am looking forward to the rest of my life.

Dean Roberts, 2023

Acknowledgements

To Ray Hamilton, for converting my drafts into a readable book. I am lucky to have worked with one of the best editors in the business and I can't thank you enough.

To Michael Konakli. They say angels come in different forms and you are definitely one of those forms.

To my CBT counsellors, for helping me to make sense of how my mind works from a broader perspective, thereby allowing me to move forward with a rationale which made sense to me.

To all the guys at Bodyworks Gym in Tottenham, thank you for the support and help with my training goals, both physically and mentally. There is no gym in the world like ours.

To Tainu 'Tre' Young. No matter if and when our paths separate or cross, you will always be my best friend and I thank you for all the times you saw something in me, especially when I doubted myself.

To Volkswagen, for producing my Bora and my Polo. Without the Bora I would have been stranded; without my Polo I would have been homeless. For me they will always be the best two cars ever made, because they kept me alive and kept me moving. They provided me with shelter, a place to sleep, a place to write and a place of peace.

www.ingramcontent.com/pod-product-compliance
Lightning Source LLC
Chambersburg PA
CBHW071300110526
44591CB00010B/725